KILLING TIMES

Killing Times

THE TEMPORAL TECHNOLOGY
OF THE DEATH PENALTY

DAVID WILLS

FORDHAM UNIVERSITY PRESS

New York 2019

Fordham University Press gratefully acknowledges
financial assistance and support provided for the
publication of this book by Brown University.

Fordham University Press has no responsibility for the
persistence or accuracy of URLs for external or third-party
Internet websites referred to in this publication and does not
guarantee that any content on such websites is, or will
remain, accurate or appropriate.

Fordham University Press also publishes its books in a
variety of electronic formats. Some content that appears in
print may not be available in electronic books.

Visit us online at www.fordhampress.com.

Library of Congress Cataloging-in-Publication Data
available online at https://catalog.loc.gov.

Printed in the United States of America

21 20 19   5 4 3 2 1

First edition

In fondest memory of Helen Tartar (1951–2014)

CONTENTS

If it were done when 'tis done, then 'twere well it were done quickly
> —Shakespeare, *Macbeth*

Introduction

I happen to begin writing this introduction on April 29, 2015. It is an everyday on planet Earth. From Indonesia comes news of eight convicted drug smugglers—two Australians, a Brazilian, an Indonesian, and four Nigerians—executed by firing squad. In the United States, the defense continues its argument against a death sentence for Boston marathon bomber Dzhokhar Tsarnaev, in response to the federal Justice Department's impassioned plea for just such a sentence. In Washington, as the Supreme Court hears arguments for and against Oklahoma's single-drug (midazolam) protocol in *Glossip v. Gross*, Justice Sonia Sotomayor opines that death by potassium chloride is akin to being burned at the stake. Although it is not in the day's papers—probably because no Westerners are being executed—one imagines the Islamic State continuing to perform executions in the territories it occupies (ten days ago, a video was released purporting to show fifteen Ethiopians subjected to such a penalty in Libya). And in Hungary, Prime Minister Viktor Orbán threatens to reinstate capital punishment in spite of the European Community ban to which his country has so far subscribed. Clearly, from West to East and back, the death penalty is very much with us.

By the time this book is published, many months, even years, will have passed since the date I just marked. The events recounted may or may not have attained a different significance.[1] But two things seem certain: First, those who read these words will have continued to live and to advance toward a death whose precise timing remains, in by far the overwhelming number of cases, unforeseen; and second, capital punishment will in one way or another, in one place or another, still be with us, inflicting on what is relatively a very limited number of humans the penalty of having their days precisely numbered.

Many years ago I told myself, and others, that I would never become a naturalized American until my adopted country abolished the death penalty. I told myself that especially during the years I lived in Louisiana, where the fact of the death penalty was and remains difficult to avoid, where executions took place regularly, where Angola Prison stands as a monument to some of the most egregious practices of the American punishment archipelago. While in Louisiana, I was for some time active in an Amnesty International chapter that divided its activities between intercessions on behalf of a persecuted Tunisian mathematics professor, of exactly my age, named Moncef Ben Salem—with whom I conversed by phone a few times in an effort to offer some moral concern and solidarity—and support for the Louisiana Coalition to Abolish the Death Penalty, whose most noteworthy member was Sister Helen Prejean.

Later I moved to New York, where in spite of George Pataki's successful reintroduction of capital punishment legislation in 1995, no execution was ever carried out before the law was held to be unconstitutional. I then went on to Rhode Island, which has not executed anyone since 1845, and which became in 1984 the first state to abolish the death penalty in the post-1976 period. One might say I have been lulled into a sense of security regarding capital punishment.

More than twenty years have passed since my mildly activist days in Louisiana, and about ten years ago a different logic led me to become an American citizen nevertheless. In 2011, following the Tunisian Spring, Moncef Ben Salem's twenty-four years of imprisonment, harassment, and collective punishment came to an end, and he was appointed Tunisia's Minister of Higher Education. I wrote to congratulate him, but we never spoke again. He died in March 2015, still having my age. Abolition did not follow on the heels of democratization in Tunisia, as has consistently been the case in recent history—from South Africa to Serbia—and the country's new constitution has retained the death penalty. Nevertheless, Amnesty International defines Tunisia as "abolitionist in practice" and there have been no executions since 1991, which includes most of the period of the pre-Spring repressive government of President Ben Ali. In December 2014, Tunisia joined 117 countries voting in favor of the UN global moratorium on the use of the death penalty.[2]

Back here, though, there is still the death penalty. As of 2017 the United States remained one of 56 retentionist countries, 142 others being abolitionist in law or practice for all, or ordinary crimes. Yet, nineteen states within the United States have abolished capital punishment, and four more have gubernatorial moratoria that currently put the practice on hold.[3] Renewed expressions of opinion concerning its unconstitutionality have been followed by more nuanced positions taken by outgoing Democrat President Obama and candidates hoping to succeed him, Hillary Clinton and Bernie Sanders. But there is still the death penalty, and an incumbent president, Donald Trump, who strongly supports it, continuing the tradition of every incumbent before him.

I record those milestones—punctual moments, the passage of years—simply to emphasize my interest, in this book, in the complex temporality of the death penalty: the slow time of judicial processes, the presumed instantaneity of the end of life; and most important, the state's imposition of a precise timetable for ending a human life, coupled in the American context with an often decades-long limbo on death row. In imposing and enforcing a precise moment of death, capital punishment has to be conceived of differently from suicide, euthanasia, murder, and even genocide. A person may decide to end his or her life on a particular date, perhaps even at a precise time on the clock, but that timing will be of his or her own choosing and executed according to his or her program; a decision—judicial or otherwise—may be made to remove the life-support system of someone who is comatose, but that person will not have been informed of such a decision in a courtroom by the machinery of state; a murder may be minutely planned and timed, but the killing will always retain for its victim something of the structure of an accident; and although genocide may be enacted by a state, and—as in the paradigm of the Nazi Holocaust—although it requires a type of precise industrial program, something about its very wholesale aspect, and necessary haste, prevents it from functioning as the same imposition and repetition of a judicial timetable as the death penalty. Of course, one could find or imagine cases that fall between those different categories of dying, which would raise the question of whether they should more accurately be called one or the other, whether murder or suicide (e.g., a murder-suicide pact), murder or euthanasia, murder or genocide. And indeed, since capital punishment inevitably raises the question of its judiciality, it risks hovering between murder and death penalty, or, as discussed in Chapter 4, can overlap with suicide.

My presumption, and my argument here, beyond all those complications, is that the death penalty is distinctive for its external, institutional, judicial, and political imposition of a time of death, a moment of death. That is what constitutes and defines the death penalty as a human invention, and it is what distinguishes it from the human slaughter of nonhuman animals, especially in industrial agriculture. Animals are put to death for human consumption, or retributively when they kill humans, but that putting to death no longer constitutes a judicially sanctioned punishment for a crime. By means of the death penalty, conversely, the human is robbed, by a socially and politically sanctioned machinery, of a mortality defined not only as knowing that one will die, but more specifically as *not knowing the hour of one's demise.* It is from such a perspective of the state's interruption of the time of life that this book seeks to analyze some of the complexities of what I will call *the temporal technology, the killing times* of the death penalty.

A further temporality, already evoked, is in operation here. It concerns the time of academic writing, the fact and implications of this book's publication by a university press, and of my having carried out research for it in the context of my employment as a university professor. However much professing via writing be an integral part of and an expectation within an academic career, such writing works according to a different rhythm from other writing (fiction or nonfiction) that is carried out as a profession. And there is inevitable, but necessary tension between professional writers and professor-writers, a tension that is itself a function of temporality, of variations in what is precisely called a *deadline.* That tension comes into play in the first instance once a professor-writer such as myself takes it upon himself to address "current events," events taking place in the current or present time. To begin, it is simply this: As I have already suggested, while I am writing according to the rhythms and protocols of academic research and publication, the present, and its current events are evolving; as I spend however long it takes me to put this book together and to have it published, more, or fewer people are being condemned to death and executed, and in evolving circumstances.

But in a second, broader sense, a tension arises from a vexed relation of academic work—and scholarship in the literature-based disciplines of the humanities in particular—to politics. The last two generations of scholarship emerging from those disciplines have been marked by a type of "right to the political," the first of whose manifestations, in my domain at least, was no doubt a text that is now rarely read, namely Roland Barthes's *Criticism and Truth* (published in English only in 1987, but in French in 1966). Barthes wrote his book in reply to a Sorbonne professor's response to his study of seventeenth-century playwright Jean Racine. Barthes was pilloried by that venerable *sorbonnard*, Raymond Picard, less for politicizing the literary than for historicizing or psychoanalyzing it, but attention to the evacuation of history and politics from cultural analysis had been a fact of his work since *Mythologies* (1957); indeed, one recognizes in his detractors' call for attention to "what is literary in literature" an objection that continues to be echoed today.[4] And whereas there existed in the French tradition a time-honored respect for the punctual interventions of the *écrivain engagé*—with outstanding examples such as the activism of Victor Hugo throughout much of the nineteenth century, Émile Zola's "J'accuse" published in 1898, and then a Camus, a Sartre, or a Foucault in the twentieth century—Barthes's gesture was very different, arguing not that a writer could, or should be involved politically, but rather that the literary is always already the political.

In 2015, the argument appeared to have been won, even if disagreement remained concerning the results of that presumed victory, and even if the 2016 presidential election proved what little distance half a century of a supposed progressive academy had covered in producing a better politically informed populace. Henceforth, though, academics working across the cultural field do not hesitate to foreground political analysis within their disciplines, and currents such as gender studies, ethnic studies, and postcolonialism very often have overt political critique as their basis. Sometimes those gestures are indistinguishable from activisms of various types, and sometimes they amount to little more than liberal leftist caricatures that risk nothing in terms of the institutional status quo, beginning with the institution of the university itself. But I would venture that what necessarily problematizes all such gestures is the temporal tension I am referring to here: The presumed efficacy of political action is related to a "punctuality" of the moment, whereas academic temporality obeys a different, slower rhythm.

How, then, to characterize an academic project that relates to the death penalty without for all that claiming to be straightforward activism? That presumes, first of all, that we can locate where activism begins and ends, and where it begins to be straightforward, which takes us back to the question of different temporalities, to the idea that activism and political action rely on an immediacy whose time is different from the time of reflection or deliberation. In trying to resolve those differences, we would be faced with the impossible task of defining the time—to cite some random examples—of Frantz Fanon's *Wretched of the Earth* versus Black September's 1972 Munich operation, or Nelson Mandela's Robben Island sojourn versus the signing of the Magna Carta. This project renounces such a task. However, on the topic of more or less activist politics, I would like to make this much clear, from the outset: I find the death penalty anathema, an inexcusably retrograde form of vengeance that has rightly been abandoned by the vast majority of countries, and it is for me a particularly troubling anachronism in the genealogy of American justice and jurisprudence, indeed of American democracy.[5] I would also add that what might be called my innate opposition to the death penalty derives less from adopting an explicit moral position—based either on sentiment or on rational argument—than from my having grown up in an ambiance of "death-penalty irrelevance." In this, my position is close to that expressed by Justice Blackmun, dissenting—as I later discuss—from the abolitionist majority in *Furman v. Georgia*:

> Having lived for many years in a state [Minnesota] that does not have
> the death penalty, that effectively abolished it in 1911, and that carried
> out its last execution on February 13, 1906, capital punishment had
> never been part of life for me. In my State, it just did not exist. So far
> as I can determine, the State, purely from a statistical deterrence point
> of view, was neither the worse nor the better for its abolition, for, as
> the concurring opinions observe, the statistics prove little, if anything.
> But the State and its citizens accepted the fact that the death penalty
> was not to be in the arsenal of possible punishments for any crime.[6]

Blackmun went on in that dissent to address the constitutionality of the death penalty and to decide that it could be upheld. As I discuss in Chapter 1, some eighteen years would pass before his historic renunciation of its machinery in *Callins v. Collins*.

I am not under the same pressure. However abolitionist my position be, deciding whether the death penalty obeys or contravenes the U.S. Constitution, or whether it is a moral punishment for certain crimes, is for me an indirect, but not primary interest. Instead, as I will progressively explain, I seek to analyze a particular conceptual framework relating to temporal aspects of capital punishment. Nevertheless, as will emerge, that analysis leads chapter by chapter to conclusions that are explicitly, even stridently critical of the death penalty—particularly as still practiced by the United States—and consequently to positions that are resolutely abolitionist.

This book will not, therefore, seek to reconcile differences between the slow time of academic research, writing, and publication, and the urgent current question that is the death penalty. I acknowledge and accept the rhythmic inconsistencies, or syncopations that come into play on one side and the other, both on the academic side and the political side. There is no simple way to resolve the tension between the exigencies of a given political instant and the extended time of academic reflection, and that tension becomes even more fraught when we consider contemporary forms of mediatic instantaneity. But one cannot help being struck by the uncanny resemblance between, on one hand, that relation of urgency—"act now!"—versus duration—"thinking and writing takes time" (and represents a type of passivity)—on the basis of which we still presume to determine political relevance, and, on the other, the temporal framework of the death penalty, where another type of insistence on instantaneous efficacy ("If we must do it, let's make it quick and painless") meets resistance in the requirements of due process and desire for the extension of human life. The death penalty itself has its rhythms, its slow and fast times, which, from the moment the sentence is passed, become *killing times*.

For example: Within another time frame of the writing of this Introduction and this book, namely the fall semester of 2015, I taught a seminar on the topics related to it. On the Wednesday of the first week of that class (September 16, 2015), Richard Glossip was destined to die following the Supreme Court's rejection of his petition during that summer. He had been on death row for some seventeen years, since his conviction for a 1997 murder. He did not die that Wednesday, but was given two week's reprieve until September 30. For the five-odd hours the class spent together during that period, we tried to imagine, to judge, to conceive of how quickly or slowly those two weeks passed for him. On September 30, the Oklahoma Department of Corrections opened its lethal injection drug shipment, received from its secret supplier, to find that potassium chloride, one of the drugs about which the Supreme Court had deliberated at considerable length while hearing his case, had been replaced by potassium acetate. Richard Glossip, having eaten a last meal for the third time, and even having shared it with his jailers—how would we measure the time of that communion?—was removed from death's antechamber. His execution was put on hold until at least 150 days beyond the completion of a grand jury inquiry initiated by the Oklahoma State Attorney General. The report of the grand jury, released on May 19, 2016, exposed "deeply troubling failures" in the exercise of the death penalty. Another independent review was conducted by the Oklahoma Death Penalty Review Commission and published on April 25, 2017. The Review Commission's members called into question whether the death penalty could be administered "in a way that ensures no innocent person is put to death" and unanimously recommended that the state extend its effective moratorium on executions pending "significant reforms."[7] For my class, then, back in fall 2015, Richard Glossip, whose execution would have inaugurated a semester-long discussion of the temporalities of the death penalty, instead survived it, leaving us at a loss how to count, measure, let alone experience the variety of artificially and more or less arbitrarily imposed times-to-death lived by him.

The enormous discrepancies, the different extents of limbo between sentence and execution would be capital punishment's most obvious slow time, at least in the United States. One can die waiting to be killed; a sentence is passed and a punishment determined, but the punishment itself is not immediately enacted and may be deferred, as in Glossip's case, for many years. Gary Alvord, sentenced by Florida in 1974, died in prison on May 21, 2013, having the macabre distinction of being the longest-serving death row prisoner in the United States (thirty-nine years). Contrast with that the desired, and often failed instantaneity of execution itself, a fast killing time. Those two rhythms or speeds far from constitute a simple opposition, and they are rendered more complex still by what now looms on the horizon of any abolition of the death penalty—at least in the United States—namely life imprisonment without parole, which, for not being currently conceived of as a death penalty but being precisely a substitute for it, introduces a whole other category of *killing time*: You are sentenced not to be killed but to a punishment that will not end until you are dead.

The specific idea of mortal time that emerges in what follows is motivated by my own reigning academic interest in what I have called the "prosthetic" relation between the human body and technology. As I have developed in three different volumes spanning almost twenty-five years, close examination of how the human relates to the technological points persistently to the fact of their inextricability, to how the human has never in fact functioned without technology, to what extent technology resides *within* the human. Such an inextricability clearly extends beyond the classic sense of prosthesis as a simple mechanical add-on to the body designed to remedy a deficiency in that body.[8] From that perspective, my interest in capital punishment is in what changes—for "prosthesis"—once the human body is attached to a lethal machine in very different ways from the use of medical prostheses designed to extend or ameliorate its life. And what comes to the fore, as I see it, as the essential element of the relation between the human and the technological in the context of the death penalty, is what may in fact be revealed as a "first" technology, namely time. In the perspective of the *timed untimely* death imposed by the death penalty, what comes into focus as original prosthesis to the human is *time* itself: not because the prosthesis called time begins with the death penalty, but because capital punishment imposes a particular version of prosthetic time, one that precisely underlines the prosthetic status of time and inscribes it as an inescapable fact of the human.

In the chapters that follow, I will seek to understand how or why the death penalty requires time as part of its machinery, how it requires the human to be tethered to time in a specifically artificial, or *prosthetic* manner; and what difference exists between the death penalty's prosthetic time and the temporal technology of the human animal in general.

Six *killing times* will be examined in this book. Chapter 1 undertakes something of an historical overview of American Supreme Court jurisprudence relating to the death penalty. I seek to provide sufficient background information for nonjurist readers, concentrating on cases that will serve as points of reference for subsequent discussion. At the same time, I emphasize that what emerges from many of those cases is the increasingly important idea that the cruel punishment referred to in the Eighth Amendment is a function of time: Capital punishment becomes cruel if it takes too long. In my view, the necessity of defining and controlling the instant has shaped jurisprudential debate regarding the death penalty in the United States from 1879 to the present. It prompts my inquiry into other temporal modalities that crisscross the same debates, and it takes me back to the pivotal moment of the post-Enlightenment period when the question had already been explicitly posed, the moment of the French revolutionary penal code and the introduction of the guillotine.

Chapter 1 also introduces another important strand of my discussion. In starting from Harry Blackmun's famous 1994 declaration, in *Callins*, that he would no longer "tinker with the machinery of death," I try to analyze some of the paradoxical effects of the technology of the death penalty that follow from what I have just described: how, by prescribing the moment of death, the death penalty presumes a concept of life separated by an ever-refinable knife edge from death; how an abolitionism such as Blackmun's presumes a natural life struggling against the unnatural machine; how the machinery of execution acts as a prosthesis to the body that plays between prolonging life and bringing it to an end.

Chapter 2 examines in detail the introduction of the guillotine in France as exemplar of a new, humanitarian, instant death penalty, whose principles continue to dominate in the West. My further contention in that chapter is that the death-dealing instant functions in tension with forms of visuality, which relate in the first instance to the dissuasive pretentions of capital punishment, but which have been complicated otherwise in the period of the photographic image, allowing Western Enlightenment principles precisely to be drawn back into comparison with the brutal practices that they claimed to eschew.

Chapter 3 pursues some of the complications raised in Chapter 2 by trying to understand to what extent, in the practice of the death penalty, a temporality of blood continues to function in the era of a purely chemical death penalty such as lethal injection—one that thinks it has made blood invisible—and how that works through what the previous chapters have emphasized in terms of the instant. It is in that chapter that I develop most explicitly the conceptual and philosophical framework of my idea of *killing time*, as specific technological interruption of mortal temporality. I discuss first the timing of Socrates's death sentence, then Heidegger's *temporalizing* time, which he contrasts with Hegel's succession of instants or "nows," before coming to read the peculiar conceptual relation that can be found in Hegel between time and blood. That analysis will allow me to argue that blood, in the form of an externalized, prosthetic time, is indeed shed in every execution.

In the final three chapters of *Killing Times*, the definitive moment of capital punishment—the incontrovertible fact of a state's deciding on the instant of a subject's death, and questions about *the quickness of the death penalty's fastest killing time*—will be measured against what might be called its "spatial" reach outside the strict context of a judicial death penalty. In Chapter 4, I discuss the suicide bomber who plays the role of an anti-subject (of the law and of the state), striking and killing in a way that robs the law and the state of its violent recourse. By preempting the moment of capital punishment, and *simultaneously* acting as his or her own judge, jury and executioner, the suicide bomber claims to reappropriate the time and instant of the death penalty in an absolute sense: committing a capital crime, short-circuiting the judicial process, and executing himself or herself in the process.

In order to understand that absolute reappropriation of the instant against the background of terrorism with which it is usually associated, I return to the historical context out of which the term "terrorist" emerged, namely the French revolution. Through discussion of an important post–World War II essay by Maurice Blanchot, I analyze the mechanism of what we call in English the Reign of Terror, as the revolutionary exercising of supreme freedom by means of the right to death, that of others and that of oneself. That analysis allows me to conclude that a structural relation exists between the appropriation of the instant of death by capital punishment and by the terrorist.

In Chapter 5, I ask how the sovereign prerogative that is enshrined in a judicial appropriation of the instant of death relates to other instances of state-sanctioned death-dealing violence, in particular the most obvious case called war. To what extent does war legitimate capital punishment or capital punishment legitimate war? Though such broader ethical and political questions are not the focus of my study, I take up here the special new *instantanization* of intercontinental space, and the special case of state killing on the edge of war represented by the drone strike. The contemporary embrace, by successive U.S. presidents and their military, of targeted killing by drone, is precisely justified on the basis of a clear distinction between judicial execution and an act of war. But, to the extent that specifics of that justification, and the process of targeted killing, remain essentially secret, no clarity will have been provided, and we are left with the simple numerical fact of a ratio of three or four, perhaps even five times as many people executed by drone strikes since 2002 as have been judicially executed since 1976. In a sense, that makes the drone strike *the* American form of execution.

Beyond that numerical evidence, the drone penalty again brings into focus two opposing time frames. The first is the long history (Enlightenment to the present) of relations between capital punishment and slavery, which is uncannily repeated as the African theater of drone operations expands across that continent loosely following medieval trade, and later slave-trade routes. Also intersecting with slavery and the death penalty on the edge of judiciality are the perverse practices of incarceration—death row or not, solitary confinement or not—that affect predominantly the African American population of the United States, but overflow into post-9/11 practices such as rendition of foreign citizens and the use of black sites. The second time frame is more specifically the moment of the instantaneous intercontinental strike, carried out by a sovereign held to no account, which, I will argue, inextricably links the American president to the "terrorist" or "militant," also acting in secret, whom he kills.

Finally, in Chapter 6, I turn to very different time and space coordinates of the death penalty, those relating to various discursive frameworks. Here I am interested less in the deliberative process of the trial itself than in the *recounting* of the crime, and of its time, by means of narrative forms such as the confession. By that means the condemned person takes back the damnable act and at the same time reaffirms it, seeking, by means of avowal or remorse, to have his or her time over again. Invitations and incitations to confess, and processes such as plea bargaining, or any weighing of the probability of a conviction against the accused's willingness to cooperate, mean that one is punished not just for a crime but also for how much of the state's time (and money) has been wasted on a trial; and by the same token, punishment is calibrated on, even requires, some form of recounting, of owning up. Punishment is thus not just a penalty but also a discursive instance: It speaks the power of the law and the justice of the penalty, and the penalty imposed is proportionate not only to a crime but also to discursive formations, such as testimony and confession, that relate to the crime; capable therefore of being modified if guilt is admitted and remorse is shown.

I examine those questions first via the strange narrative *I, Pierre Rivière, having slaughtered my mother, my sister, and my brother*, published in a collective text edited by Michel Foucault in 1973.[9] Rivière's narrative account of his 1835 crime, which he intended to write as an advance justification for committing it, uncannily becomes part of that crime; yet at the same time, once he does write it—following the advice of the justice system—it is used both as evidence for the prosecution and as a defense based on the emerging doctrine of extenuating circumstances and the new potential of an insanity plea. And Rivière's memoir—in its peculiarity, but also in its principle—shows how the strict form of a confession overflows into narrative fiction. That leads me to discuss work by one who might be called the literary writer of the law, and of the death penalty, par excellence, namely Franz Kafka.

The ultimately penalty reinforces or concentrates the desire for recounting that is a function of any judicial deliberative, and due, process. By the same token any penalty—and, in the most extreme way, the death penalty—wishes to bring recounting to an end, as if to discount it, in order to provide the closure that is a much vaunted justification for carrying out a death sentence. The death penalty seeks to end both the time of the crime and the time of punishment. Yet, by preempting any further utterance by the one condemned, capital punishment itself becomes the voice of that convict, stating his or her guilt, perhaps remorse, as well as the justice of the punishment. In the very moment when the death sentence deprives of discourse, therefore, it multiplies those discourses; by disallowing anything anymore being said to the contrary, the instant of execution is the inaudible or impossible cacophony of all those voices that will have been heard through it and imposed on it, like a machine, and, through its machinery, on its victim.

Still more uncannily, I would suggest, that moment of closure remains all the more illusory, and is kept forever open by the discourse of its own potential failure: the possibility of punishing someone innocent. A death penalty that kills someone innocent does not just commit its own crime of murder but has its sentence drowned out by the more powerful voice of that innocence; its instant and end of time is countermanded by the infinite value and unsilenced cry of innocence.

French philosopher Jacques Derrida conducted a two-year seminar series on the death penalty in 1999–2001. In the ninth and tenth sessions of the first year he brings into focus the difference between a mortality that means knowing we will die one day, and the specific circumstances of being condemned to death: "The mortal that I am knows that he is condemned to die, but even if he is sick, incurable, or even in the throes of death, the mortal that I am does not know the moment, the date, the precise hour that he will die."[10] On the other hand, "the concept of the death penalty supposes that the state, judges, society, the bourreaux and executioners, that is, third parties, have mastery over the *time of life* of the condemned one" (*DP I*, 220, my emphasis). In is on the basis of that seemingly simple insight— how the everyday time of life that can end at any time is transformed into a particular time at which a man or woman will be killed, a *killing time*— that I develop the discussions that follow. Many elements of this book are inspired by the analyses in Derrida's two volumes. In certain chapters I return in more depth to questions he raises; at other times my references are more oblique or implicit as I examine *killing times* according to my own logic. But the idea, developed by Derrida, that "if there is some torture, torturing, cruelty in the process of the condemnation to death . . . [it] is indeed, beyond everything, beyond the conditions of detention, for example, and so many other torments, the experience of time" (220), remains my major premise throughout. And, coupled with the fact that the death penalty "provides the only example of a death whose instant is calculable by a machine, by machines" (257), it forms the basis for my interpreting the death penalty's interruption of ordinary mortal temporality as a form of technologization.

To recap: The argument of this book will be that the death penalty exposes the technicity or *prostheticity* of mortal time, something that we experience as a disruption of that time. Time—at least human time—comes into play as a function of mortality. We know there is time because we know that, at our end of it, we will die; we come to understand the passage of time, its hours and days, years and decades, as an inexorable movement toward death. From that point of view time already carries within itself a technological or prosthetic element, that of an impersonal or external machine to whose automatism we remain tethered. Time is something that we experience as already in train the moment we are born, and it is a train that we cannot escape riding until the moment we die. But as long as we do not know for how long we will remain alive, as long as we presume to survive each next moment, we are able in a sense to subject time to the rhythm of our individual lives, to escape its control or outrun it—as it were, to naturalize it.

On the other hand, once death is artificially announced, imposed, foreseen, and forecast, once a decision is reached and a sentence of death is passed precisely in opposition to the "natural" temporal flow of mortality, then the technological structure of time returns with a formidable vengeance. Time suddenly appears as the autonomous machine that it in fact is, functioning outside of our growing and aging bodies; and what remains of one's life becomes or comes to obey a very different type of countdown. Not only, therefore, is the life of one condemned to death cut short by what Blackmun called "the machinery of death," but the temporality of mortality also comes to be experienced in its technological force; it is as if a mechanical or technologized time were taking over that life and putting it on its own schedule in a way that could never be the case for ordinary mortals living out their days in the expectation that one of those days—yet to be revealed—will be their last.

Killing Times will argue, therefore, that the contrived interruption of a life constituted by the death penalty throws into relief the technological status of human mortality. Once the end of life is determined and organized, made by a death sentence to arrive prematurely, then what seemed to be the natural linearity and teleology of that life—the presumption that life will continue uninterrupted until some undetermined moment—is denaturalized. Now, two things must be noted here, before being developed in later discussions. First, the "denaturalization" just mentioned comes into play in the case of, for example, a terminal illness as well as a judicial death sentence; but, I would maintain, the form of that interruption is nevertheless different in each case, and its particular status as a technological interruption is more pronounced when the state pronounces, as it were arbitrarily, a specific date and time for ending a life. Second, and more important, the recognition of a denaturalized or technological time to which I just referred occurs in strikingly different registers or modes for us ordinary mortals and for those who are sentenced to death. It is experienced somewhat abstractly or, one might say, ontologically by all of us, but it is of course a reality and psychological torment for those who are condemned to death, required to live, experience, indeed suffer it, on an incomparably different existential level.

The death penalty further disturbs temporal linearity by means of the different rhythms, suspensions, and accelerations to which I referred earlier. As practiced, but also as constituted, it makes the time of a life run quickly toward death, but that does not happen according to a coherent progression. I say "as practiced" because, as I have already mentioned, due process requires not just a certain set of procedures—hearings, trial, jury deliberation—before a death sentence, but another set—appeals, stays—following the sentence as it proceeds toward being carried out. But I say "as constituted" because even in the case of a summary execution, where the sentence is carried out more or less immediately after its passing, the time, however brief, between judgment and execution, is a time out of joint: The mortal flow has nevertheless been irrevocably disrupted, subject to the different law, schedule, and mechanism just described. In English we speak of the time of deferment as of a "stay (of execution)," during which time is understood to stand still; in French it is a *sursis*, from the Latin *supersedere*, whence our verb "to supersede," one time taken over by another, literally one time sitting on top of another, which I interpret as technological time sitting atop of some presumed sense of natural mortal time.

The time is now 5:49 P.M. on September 21, 2018.

CHAPTER I

Machinery of Death or Machinic Life

In February 1994, the lone dissenting voice of Justice Harry A. Blackmun expressed from the bench of the U.S. Supreme Court opposition as a matter of principle to the constitutionality of capital punishment in America. In *Callins*, Blackmun famously declared:

> On February 23, 1994, at approximately 1:00 A.M., Bruce Edwin Callins will be executed by the State of Texas. Intravenous tubes attached to his arms will carry the instrument of death, a toxic fluid designed specifically for the purpose of killing human beings. The witnesses, standing a few feet away, will behold Callins, no longer a defendant, an appellant, or a petitioner, but a man, strapped to a gurney, and seconds away from extinction.
>
> Within days, or perhaps hours, the memory of Callins will begin to fade. The wheels of justice will churn again, and somewhere, another jury or another judge will have the unenviable task of determining whether some human being is to live or die. . . .
>
> Twenty years have passed since this Court declared that the death penalty must be imposed fairly, and with reasonable consistency, or not at all . . . and, despite the effort of the States and courts to devise

legal formulas and procedural rules to meet this daunting challenge, the death penalty remains fraught with arbitrariness, discrimination, caprice, and mistake. . . .

Having virtually conceded that both fairness and rationality cannot be achieved in the administration of the death penalty . . . the Court has chosen to deregulate the entire enterprise, replacing, it would seem, substantive constitutional requirements with mere esthetics, and abdicating its statutorily and constitutionally imposed duty to provide meaningful judicial oversight to the administration of death by the States.

From this day forward, I no longer shall tinker with the machinery of death. For more than 20 years I have endeavored—indeed, I have struggled—along with a majority of this Court, to develop procedural and substantive rules that would lend more than the mere appearance of fairness to the death penalty endeavor. Rather than continue to coddle the Court's delusion that the desired level of fairness has been achieved and the need for regulation eviscerated, I feel morally and intellectually obligated simply to concede that the death penalty experiment has failed.[1]

As Blackmun states, in the twenty-odd years since *Furman* (1972) had struck down capital punishment and *Gregg* (1976) had reinstated it, he had been struggling—in complicated ways to which I shall return—with the question of the death penalty's constitutionality.[2] When he dissented in 1994, the Court's two reliable abolitionists, Justices Brennan and Marshall, were no longer there to accompany him, having retired in 1990 and 1991 respectively. Blackmun would himself retire from the Court a few months after *Callins*, having served for nearly twenty-four years following his appointment in 1970 by Richard Nixon. It would take another fourteen years for something of his frustration to be expressed once again, in somewhat muted form, by Justice John Paul Stevens—who nevertheless found his hands tied and so concurred—in *Baze* (2008).[3] Stevens in turn retired in 2010. It would take another seven years, twenty-one years after *Callins*, for full-fledged statements on the unconstitutionality of the death penalty to form the basis of the dissenting opinion by Justice Breyer, joined by Justice Ginsburg, in June 2015 in *Glossip*.[4]

In this chapter I focus, however inexhaustively, on that evolution of challenges to the constitutionality of the death penalty. My discussion will concentrate on the Eighth Amendment prohibition against cruel and unusual punishment: "Excessive bail shall not be required, nor excessive fines imposed, nor cruel and unusual punishments inflicted." Briefly, the major history of Supreme Court deliberations concerning Eighth Amendment defenses in capital cases begins in the context of Utah's introduction of a firing squad in 1879, followed by New York State's use of the electric chair in 1890. Two important noncapital cases, *Weems* in 1910 and *Resweber* in 1947, revived the debate, which came to be presented as a civil rights issue in the 1960s, leading ultimately to *Furman*, which ruled against the death penalty in 1972. That decision caused states to overhaul their statutes both in terms of amending trial and sentencing practices and in seeking demonstrably painless methods of execution. The subsequent reforms were considered adequate by the Supreme Court majority in *Gregg*, at which point the tinkering that Blackmun speaks of began in earnest, continuing still: through *Callins* (1994) and, among other cases, *Baze* (2008) and *Glossip* (2015).

Before returning to discuss further the issues—especially issues of temporality—pertinent to those cases, I wish to underscore another element of Blackmun's *Callins* dissent, which relates differently but no less centrally to the ideas I will develop. The catchphrase that his opinion has made famous—"I no longer shall tinker with the machinery of death"—assumes a necessary link between capital punishment and a cruelty or inhumanity that works through the schematics or thematics of a mechanical operation. The presumption is that whereas death kills, a machinery of death, a death-dealing machine, a technological apparatus, kills inhumanly and therefore inhumanely. To paraphrase: *Intravenous tubes carry the instrument of death, a toxic fluid, into a man strapped to a gurney . . . the wheels of justice churn, the Court abdicates its responsibility, [but] I no longer shall tinker with the machinery of death.* Blackmun paints a stark contrast between, on one side, human beings, the witnesses, a man, and on the other, an impersonal state with its instruments, justice with its wheels, death via machines. According to his logic, that of a well-known and well-worn mythology and ideology—with which it is difficult not to be in sympathy, but whose complexities nevertheless call for analysis—cruelty follows where human agency and responsibility cede ground to a type of implacable mechanistic automatism.[5] While I therefore concur fully with the sentiment expressed by Blackmun regarding the machinery of state killing, it will be my contention that the specific technological intervention into life in order to end it that is constituted by the death penalty does not simply bring about the mechanical interruption of life, but in fact stages the unstable and problematic relation that life will always have maintained with the machine.

Specifically, a primary, if not the primary relation between human life and technology is established by means of time, by means of time as something that is in itself technological. It is not the explicit focus of Blackmun's argument, but in the jurisprudential history to which he refers—to accentuate his own struggle with the machinery of death with which he no longer will tinker—time is of paramount, if not always explicit interest. That interest begins with his very mention of a twenty-year endeavor, and it is reinforced by the use of the verb "tinker," meaning not just "to work upon a thing by making small repairs" or "to work in a bungling way," but also "to putter aimlessly," in other words to dally or waste one's time in the effort. Beyond that, however, time is the inescapable index of cruelty from *Weems* (1910) to *Glossip* (2015): fifteen years in chains for defrauding the government in the first case, time that does or does not allow pain to be felt in the second. Thus, if we were to follow in reverse the generational development of constitutional challenges to the death penalty we would have to go back through *Resweber* in 1947, which is twenty-five years prior to *Furman* (1972), and before that to *Weems* in 1910, thirty-seven years before *Resweber*, and indeed, twenty to thirty years before that, to *Kemmler* and *Wilkerson*.[6]

Within that history, the machinery of death appears to function, or malfunction, according to three principles: There is a threat of breakdown producing pain and cruelty, the risk of a vulnerable human being left to suffer because of an unreliable machine; there is a principle of perfectibility—a progressively more reliable and more humane machine— that answers to the doctrine of evolving standards; and there is supervisory oversight deemed acceptable or unacceptable in proportion as it cedes to nonsovereign, international pressure. Throughout that history, attention to time will be a constant, beginning in a not insignificant manner with the time of history, especially the history of the West in the post-Enlightenment period. During that period of some two and a half centuries, the concept of capital punishment will have explicitly separated itself from the practice of torture. In rejecting torture, the death penalty will become a function of the recognized human right not to have pain inflicted, either for its own sake or for the sake of some reason of state; the right not to have pain inflicted and the right not to have to *endure* pain, implicitly defined thereby through the concept of *duration*, the passage of time. In the attention paid to different methods of execution such as are periodically reviewed by this or that Supreme Court Justice, the background or foreground question is consistently some idea of time. As Kant argues in his 1781 *Critique of Pure Reason*—one of the founding texts of the Enlightenment—time is sensibility, perhaps we could say "feeling" itself: "time is . . . a pure form of sensible intuition. . . . All objects of the senses are in time, and necessarily stand in relations of time. . . . If one removes the special condition of our sensibility from it, then the concept of time disappears."[7]

The Court's first important decisions regarding the Eighth Amendment in the context of the death penalty arose precisely from the shift away from hanging, which was the preferred method of execution in the United States throughout much of the nineteenth century. When called to consider the constitutionality of execution by firing squad in *Wilkerson*, the Court referred to Blackstone's *Commentaries on the Laws of England*, which mentioned how "terror, pain or disgrace" could be superadded to punishment for "very atrocious crimes," leading to such cases as being "emboweled alive, beheaded, and quartered . . . public dissection . . . burning alive." However, those excesses, to the extent that they "savored of torture or cruelty," were mitigated by the "humanity of the nation" (*Wilkerson*, 135). That humane doctrine is what guided the Court in concluding that although such "punishments of torture" (ibid.) are forbidden by the Eighth Amendment, the firing squad, used for example by the military, is acceptable. The point is explicitly made, however, that "difficulty would attend the effort to define with exactness the extent of the constitutional provision which provides that cruel and unusual punishments shall not be inflicted" (135–36). Simply put: How much punishment is permissible, and precisely when—or after how long—does it become cruel? Such a difficulty, which I shall persistently take to be a difficulty with time, and—more especially as history progresses—with the instant, remains to this day.

The problem of determining just how much pain or suffering the Constitution allows returns very soon thereafter, with New York State's introduction of electrocution in 1890. Though the case of the first convict condemned to that form of execution, William Kemmler, was decided less on the question of the Eighth Amendment than over the right of New York State to decide its own standards and forms of punishment, the cruelty issue nevertheless came into play in explicit terms. The New York Court of Appeals had determined that electrocution "must result in *instantaneous, and consequently in painless* death" (*Kemmler*, 443–44, my emphasis). In that respect, it was in agreement with the intent of the governor, who, in his message to the legislature on January 6, 1885, expressed a desire to move beyond the "present mode of executing criminals by hanging [that] has come down to us from the dark ages" in favor of "a means for taking the life of such as are condemned to die in a less barbarous manner" (444); as a result, he appointed the commission that would subsequently find electrocution to represent precisely the desired advance out of barbarism.[8]

While seconding the New York Court of Appeals, the Supreme Court nevertheless saw fit to refer to *Wilkerson*, and it quoted in particular the difficulty just mentioned of "defin[ing] with exactness the extent" of the Eighth Amendment provision. It added: "Punishments are cruel when they involve torture or a lingering death; but the punishment of death is not cruel within the meaning of that word as used in the constitution. It implies there something inhuman and barbarous, something more than the mere extinguishment of life" (447). *Kemmler* decides, therefore, that death itself is not cruel, but that a lingering death would be; mere extinguishment of life is constitutionally permissible, and a supposed *instantaneous* death by electrocution fulfills that condition. The difficulty thus moves from the broad question of defining what is cruel and unusual to unending debate about how to mechanically induce an instantaneous death. Once Justice Brennan contends in *Furman* that "death is an unusually severe punishment, unusual in its pain, in its finality, and in its enormity. . . . It appears that *there is no method available that guarantees an immediate and painless death*" (*Furman*, 287, my emphasis), the efficacy of technology has folded into it—as if it didn't always—the matter of speed as a function of time. Technology in general is, after all, about nothing more than gaining speed and saving time, from the first stones for hewing, and flints for cooking, to the memory of a computer or bandwidth of a server.

Hanging had been seen as an advance over methods of execution that involved bloodshed—an attendant question that I return to in a later discussion—but it came to be considered "barbarous" in comparison to electrocution, and hence a failure when it came to the question of speed. The improvement represented by electrocution resides explicitly in its instantaneity. Yet, by presuming to close off discussion concerning the definition of "cruel and unusual," introducing instead the concept of the instant, *Kemmler* in fact opens an insoluble debate that returns in *Glossip* 125 years later. *How instant is instant?* If lingering, torturous death can be superseded by hanging, and hanging can be superseded by the presumed instantanization of electrocution, and electrocution can then be superseded by lethal injection, at what point will the death penalty have arrived at the perfection it seems in this way to seek? How, in that context, will the choice of midazolam over sodium thiopental as the first, sedating drug of a lethal cocktail, as debated in *Glossip*, be able to refine the instant of death? We can therefore say that the same temporal perfectibility of capital punishment continues to be posited, as an argument against its cruelty, from *Resweber* to *Baze* and *Glossip*. And the same frustration concerning the inability to bring that debate to a close infects not only questions attending this or that method of execution but also the status of the death penalty vis-à-vis the Eighth Amendment. When Stevens concurs with the majority to reject the *Baze* petitioners' arguments against the cruelty of Kentucky's concoction of sodium thiopental, pancuronium bromide, and potassium chloride, he nevertheless offers this wistful assessment: "When we granted certiorari in this case, I assumed that our decision would bring the debate about lethal injection as a method of execution to a close. It now seems clear that it will not. . . . Instead of ending the controversy, I am now convinced that this case will generate debate not only about the constitutionality of the three-drug protocol . . . but also about the justification for the death penalty itself" (*Baze*, 71).

The next important case after *Kemmler* was *Weems*, in 1910. It is, of course, a strange bedfellow to those capital cases, for it is not about the death penalty; however it is all about time and the possibility of pain that attends the duration of a punishment. In fact, it is striking that the Supreme Court allows the cruelty of pain, which *Wilkerson* and *Kemmler* presumed to understand as the barbarisms of torture or other physical punishment, to apply to debate concerning the length of a prison sentence: fifteen years hard labor for defrauding the government of 612 pesos (in the Philippines, then under US jurisdiction). What introduces discussion of cruelty is the fact of the sentence being *cadena temporal*, which meant that Weems would have to spend all his *time* in chains, and he indeed argued that "the cruelty of pain" might therefore obtain. But it also seems that cruel pain was necessarily implied by long time, so that the Eighth Amendment question could not *not* be addressed once it had been introduced: "It may be that even the cruelty of pain is not omitted. He must bear a chain night and day. He is condemned to painful as well as hard labor" (*Weems*, 366). According to that reasoning the chain might be cruel because it has to be worn *all the time*. Thus, although the majority cannot determine the "exact measure" of "what painful labor may mean" (366), it is inexorably drawn into a conceptual overlapping of the duration of the sentence and the pain caused by the chain, and, as a result, into adjudicating the difference between Eighth Amendment claims relating to methods of execution and the more general precept of a punishment that "should be graduated and proportioned to the offense" (367). In other words, the "cruelty" referred to in the Eighth Amendment henceforth evokes at one and the same time the extremity of punishment and the duration of punishment. As a result, the paradigm for both is taken, as if automatically, to be the death penalty.

By returning to the "difficulty" of *Wilkerson*, *Weems* is unable to extricate itself from the quandary presented by that case: "What constitutes a cruel and unusual punishment has not been exactly decided. It has been said that ordinarily the terms imply something inhuman and barbarous—torture and the like" (368), yet "no case has occurred in this court which has called for an exhaustive definition" (369). The majority therefore seeks guidance in an 1866 Massachusetts case (*Pervear*) before finding itself required to return to *Wilkerson* and *Kemmler*, citing in particular the passages I have quoted. And if case law is lacking, "the law writers" are similarly "indefinite" (371) telling us that the Eighth Amendment language comes from the 1688 English Bill of Rights relating to "such violent proceedings as had taken place in England in the arbitrary reigns of some of the Stuarts," which "would seem to be wholly unnecessary in a free government" (ibid.).

If the majority finds it necessary to focus on the interpretation of the amendment, that focus becomes all the more sharp in the dissent of Justice Edward Douglass White, who considers that "it is impossible to fix with precision the meaning" (385) of the Eighth Amendment, but that that meaning does not sustain its being applied to the case of *Weems*. His reasoning, based on examination of English practice and the bills of rights or constitutional previsions of states such as Virginia, relies precisely on the absence of blood in *Weems*, for he understands the word "cruel" in the Eighth Amendment to refer explicitly to "the atrocious, sanguinary, and inhuman punishments which had been inflicted in the past upon the persons of criminals" (390), and to forbid only "unnecessary bodily suffering through a resort to inhuman methods for causing bodily torture" (409). For that reason, White determines, the death penalty itself, previously imposed by cruel means, survived as a punishment once those cruel means of execution came to be rejected: "To illustrate. Death was a well-known method of punishment, prescribed by law, and it was, of course, painful, and in that sense was cruel. But the infliction of the punishment was clearly not prohibited by the word 'cruel,' although that word manifestly was intended to forbid the resort to barbarous and unnecessary methods of bodily torture in executing even the penalty of death" (ibid.).

The presumption of a death penalty whose punishment would consist in nothing more than death is later made explicit, in *Resweber*, the 1947 case of a Louisiana man whose first electrocution failed because of problems with the machinery, and who therefore argued that having to face the process a second time would be cruel and unusual. The Court rejected his petition, finding that "even the fact that petitioner has already been subjected to a current of electricity does not make his subsequent execution any more cruel in the constitutional sense than any other execution" (464).

The majority repeats the presumption of previous cases, that "the cruelty against which the Constitution protects a convicted man is cruelty inherent in the method of punishment, not *the necessary suffering involved in any method employed to extinguish life humanely.* The fact that an unforeseeable accident prevented the prompt consummation of the sentence cannot, it seems to us, add an element of cruelty to a subsequent execution" (ibid., my emphasis). According to that logic, suffering is "necessary" in any execution, which brings the question back to a quantification based on time: Prompt consummation of the sentence is humane, as is accidental nonpromptness; only purposeful nonpromptness would be unconstitutional.

However, the notable dissent of four justices argues otherwise, entertaining precisely a difference between instantaneous death and death meted out in installments: "The contrast is that between instantaneous death and death by installments. Electrocution, when instantaneous, *can* be inflicted by a state in conformity with due process of law" (474). Because *Kemmler* had determined the constitutionality of the electric chair as more humane than previous methods by reason of its instantaneity, the dissenting justices found that the constitutional standard failed once the instantaneity of execution was again put in question: "The all-important consideration is that the execution shall be *so instantaneous and substantially painless that the punishment shall be reduced, as nearly as possible, to no more than that of death itself.* Electrocution has been approved only in a form that eliminates suffering" (ibid., my emphasis). That formulation concerning *a death penalty that involves no punishment other than death* has echoed throughout the ensuing seventy years. But however much it might represent a laudable ideal, it is fraught with ambiguities. The determination of the dissenting justices in *Resweber* was based on their reading of the Louisiana law that prescribed and defined electrocution as "causing to pass through the body of the person convicted a current of electricity of sufficient intensity to cause death, and the application and *continuance of such current* through the body of the person convicted *until such person is dead*" (474–75, my emphasis), a definition that was for them restricted to a single uninterrupted event. Yet even a surface reading of that statute uncovers the relative sense of instantaneity, indeed the necessity of duration involved in "the application and continuance of such current . . . until such person is dead." That relativity—of a continuous instant—carries over into the dissenting justices' use of the term "so instantaneous . . . that," which we have to read as "as instantaneous as we can make it," a formula that carries with it the presumption and expectation of a better, more perfected technology waiting always around the corner.

A different version of the temporal quandary pervades the reasoning that brings the dissent to its conclusion:

> If the state officials deliberately and intentionally had placed the relator in the electric chair five times and, each time, had applied electric current to his body in a manner not sufficient, until the final time, to kill him, such a form of torture would rival that of burning at the stake. Although the failure of the first attempt, in the present case, was unintended, the reapplication of the electric current will be intentional. How many deliberate and intentional reapplications of electric current does it take to produce a cruel, unusual and unconstitutional punishment? While five applications would be more cruel and unusual than one, the uniqueness of the present case demonstrates that, today, two separated applications are sufficiently "cruel and unusual" to be prohibited. If five attempts would be "cruel and unusual," it would be difficult to draw the line between two, three, four and five. It is not difficult, however, as we here contend, to draw the line between the one continuous application prescribed by statute and any other application of the current. (476)

The number five is arbitrarily chosen in order to take our imagination back to a death sentence—burning at the stake—in which the time of execution is extended so far that it constitutes torture and barbarity. The stake remains the figure for time-extended execution from *Kemmler* (446) through *Resweber* to *Glossip*, where Justice Sotomayor, in dissenting, considered that the Court "leaves petitioners exposed to what may well be the chemical equivalent of being burned at the stake" (Sotomayor dissenting in *Glossip*, 2). In contrast, at the positive, enlightened and progressive end of the scale, in 1947, there is an instantaneous execution, represented since 1890 and *Kemmler* by electrocution. But once that execution fails, and has to be repeated, we necessarily head back down the road toward barbarism. One might imagine a progressive scale where hanging corresponded to two attempts at electrocution, beheading to three, garroting to four, and so on.

Wilkerson, *Kemmler*, and *Resweber* come in this way to constitute something of a holy trinity of Supreme Court decisions concerning the Eighth Amendment. When Ruth Bader Ginsburg, joined by Justice Souter, dissents in *Baze* in 2008, she notes that those three cases are all that American jurisprudence has to lean on to determine the cruelty, or not, of a particular method of execution, but that "no clear standard for determining the constitutionality of a method of execution emerges from these decisions" (*Baze*,

115). And indeed, arguments in *Baze* will show, in one sense, how little has been resolved in the 130 years following *Wilkerson*. What has changed radically however, is that the electric chair and other methods that were at the center of the debate from 1879 to 1947 and beyond, have been replaced by lethal injection and by its attendant new temporal order. That new order might be called *machinic* mechanics: Methods of execution that were, perhaps less and less, but still unavoidably, reliant upon human competence—the skill of the beheader, the hangman, or the rifleman—are replaced by a fluid mechanics, whose technologies of flow were of course already implied by the application of an electric *current*, but which are even more strikingly in force once it is a matter of drugs that course in concert with the natural circulation of the blood. When properly executed, death by lethal injection will supposedly have the natural time of the body; it will be a death brought about in concert with the fluid time of blood. How that indeed functions in conceptual terms will be analyzed in Chapter 3.

However, that new order is in question in *Baze* to the extent that the petitioners return to the risks of human error; they try, at least implicitly, to keep lethal injection in the same "barbarous" company as preceding methods of execution. For the majority, the standard that was progressively met by firing squad and by electrocution has been refined as perfectly as is currently possible within the death penalty's constitutional parameters: *Gregg* has ruled the death penalty constitutional, and it therefore "necessarily follows that there must be a means of carrying it out. Some risk of pain is inherent in any method of execution—no matter how humane—if only from the prospect of error in following the required procedure. It is clear, then, that the Constitution does not demand the avoidance of all risk of pain in carrying out executions" (*Baze*, 47). But if some pain over and above that required for the mere extinguishment of life is permissible, it is also clear that, beyond a certain, undefined level, pain becomes constitutionally impermissible.[9] The petitioners in *Baze* argue in turn that the procedures followed by the state of Kentucky create such an "unnecessary risk" of pain (47). The risk is seen to derive from the specifics of administering Kentucky's three-drug protocol, specifically that the first drug to be administered, sodium thiopental, will not sufficiently sedate to prevent the acknowledged pain of the second and third drugs (pancurium bromide and potassium chloride). The majority's rejection of that argument and acceptance of the protocol will lead to the new challenge of *Glossip*, once supplies of sodium thiopental dry up and Oklahoma decides to substitute, for that barbiturate, the milder sedative midazolam.

The matter of pain-inducing time, or duration, does not appear to be at issue in *Baze*, but it is implied first by the question of whether the barbiturate will do its job within the period allocated before the second and third drugs flow; in other words, whether the procedure will have to be prolonged, and extend beyond its planned time. Related to that, the question of time is implied in the second place by questions concerning how the required state of sedation is determined, including "rough-and-ready tests for checking consciousness—calling the inmate's name, brushing his eyelashes, or presenting him with strong, noxious odors" (*Baze*, 60), tests that introduce delay and the possibility of human error. More important, however, the fact of the three-drug protocol returns us to the idea of an execution that consists of not one event but a sequence of three events whose enumerative logic constitutes, by definition, delay and a division of the instant. Though the petitioners do not make that point, their suggestion that a single drug would be preferable can be understood to imply it. For, however smoothly the process may be administered, we risk returning to the dilemma, posed in the *Resweber* dissent, of drawing the line between one application and multiple applications of a penalty. The differences are of course substantial between a "continuous" administering of three different drugs, and one versus two, three, four or five applications of electric current, but questions of what constitutes an instant, whether a continuity can remain instantaneous, and at what point the instant or the continuity should be considered to have been interrupted, are nevertheless reposed in stark profile.

When Ginsburg dissents in *Baze* and reviews the trinity of precedents available for ruling on the Eighth Amendment test regarding capital punishment, she emphasizes how "the age of the opinions limits their utility as an aid to resolution of the present controversy. . . . Wilkerson was decided 129 years ago, Kemmler 118 years ago, and Resweber 61 years ago. Whatever little light our prior method-of-execution cases might shed is thus dimmed by the passage of time" (*Baze*, 116). On one level Ginsburg's reference to the age of opinions and their corresponding limited utility is something of a heresy vis-à-vis the doctrine of precedent, since subsequent cases have continued to rely on those decisions. On the other hand, her comment focuses on how much presumptions concerning technological progress have informed interpretations of the Eighth Amendment and the application of the death penalty since 1879 (or indeed, since the 1791 Bill of Rights); and furthermore, how much the question of a time that produces pain overlaps with a different chronology, namely that implied by the doctrine of evolving standards of decency.

That doctrine—already presaged in *Kemmler*'s 1890 adoption of electrocution in order to reject the "barbarous" "dark ages"—was first expounded in *Trop* (1958), which held that loss of citizenship was too harsh a punishment for a soldier who deserted briefly in Morocco in 1944. The majority held in that case that the Eighth Amendment "must draw its meaning from the evolving standards of decency that mark the progress of a maturing society."[10] The relevance of the doctrine to capital punishment is already clear here, since the *Trop* majority begins by insisting that although capital punishment "cannot be said to violate the constitutional concept of cruelty . . . it is equally plain that the existence of the death penalty is not a license to the Government to devise any punishment short of death within the limit of its imagination" (*Trop*, 99). The *Trop* case will come into special focus through a series of decisions made over a twenty-year period between 1988 and 2008, which were also the years during which Justice Antonin Scalia emerged as the Court's most vocal—and often eloquent—exponent of an originalist understanding of the Constitution, an understanding with which the evolving standards doctrine is, at bottom, in contradiction. Simply put, for any absolute originalist, the Constitution functions as a timeless document that cannot be subject to standards that evolve over the years. In his rebuttal to Blackmun's *Callins* dissent, Scalia argues that Blackmun's quandaries have been "invented without benefit of any textual or historical support" (*Callins*, 1142), and that, if an electorate and its legislators judge that the death penalty is warranted, calling that judgment into question by "false, untextual, and unhistorical" (1143) means is impermissible. Paradoxically, that was Blackmun's very position in *Furman*, when he decided that his task was not to legislate (*Furman*, 410–11), but at the same time he was led to believe that our being "less barbaric than we were in 1879, or in 1890, or in 1910, or in 1947, or in 1958, or in 1963, or a year ago, in 1971, when Wilkerson, Kemmler, Weems, Francis, Trop, Rudolph, and McGautha were respectively decided" (410) necessarily reflects back on how to read the text of the Constitution.

For the *Trop* majority, the need for historical context is clear from the outset. The evolving standards doctrine is inextricably dependent on the idea that "the provisions of the Constitution are not timeworn adages or hollow shibboleths. They are vital, living principles" (*Trop*, 103). Tellingly, Blackmun's *Furman* dissent finds a similar inspiration in Thomas

Jefferson's oft-quoted 1810 letter to Samuel Kercheval regarding the
idea for regular review of the proposed Virginia constitution:

> Some men look at constitutions with sanctimonious reverence, and
> deem them like the ark of the covenant, too sacred to be touched.
> They ascribe to the men of the preceding age a wisdom more than
> human, and suppose what they did to be beyond amendment. I knew
> that age well; I belonged to it, and labored with it. It deserved well of
> its country. It was very like the present, but without the experience of
> the present; and forty years of experience in government is worth a
> century of book-reading; and this they would say to themselves were
> they to rise from the dead. . . . I know . . . that laws and institutions
> must go hand in hand with the progress of the human mind. As that
> becomes more developed, more enlightened, as new discoveries are
> made, new truths disclosed, and manners and opinions change with
> the change of circumstances, institutions must advance also, and
> keep pace with the times. We might as well require a man to wear
> still the coat which fitted him when a boy, as civilized society to
> remain ever under the regimen of their barbarous ancestors.
> (Quoted in *Furman*, 414)

References to evolving standards thus became a staple of death penalty jurisprudential discussions, and the debate consistently evokes the pressure
that such a doctrine puts on the Constitution. Dissenting in *McGautha* in
1971, Justice Douglas complained of the irreconcilability of the Court's
"wooden position" with the "evolving gloss of civilized standards," finding that "the vestiges of law enshrined today have roots in barbaric procedures"; concurring in *Kennedy* in 2008, Justice Kennedy affirmed that
"evolving standards of decency must embrace and express respect for the
dignity of the person" and that "when the law punishes by death, it risks
its own descent into brutality"; and that same year in *Baze*, Justice Stevens
stated that "our society has moved away from public and painful retribution towards ever more humane forms of punishment. In an attempt to
bring executions in line with our evolving standards of decency, we have
adopted increasingly less painful methods of execution, and then declared
previous methods barbaric and archaic."[11] Different brethren weighed in
consistently, especially in the period 1988–2008, over the point to which
standards had or had not evolved and the role of the Court in determining
where to situate evolutionary progress at this or that moment in time.

The most relevant cases were *Thompson* (1988), *Stanford* (1989), *Atkins*
(2002), *Roper* (2005), and *Kennedy* (2008).[12] By 2008 the Court seemed

irrevocably to have decided that American society henceforth found the death penalty to be cruel and unusual punishment if applied to a juvenile or a mentally retarded person, or for the crime of rape. But the progression toward that new standard was far from uniform and uninterrupted. Nevertheless, the opinion that has so far triumphed, is, as the language of *Trop* made explicit, *progressist* or perhaps activist. It gives the Court the right to determine the maturity of society at a given point in time. Writing for the majority in *Roper*, Kennedy assumes that right without question: "the Constitution contemplates that in the end *our own judgment will be brought to bear* on the question of the acceptability of the death penalty under the Eighth Amendment" (563, my emphasis). And that statement is already a reaffirmation, for Kennedy is returning in *Roper* to a principle established by a 6–3 majority three years earlier, in *Atkins*—concerning not a juvenile but a "mentally retarded criminal"—and before that, to the judgment of a decidedly more liberal Supreme Court in *Coker* (1977), which prohibited the death penalty for the crime of rape, which is the question again before the Court in *Kennedy*.[13]

In *Roper*, Stevens, joined by Ginsburg, saw fit to include a single-paragraph concurring opinion that did nothing more than drive home the principle of the sovereign judgment of the Court:

> Perhaps even more important than our specific holding today is our reaffirmation of the basic principle that informs the Court's interpretation of the Eighth Amendment. If the meaning of that Amendment had been frozen when it was originally drafted, it would impose no impediment to the execution of 8-year-old children today. . . . The evolving standards of decency that have driven our construction of this critically important part of the Bill of Rights foreclose any such reading of the Amendment. In the best tradition of the common law, the pace of that evolution is a matter for continuing debate; but that our understanding of the Constitution does change from time to time has been settled since John Marshall breathed life into its text. (587)

That opinion is shared by Justice O'Connor, even as she dissents from the judgment for reasons explained below: "It is by now beyond serious dispute that the Eighth Amendment's prohibition of 'cruel and unusual punishments' is not a static command. Its mandate would be little more than a dead letter today if it barred only those sanctions like the execution of children under the age of seven that civilized society had already repudiated in 1791" (589). The anathema of executing children as young as seven or eight functions as the bellwether assertion of societal evolution.

No member of the Court is about to argue in 1988, or in 2005, that the good citizens of this or that state may in their wisdom perform such a barbarism as was permitted when the Eighth Amendment was adopted in 1791. *Stanford* returns to that standard in 1989, and indeed it is Scalia who notes that "the common law set the rebuttable presumption of incapacity to commit any felony at the age of 14, and theoretically permitted capital punishment to be imposed on anyone over the age of 7" (368), on his way to accepting that the amendment has rightly been interpreted with the flexibility advocated in *Gregg*: "They are correct in asserting that this Court has 'not confined the prohibition embodied in the Eighth Amendment to barbarous methods that were generally outlawed in the 18th century,' but instead has interpreted the Amendment 'in a flexible and dynamic manner'" (*Stanford*, 369). Of course, as I will explain further, the focus on the unacceptability of executing a child does not represent contemporary horror at such treatment of the innocent without also implying a relation between ontogenetic and phylogenetic maturation: The idea that a child is considered too young to be executed because he or she has not yet reached the age of reason and responsibility is a function of the supposition that humankind in general, or a given society within it, has matured beyond the barbarisms of two centuries ago. It is unclear whether that vaguely reciprocal relation between the evolving criminal responsibility of an individual human and evolving standards of decency of humankind is registered by those who, on both sides of the originalist debate, make reference to that element of 1791 law, but it is possible to interpret the consistency of the reference as an unease concerning where, along the jurisprudential evolutionary scale, this or that state electorate or legislature resides, and concerning how it is that serious discrepancies exist between the standards obtaining in one populace and another.

In 1988, therefore, in *Thompson*, first of that twenty-year series of cases just mentioned, a 5–3 majority found, by means of an arithmetic that the dissenters would consider rather dubious, that a person who committed murder at the age of fifteen could not be executed. The arithmetic consisted in counting eighteen states that did not permit imposition of the death penalty for juveniles, and adding to those eighteen another fourteen states that had no death penalty at all, to constitute a majority of thirty-two out of fifty states. According to the *Thompson* majority, that indicated a national trend against capital punishment for minors, and by extension an indication of the point to which standards of decency had evolved. Sandra Day O'Connor concurred, but added an opinion that challenged her colleagues' arithmetic and seriously questioned whether any satisfactory determination of where American society stood on executing a juvenile had in fact been made. Her translation of the *Trop* doctrine into that of a "national consensus" may have removed from it the explicit temporal terms of *"evolving* standards . . . the *progress* of a *maturing* society" (my emphasis), but the substance of her dissent reaffirmed her resistance to progressist assumptions, concluding that "the ultimate moral issue at stake in the constitution question [is] to be addressed in the first instance by those best suited to do so, the people's elected representatives" (*Thompson,* 858–59). In that way she rejected the notion of a teleological, linear chronology of maturation by asserting that whereas American society appeared to have matured beyond capital punishment in general in 1972, it clearly returned, or regressed back to it, starting in 1976. As a result she would give no blanket approval to the new standard and a year later she herself effectively "regressed" by joining, in *Stanford,* a majority (5–4) that rejected a similar petition for two men sentenced for crimes committed when they were aged sixteen and seventeen. The same objection to the Court's assessment of society's standards would also lead her to dissent in *Roper* (2005), by which point, however, the Court had swung back (5–4), seemingly definitively, against the death penalty for persons under the age of eighteen.

A much starker opposition to the progressist majority in *Roper* was expressed by Scalia. In his *Thompson* dissent he had already objected that, in his view, even granting a certain evolution, society cannot be said to have progressed to the point where it prohibits the death penalty for a juvenile *in all cases,* which is effectively what he found the Court to be doing by accepting the petitioner's argument. He then went on to question the principle of the evolving standards doctrine in terms to which he would return in subsequent cases:

> Of course, the risk of assessing evolving standards is that it is all too easy to believe that evolution has culminated in one's own views. To avoid this danger, we have, when making such an assessment in prior cases, looked for objective signs of how today's society views a particular punishment. . . . The most reliable objective signs consist of the legislation that the society has enacted. It will rarely, if ever, be the case that the Members of this Court will have a better sense of the evolution in views of the American people than do their elected representatives. (*Thompson,* 865)

By that reasoning, since Oklahoma had enacted legislation allowing a capital sentence for a minor, and since there was no federal legislation counteracting Oklahoma's law, the law of that state should stand. Scalia considered the majority's interpretation of the doctrine to represent but a tiny sample of the socius, nothing more than five brethren constituting "a majority of the small and unrepresentative segment of our society that sits on this Court. On its face, the phrase 'cruel and unusual punishments' limits the evolving standards appropriate for our consideration to those entertained by the society, rather than those dictated by our personal consciences" (873).

Thanks to O'Connor's swing vote, Scalia's minority opinion became that of the majority in *Stanford* (1989) (rejecting the Eighth Amendment defense for crimes committed at sixteen or seventeen years, in contrast to that committed by a fifteen-year-old in *Thompson*). Writing that majority opinion, Scalia repeats his view that "in determining whether a punishment violates evolving standards of decency, this Court looks not to its own subjective conceptions, but, rather, to the conceptions of modern American society as reflected by objective evidence" (*Stanford*, 361, 362). The majority in *Thompson*, and the minority in *Stanford*, he declares, were asking the Court's members to act, not as "judges of the law" but as "a committee of philosopher-kings" (379). The only means to avoid such an undemocratic exercise of power is to allow any decision concerning what is cruel and unusual to be made by "the citizenry of the United States. It is they, not we, who must be persuaded. For as we stated earlier, our job is to identify the 'evolving standards of decency'; to determine, not what they should be, but what they are. We have no power under the Eighth Amendment to substitute our belief in the scientific evidence for the society's apparent skepticism" (378).

When Scalia is subsequently required to suffer the rebuke of a new majority, first in *Atkins* and then again in *Roper*, he is barely able to contain his ire, asserting that "*Stanford v. Kentucky* should be deemed no longer controlling on this issue" (*Roper*, 574). In his *Atkins* dissent he intones: "Today's decision is the pinnacle of our Eighth Amendment death-is-different jurisprudence. Not only does it, like all of that jurisprudence, find no support in the text or history of the Eighth Amendment; it does not even have support in current social attitudes regarding the conditions that render an otherwise just death penalty inappropriate. Seldom has an opinion of this Court rested so obviously upon nothing but the personal views of its members" (*Atkins*, 337–38). He proceeds to list step by step what he considers to be the progressively imposed impediments to capital punishment, steps that amount to its "incremental abolition by this Court" (353). Three years later, in *Roper*, his frustration leads him to suggest that his brethren have abandoned, rather than interpreted the Constitution:

What a mockery today's opinion makes of Hamilton's expectation, announcing the Court's conclusion that the meaning of our Constitution has changed over the past 15 years—not, mind you, that this Court's decision 15 years ago was *wrong*, but that the Constitution *has changed*. . . . Worse still, the Court says in so many words that what our people's laws say about the issue does not, in the last analysis, matter. . . . On the evolving-standards hypothesis, the only legitimate function of this Court is to identify a moral consensus of the American people. By what conceivable warrant can nine lawyers presume to be the authoritative conscience of the Nation? (*Roper*, 608, 616)

Between the view that the Court's "own judgment will be brought to bear on the question of the acceptability of the death penalty under the Eighth Amendment" and the idea that such a view means setting aside the Constitution, the gulf is indeed wide. My interest is by no means in trying to adjudicate between those opposing positions. Rather, I would have us reflect on the effect of a divergent set of temporal frames for the evolving standards of a maturing society on the conception of a *penalty*, particularly the death penalty, on its time and its attendant *pain*. In other words, as I suggested earlier, how should we understand the temporal modalities of a death penalty that is rejected for eight-year-olds but accepted for sixteen-, seventeen-, or eighteen-year-olds as a question of ontogenetic maturity, against the backdrop of a problematic assessment of the phylogenetic maturity of American society, especially when a judge who argues that the relevant fifteen-year-old is mature enough seems simultaneously to argue that the relevant society isn't? On one level there is nothing incongruous to be found there, and indeed the incommensurabilities between ontogenetic and phylogenetic evolution are obvious. However, when a court decides, based on where a society stands on the question, whether to execute a juvenile, a strange intersection of competing temporalities is at work: a juridical decision is made concerning the termination of life, that is to say the preempting of the maturing process of an individual, based on an assessment of the moral or "criminal" maturity of that individual, but that assessment itself relies on determining the current point within the evolutionary progress, or the current point of maturity, of the society to which that individual belongs.[14]

According to the logic of evolving standards as expressed in *Thompson*, *Stanford*, *Atkins*, and *Roper*, the juvenile lives if the society has matured or evolved enough to think he or she is not mature enough. Yet the converse is not necessarily true: if that individual is executed, it cannot be objectively determined whether it is because the society has sufficiently evolved to decide that that should be the case, or because it has not sufficiently evolved to decide that that should *not* be the case, and therefore continues to make its decision in favor of the death penalty from some regressive punitive standpoint. Certainly, the fact that the doctrine of evolving standards is consistently evoked as a function of progress away from barbarism—you can no longer hang, draw, and quarter; you can no longer execute an eight-year-old; you can no longer strip someone of citizenship for desertion; you cannot execute minors or the intellectually impaired—suggests that the more evolved and mature a society, the more permissive it will be. And indeed, Scalia does not appear to contest that, merely arguing that the Court must not get ahead of the electorate.

Yet that intersection of different scales of evolution or maturity is complicated further. As long as the decision is made on the basis of an Eighth Amendment defense—which is the case for *Thompson*, *Stanford*, *Atkins*, and *Roper*—it necessarily concerns, as we have already seen, the duration of punishment as a function of pain. That would be, in the first instance, because, as I maintain in general here, there is no watertight separation between the concepts of duration and of punishment. But a more specific reason is this: Though it may appear, in cases of juveniles or the intellectually impaired, simply to be a matter of whether certain classes of persons should be subject to a judicial system's harshest penalty, Eighth Amendment death penalty jurisprudence from *Wilkerson* to *Baze* consistently makes the fact of capital punishment a question of suffering understood as pain endured. By being society's harshest punishment the death penalty represents what is most to be *endured*, and we need to understand that word not just in the sense of the passivity of suffering, something one has to undergo, but also in the sense that one suffers, through one's suffering, the passage of time. Hence the evolving standards doctrine as a function of Eighth Amendment death penalty cases apposes the long, gradual, even interminable evolution of a society toward maturity and the concentrated, ever briefer instant of execution. On the face of it a long evolved, mature society wants an ever briefer instant of execution; and, for juveniles and the mentally impaired, it wants an instant so brief as to no longer exist. Yet at least part of the reason for wanting such an instant not to exist for certain classes of person is the idea that such an instant, however brief, remains interminable and immeasurable—because unbearable, intolerable, indeed insufferable.

What does it even mean, finally, for a society's standards of decency to evolve, for a society to progress toward maturity? How could we define or describe the temporality of such progress, its pace or rhythm, progressions and regressions, let alone measure it? How would we know what point along the road to maturity we had reached at any given moment? For the presumption that each new step represents progress comes from a type of retrovision, a tautological form of hindsight: We don't do it any longer, and time has moved forward, so we must have evolved.

Within that framework, what does it mean that what defines a constitutionally permissible amount of pain evolves over time? Is that a physiological, psychological, sociological, or moral judgment? Now that we are more mature, do we feel pain more keenly, our own pain or that of others? Does our valuing life more, or expecting it to be better and longer—if that is what this progress means—determine our level of evolution? Have we now arrived at a more evolved means of relating crime to punishment (indeed, should we even be discussing questions of punishment without examining, just as microscopically, the whole conceptual framework within which we define, and change our definitions of crime)?

Further, how are we to compare the progress from the methods cited in *Wilkerson*—disemboweling, beheading, quartering, public dissection, burning alive—to that of the late nineteenth to the twenty-first centuries, during which time, as Justice Roberts presumes in *Baze*, we have progressed via "the firing squad, hanging, the electric chair, and the gas chamber . . . to more humane methods, culminating in today's consensus on lethal injection?" (62) How much more evolved or mature is a society that exchanges the stake for the gallows, than one that exchanges the electric chair for lethal injection? Should those examples of progress be somehow correlated with how many years it took a given society to reach each point? Or somehow factored into a logarithm of accelerating evolution? Were we to have such determinations at our disposal, could we then calculate how long it will be before a state governor—just as the governor of New York did prior to *Kemmler*—calls for a less barbarous means of execution than lethal injection? For should we not presume, according to the logic of the doctrine, that such a solution waits around some future corner? Should we not imagine—on the basis of the evolving standards doctrine—a future moment when lethal injection appears as barbarous as quartering, or when the difference between it and still to be invented methods of execution is like quibbling over the stake versus disemboweling versus public flaying or dissection?

Indeed, for this is where the logic of evolving standards finally leads us, is the future to be imagined that of a society evolved or mature enough to abolish the death penalty? Is that the progress toward some ultimate or ideal maturity—let's call it "adulthood"—that American society, at least since *Wilkerson*, or since *Trop*, is currently striving for? If we look at *Kennedy* as the culminating case in the twenty-year period during which these issues were debated and decided, societal progress toward no death penalty at all does seem to be what is implied. In that case the Court struck down (5–4), on Eighth Amendment grounds, a Louisiana law imposing the death penalty for rape of a child. Tellingly perhaps, Scalia, while joining the dissent written by Justice Alito—repeating the argument that the national consensus presumed by the majority does not exist—did not add this time an opinion of his own. However, when Louisiana asked for a rehearing on the grounds that the majority should have taken military law into account, and the majority rejected that request, Scalia felt obliged to add a statement that again outlined his position in the strongest terms:

> The majority opinion, after an unpersuasive attempt to show that a consensus against the penalty existed, in the end came down to this: The Constitution contemplates that in the end our own judgment will be brought to bear on the question of the acceptability of the death penalty under the Eighth Amendment. . . . The proposed Eighth Amendment would have been laughed to scorn if it had read "no criminal penalty shall be imposed which the Supreme Court deems unacceptable." But that is what the majority opinion said.[15]

In Scalia's eyes, evolving standards has come to mean the incremental abolition that he feared six years earlier in *Atkins*. And there is much in the majority opinion in *Kennedy* to support that view, which, as I have just suggested, cannot not be the teleology of the doctrine. In the first place the death penalty is understood to include its own retrograde logic, the idea that capital punishment provides by definition a downhill slope away from well evolved decency: "When the law punishes by death, it risks its own sudden descent into brutality, transgressing the constitutional commitment to decency and restraint" (*Kennedy*, 420). For that reason much of the majority's argument turns around the view that letting this sentence stand amounts to an expansion of the death penalty, whereas social evolution has been proceeding precisely in the opposite direction: "Evolving standards of decency that mark the progress of a maturing society counsel us to be most hesitant before interpreting the Eighth Amendment to allow the extension of the death penalty, a hesitation that has special force where no life was taken in the commission of the crime" (435). But that is to deny the evidence introduced by O'Connor, in *Thompson*, of nonlinear progress toward maturity, and the dissent here argues without difficulty that there is widespread increase in legislative action in favor of retributive penalties for sexual crimes. It is therefore clear from the conclusion of Justice Kennedy's majority opinion that, once the Eighth Amendment is informed by the doctrine of evolving standards, the risk that the death penalty will provoke a "descent into brutality" has as its converse risk—or ideal outcome, depending on one's standpoint—a moral ascent into abolition: "Our determination that there is a consensus against the death penalty for child rape raises the question whether the Court's own institutional position and its holding will have the effect of blocking further or later consensus in favor of the penalty from developing. The Court, it will be argued, by the act of addressing the constitutionality of the death penalty, intrudes upon the consensus-making process" (446). But, the majority argues—in terms that allow the full implications of an incremental abolition to be conveyed—that is to misunderstand the doctrine, its effect on the Eighth Amendment, and by extension on the death penalty:

> These concerns overlook the meaning and full substance of the established proposition that the Eighth Amendment is defined by "the evolving standards of decency that mark the progress of a maturing society." . . . This principle requires that use of the death penalty be restrained. The rule of evolving standards of decency *with specific marks on the way to full progress and mature judgment* means that resort to the penalty must be reserved for the worst of crimes and limited in its instances of application. In most cases justice is not better served by terminating the life of the perpetrator rather than confining him and preserving the possibility that he and the system will find ways to allow him to understand the enormity of his offense. (446–47, my emphasis)

For now, therefore, the only capital crime will be murder, but *Kennedy*'s marking a point along the line of progress must henceforth be understood as one milestone "on the way to full progress and mature judgment," and it logically signals ahead toward absolute abolition.

Justice Clarence Thomas expresses that very fear, or suspicion, in his concurring opinion in *Baze*:

> It is not a little ironic—and telling—that lethal injection, hailed just a few years ago as the humane alternative in light of which every other method of execution was deemed an unconstitutional relic of the past, is the subject of today's challenge. It appears the Constitution is "evolving" even faster than I suspected. And it is obvious that, for

some who oppose capital punishment on policy grounds, the only
acceptable end point of the evolution is for this Court, in an exercise
of raw judicial power unsupported by the text or history of the
Constitution, or even by a contemporary moral consensus, to
strike down the death penalty as cruel and unusual in all circumstances. In the meantime, though, the next best option for those
seeking to abolish the death penalty is to embroil the States in
never-ending litigation concerning the adequacy of their execution
procedures. (104–5)

But he also points again to something that has been implicit or explicit in
much that I have already cited, namely the problem of determining which
segment of society—precisely which society—is to be taken into account
when deciding on evolving standards. What is the community to which
reference should be made? In *Thompson* and in *Stanford*, Scalia cites "elected
representatives" as well as "the citizenry of the United States," as opposed
to "the small and unrepresentative society that sits on this Court." Originalism therefore goes hand in hand with statism, or even nativism, in presuming an organic relation between a politically circumscribed community
and the laws that community enacts, which comes to be disturbed by the
edicts of a larger social body, such as the federated United States, not to
mention conventions developed on an international level.[16]

For if, by the time of *Baze* and *Glossip*, the very constitutionality of the
death penalty has, through Eighth Amendment jurisprudence, again become the issue, it is also the case, as we shall now see, that the decency of
the evolving standards doctrine has effectively been transformed from a
moral issue into a human right. Already in *Weems*, before the doctrine received the explicit form provided by *Trop*, there was agreement that the
Eighth Amendment "may therefore be progressive, and is not fastened to
the obsolete, but may acquire meaning as public opinion becomes enlightened by a humane justice" (*Weems*, 378). *Trop* itself made things abun-
dantly clear by invoking the virtual unanimity of the "civilized nations of
the world" against imposing statelessness as a punishment. More generally, it stated: "The basic concept underlying the Eighth Amendment is
nothing less than *the dignity of man*. While the State has the power to punish, the Amendment stands to assure that this power be exercised within
the limits of civilized standards" (*Trop*, 100, my emphasis). Almost a century
after *Weems*, Kennedy will opine that "evolving standards of decency must
embrace and express respect for the dignity of the person" (*Kennedy*, 420);
and later, that "it is an established principle that decency, in its essence,

presumes respect for the individual" (435). By means of reference to principles of humaneness, human dignity and civilization, the doctrine and the
amendment borrow, explicitly or implicitly, from the discourses of the European Enlightenment, and by extension from the discourse on rights
that issued from the Enlightenment, particularly by means of the American and French revolutions. There is nothing unusual about that, and the
respective dates of the French Declaration of the Rights of Man in 1789,
and the American adoption of the Bill of Rights in 1791 serve to confirm
the link. But linking the Eighth Amendment to human rights internation-
alizes it, and necessarily exposes American jurisprudence to the test of
sovereignty vis-à-vis standards determined by other countries, or indeed
by humanity in general. I bring that question into the picture I am drawing here in order to inscribe the American practice of the death penalty—
at least from an Eighth Amendment perspective—within the timeframe
of a post-Enlightenment Europe, and to announce the particular contex-
tual comparison that I will emphasize in my next chapter with the history
of capital punishment in France. But it is more immediately relevant, with
respect to the cases just discussed, to the applicability or inapplicability of
international standards of decency and humane progress to America's death
penalty. *Trop*'s phrase "dignity of man" is explicitly evoking a human right,
not one limited to this or that restricted *sociua* within a given country.
However contentious its presumption be that the dignity of man and of
civilization has been determined by the European Enlightenment, it nevertheless implies that any consensus concerning standards should be universal, and thereby implicates the United States in a worldwide presumption
of progress beyond the cruel practices of a sort of foreign yesteryear.

For the majorities in *Thompson*, *Atkins*, and *Roper*, such international
comparisons have been a constant of the evolving standards doctrine. One
could indeed go back as far as *Wilkerson* for deference to practices of other
nations, for that decision seeks not to exceed "corresponding rules [that]
prevail in other countries" (*Wilkerson*, 99). *Thompson* will similarly attempt
to remain "consistent with the views expressed by . . . other nations that
share the Anglo-American heritage, and by the leading members of the
Western European Community" (*Thompson*, 815); and *Atkins* will note that
"within the world community, the imposition of the death penalty for
crimes committed by mentally retarded offenders is overwhelmingly dis-
approved" (*Atkins*, 317n). *Roper* therefore takes it as read, stating that "at
least from the time of the Court's decision in *Trop*, the Court has referred
to the laws of other countries and to international authorities as instructive for its interpretation of the Eighth Amendment's prohibition" (*Roper*,

575), and citing *Atkins, Thompson, Enmund,* and *Coker.*[17] The majority opinion adds to its argument by referring to the United Nations Convention
on the Rights of the Child (ratified by the whole world except for the United
States and Somalia), and *amicus* briefs by persons or organizations including the European Union, the Human Rights Committee of the Bar of
England and Wales, the American Convention on Human Rights, and
the African Charter on the Rights and Welfare of the Child. Further, the
opinion states: "only seven countries other than the United States have
executed juvenile offenders since 1990: Iran, Pakistan, Saudi Arabia, Yemen,
Nigeria, the Democratic Republic of Congo, and China. Since then each
of these countries has either abolished capital punishment for juveniles or
made public disavowal of the practice," which allows it to conclude that
"the United States now stands alone in a world that has turned its face
against the juvenile death penalty" (577). That same opinion, however, acknowledges the objections that will be made to such internationalist presumptions by appearing to forestall them with the conciliatory remark at
its conclusion: "Not the least of the reasons we honor the Constitution,
then, is because we know it to be our own. It does not lessen our fidelity to
the Constitution or our pride in its origins to acknowledge that the express affirmation of certain fundamental rights by other nations and peoples
simply underscores the centrality of those same rights within our own heritage of freedom" (578).

Perhaps predictably, then, Scalia is as consistent in dissenting from that
view as the Court is in affirming it. In *Thompson* he considers the "plurality's reliance upon Amnesty International's account of what it pronounces
to be civilized standards of decency in other countries" to be "totally inappropriate as a means of establishing the fundamental beliefs of this Nation. That 40% of our States do not rule out capital punishment for
15-year-old felons is determinative of the question before us here, even if
that position contradicts the uniform view of the rest of the world. We must
never forget that it is a Constitution for the United States of America that
we are expounding" (*Thompson,* 878). While conceding that "the practices
of other nations, particularly other democracies, can be relevant to determining whether a practice uniform among our people is not merely an historical accident," what counts is "a settled consensus among our own
people" (ibid.). Similarly, in *Roper,* where his position is repeated in increasingly adamant, and impatient terms: "The Court thus proclaims itself sole
arbiter of our Nation's moral standards—and in the course of discharging
that awesome responsibility purports to take guidance from the views of
foreign courts and legislatures. Because I do not believe that the meaning

of our Eighth Amendment, any more than the meaning of other provisions of our Constitution, should be determined by *the subjective views of five Members of this Court and likeminded foreigners*, I dissent" (*Roper*, 608, my emphasis). Decrying the fact "the views of other countries and the so-called international community take center stage" (622), Scalia insists that the premise that "American law should conform to the laws of the rest of the world—ought to be rejected out of hand" (624).

Scalia is right to point to the selective invoking of foreign examples by the Court. Indeed, there is something of a converse tradition, namely of making international comparisons precisely in order to reject "various barbarous and cruel punishments inflicted under the laws of some other countries," such as Thomas evokes, quoting an 1832 commentary, in his concurring *Baze* opinion (98). One might even surmise that the majority opinion in *Weems*, which introduced the terms of Eighth Amendment debate of the last hundred years or so, was in part formed in reaction to a "Spanish" punitive excessiveness that prevailed in the Philippines at the time of that case. Given those selective invocations—of foreign practices preferred when the comparison puts U.S. practice in a more punitive light, but rejected when other countries set a bad example—Scalia is able, as he does in *Roper*, to offer his brethren a simple choice between following or rejecting international precedents: "The Court's parting attempt to downplay the significance of its extensive discussion of foreign law is unconvincing. 'Acknowledgment' of foreign approval has no place in the legal opinion of this Court *unless it is part of the basis for the Court's judgment—* which is surely what it parades as today" (*Roper*, 628).

Now, on the one hand, debate concerning the relevance of international comparisons does not add anything to my foregoing analysis of evolving standards doctrine, and indeed what I have already advanced concerning the time of development of the relatively timeless document that is the Constitution. Appealing to standards set by other countries simply expands the context of that analysis, it would appear, in *spatial* rather than the *temporal* terms that are my emphasis here. On the other hand, however, that added context does mean that everything that has been said about the problematic functioning, and measurement, of standards of decency is further complicated once it is presumed that the United States is somehow maturing in parallel with at least some other countries, and with a supposed universal conception of both the human and the humane.

International comparisons are given special status when it comes to the English justice system from which U.S. jurisprudence has inherited most directly. The Supreme Court opinions relating to the Eighth Amendment that have been discussed so far often allude to origins of American jurisprudence in English law, notably the language of the Amendment itself that was borrowed from the English Bill of Rights of 1689. As the majority in *Kemmler* put it:

> The provision in reference to cruel and unusual punishments was taken from the well known act of parliament of 1688, entitled "An act for declaring the rights and liberties of the subject, and settling the succession of the Crown," in which, after rehearsing various grounds of grievance, and, among others, that "excessive bail hath been required of persons committed in criminal cases, to elude the benefit of the laws made for the liberty of the subjects, and excessive fines have been imposed, and illegal and cruel punishments inflicted," it is declared that "excessive bail ought not to be required, nor excessive fines imposed, nor cruel and unusual punishments inflicted." (*Kemmler*, 446)

And although *Trop* wrestles with "the exact scope of the constitutional phrase 'cruel and unusual,'" its majority is nevertheless confident "the basic policy reflected in these words is firmly established in the Anglo-American tradition of criminal justice. The phrase in our Constitution was taken directly from the English Declaration of Rights of 1688, and the principle it represents can be traced back to the Magna Carta" (*Trop*, 99–100). But already in *Weems* there is debate—worked through by the majority opinion with reference to "law writers" and to Virginia and Pennsylvania conventioneers—about the likelihood of the tyranny of the Stuarts being repeated, or whether, in general, "power might be tempted to cruelty" (*Weems*, 374).

The question is discussed extensively in White's Weems dissent, referred to earlier, which considers the Eighth Amendment "as to its origin in the mother country, and . . . its migration and existence in the states after the Revolution" (389). For White, "in England it was nowhere deemed that any theory of proportional punishment was suggested by the Bill of Rights, or that a protest was thereby intended against the severity of punishments, speaking generally" (393). That interpretation was supposedly followed by a number of state constitutions or bills of rights (Maryland, North Carolina, Massachusetts, New Hampshire), which seemed to assume that "the cruel bodily punishments of former times" (395) were no longer an issue. White concludes that he can "deduce no ground whatever which, to my mind, sustains the interpretation now given to the cruel and unusual punishment clause" (409).

A strikingly similar fault-line to that of 1910 will therefore reappear in *Roper*, close to a century later. For the majority in that case, "the United Kingdom's experience bears particular relevance here in light of the historic ties between our countries and in light of the Eighth Amendment's own origins. . . . As of now, the United Kingdom has abolished the death penalty in its entirety; but, decades before it took this step, it recognized the disproportionate nature of the juvenile death penalty; and it abolished that penalty as a separate matter" (577). Scalia's dissenting rebuttal is as follows:

> The Court's special reliance on the laws of the United Kingdom is perhaps the most indefensible part of its opinion. It is of course true that we share a common history with the United Kingdom, and that we often consult English sources when asked to discern the meaning of a constitutional text written against the backdrop of 18th century English law and legal thought. . . . [But] the Court undertakes the majestic task of determining (and thereby prescribing) our Nation's current standards of decency. It is beyond comprehension why we should look, for that purpose, to a country that has developed, in the centuries since the Revolutionary War—and with increasing speed since the United Kingdom's recent submission to the jurisprudence of European courts dominated by continental jurists—a legal, political, and social culture quite different from our own. (626–27)

In this way the paradoxes of an originalism such as Scalia explicitly owns in *Roper*—"the Court has, however—I think wrongly—long rejected a purely originalist approach to our Eighth Amendment" (626)—come into clear focus concerning what that amendment has inherited from the British. We share a common history, he says, and the Constitution was written against the backdrop of eighteenth-century English legal thought; as a result he would be in agreement that we don't want to continue the egregious practices of the Stuarts. But by the same token, if eighteenth-century English law condoned capital punishment on principle, and for juveniles, so should we. His assessment of the passage of time from the late eighteenth century to the early twenty-first century is that the period manifests an increasing divergence, such that American standards of decency can no longer be measured against English standards. But if American jurisprudence has, progressively over the past two hundred years, been weaned from its reliance upon English jurisprudence, it has also been, from its inception, in a relation of rupture with respect to English law. From the Declaration of Independence through the Constitution to the Bill of Rights, American law, however much it might have referred to English precedents, repeatedly *performed*—in the manner of a speech act—its own autonomy. Scalia, as originalist, organicist, and ultimately nativist, appeared willing to situate that rupture in spatial terms via a continental divide whereby England, having recently floated over to join Europe, ceded its right to influence American legal thinking. However, that is to ignore or forget the "divergence" implicit in any inheritance and the impossibility of limiting the context within which such a divergence will operate. As will have always been the case, American law measures itself, and the evolution of its standards (for example those of decency), against its own context, against the context of other traditions presumed to be germane to it (for example those of so-called Anglo-American countries), and against the context of so-called foreign traditions. As we have seen, that will have always been so, and neither the time nor the space coordinates of those contexts can be easily determined.

If the time of *evolving* standards evokes the life sciences, it is perhaps because evolution obeys a temporality that is both uneven in its speed, and characterized by discontinuities and ruptures. Within that temporal framework, human decency will on the one hand be subject to similar vagaries, but on the other hand, its presumptions of a universal humanity will similarly be rendered very fragile, whatever our universe be. And that will be, to this day, more than twenty years beyond Blackmun's *Callins* dissent, the malfunction that, as he describes it, causes Supreme Court Eighth Amendment debate, and the U.S. state machinery of death, to splutter, if not stall.

This book argues that tensions among different temporal elements within American death penalty jurisprudence—the desire for an instantaneous, painless death penalty; the presumption that certain classes of individual have not grown into the rational maturity on the basis of which they might be subjected to such a penalty; and fierce debate over how to measure at what point American society (its voters, its legislators, its judiciary) stands along the road to a progressively more decent humanity—operate in conjunction with something like a *machinic* or technological time. That machinic time—automatic, instantaneous, mechanically, and repetitively applied—emerges, paradoxically, through an interpretation of Blackmun's own long-term maturation of jurisprudential thinking, referenced in *Callins*, toward an adamant rejection of the death penalty. In describing the "endeavor" and "struggle" (*Callins*, 1141) of more than twenty years, he is referring more or less to his whole tenure as a Supreme Court justice, a tenure marked most notably by his movement from conservative to liberal positions, and, more notably still, by his authoring the *Roe v. Wade* decision that allowed abortion as a constitutional right in 1973. But "more than 20 years" is ostensibly a reference to the *Furman* decision in 1972, by a 5–4 majority, that the death penalty as applied in the United States contradicted the Eighth Amendment prohibition against cruel and unusual punishment.

In 1972, Blackmun had voted with the dissenting minority, fearing that the Court had "overstepped" (*Furman*, 414) by preempting the prerogative of the legislative branch. Thus, even though he concludes by stating "I may rejoice at the Court's result" (ibid.) and begins with the position that "were I a legislator, I would vote against the death penalty" (406), when he comes back to that point it is precisely to reaffirm that "I do not sit on these cases, however, as a legislator. . . . Our task here, as must so frequently be emphasized and reemphasized, is to pass upon the constitutionality of legislation that has been enacted and that is challenged. This is the sole task for judges. We should not allow our personal preferences as to the wisdom of legislative and congressional action, or our distaste for such action, to guide our judicial decision" (410–11). In that respect, his position is not so far from that of O'Connor, or Scalia in *Thompson* and *Stanford*, or even Thomas in *Baze*: He both argues that the Court should not legislate, and, as we shall shortly see, expresses surprise that standards could have evolved so fast.

Yet Blackmun's opinion is prefaced by his noting that it consists of "only the following, somewhat personal, comments" (405), and he includes more than passing reference to his being alone among his contemporary brethren to have made a struggle with the death penalty a matter of "judicial record," citing in particular cases from 1962 to 1968 decided during his tenure on the U.S. Court of Appeals for the Eighth Circuit. Indeed, the personal side of his *Furman* opinion could not be more explicit:

> Cases such as these provide for me an excruciating agony of the spirit.
> I yield to no one in the depth of my distaste, antipathy, and, indeed,
> abhorrence, for the death penalty, with all its aspects of physical
> distress and fear and of moral judgment exercised by finite minds.
> That distaste is buttressed by a belief that capital punishment
> serves no useful purpose that can be demonstrated. For me, it violates
> childhood's training and life's experiences, and is not compatible with
> the philosophical convictions I have been able to develop. (405–6)

He continues, in the passage quoted in my Introduction, to recount Minnesota's now century-old exclusion of the death penalty from "the arsenal of possible punishments for any crime" (406).

In *Furman*, therefore, Blackmun sides with the majority on moral grounds but dissents on legal grounds. He makes clear that he will put his personal opinions aside and decide juridically, interpreting the constitution in the way that his training, and position demand. From that perspective, and given his explicit statement that "we should not allow our personal preferences . . . to guide our judicial decision" (411), it is ironic that, in the scathing rebuttal addressed to his *Callins* dissent by Scalia, Blackmun is accused precisely of reading his "convictions . . . into a Constitution that does not contain them" (1142) and of referring often to his "'intellectual, moral, and personal' perceptions, but never to the text and tradition of the Constitution" (1141). In fact, one could say that Scalia perversely misrepresents Blackmun's opinion, which argues over fifteen pages how the text and tradition of the Constitution have been interpreted in case after case dealing with the constitutionality of the death penalty.

More specifically, though, Blackmun refers in detail to the dissenting position he had taken in *Furman*, based on his objection to the Court's abrupt change of heart. For, while agreeing that *Weems* provided a foretaste of the *Trop* evolving standards doctrine—"the Eighth Amendment's prohibition against cruel and unusual punishments 'may acquire meaning as public opinion becomes enlightened by a humane justice'" (*Furman*, 409, quoting *Weems*, 378)—he objected in 1972 to the "suddenness of the Court's perception of progress in the human attitude since decisions of only a short while ago" (*Furman*, 410). That "short while ago" was a reference to *McGautha* (1971), which turned on whether a jury should have the authority to impose the death penalty without clear guidelines concerning the appropriateness of such a sentence, and in particular, whether the Constitution was better served by having a single jury decision concerning both guilt and penalty or the bifurcated system of trial phase and penalty phase that is in use today. With respect to *McGautha*, Blackmun notes in *Callins* that "although the Court did not deny that serious risks were associated with a sentencer's unbounded discretion, the Court found *no remedy in the Constitution for the inevitable failings of human judgment*" (*Callins*, 1146, my emphasis). He therefore agreed that judicial judgment, all the way to a death sentence, was necessarily a human and thus potentially fallible judgment. For that reason he is surprised that only a year later, in *Furman*, the Court "reversed its course completely" (ibid.) as "concurring Justices argued that the glaring inequities in the administration of death, the standardless discretion wielded by judges and juries, and the pervasive racial and economic discrimination, rendered the death penalty, at least as administered, 'cruel and unusual' within the meaning of the Eighth Amendment" (1146). As he reads it, then, the *Furman* majority sought by mechanistic—one might even say "prosthetic"—means to repair the effects of what looked, to that majority, like human fallibility run rampant.

In *Callins* Blackmun goes on to explain that in spite of his *Furman* dissent in favor of capital punishment, he now agrees "that *Furman*'s essential holding was correct. Although most of the public seems to desire, and the Constitution appears to permit, the penalty of death, it surely is beyond dispute that if the death penalty cannot be administered consistently and rationally, it may not be administered at all. . . . Since *Gregg*, I faithfully have adhered to the *Furman* holding and have come to believe that it is indispensable to the Court's Eighth Amendment jurisprudence" (1147, 1148). It would be my argument that once his own change of heart means rejecting the constitutionality of the death penalty because he refuses any longer to "tinker with the machinery of death," we can interpret his *Furman* dissent as intuiting a hasty, radical jurisprudential change. However much he may have reconciled himself to that change post-*Furman*, it reappears in *Callins* as precisely the abrogation of the human in favor of the machine. From that point of view what he saw as the suddenness of the Court's reversal of course between *McGautha* (1971) and *Furman* (1972) is understood precisely as the suddenness of a machinic revolution instituting a new temporal order.

We can understand Justice Harlan's majority opinion in *McGautha* to be based on a perception that only so much, in terms of human effort and foresight, could be expected when it came to drafting sentencing guidelines in capital cases: "To identify before the fact those characteristics of criminal homicides and their perpetrators which call for the death penalty, and to express these characteristics in language which can be fairly understood and applied by the sentencing authority, appear to be *tasks which are beyond present human ability*" (*McGautha*, 204, my emphasis). And further: "For a court to attempt to catalog the appropriate factors in this elusive area could inhibit rather than expand the scope of consideration, for *no list of circumstances would ever be really complete*" (208, my emphasis). Harlan thereby implies—before the information age, of course—that for the system to work there would need to be some superhuman program or machine able to deal with all the variables; and that is too much to ask. But that is precisely what will be asked of the states just a year later in *Furman*, which gives rise to Blackmun's dissent: Find a way around the arbitrariness, the *Furman* decision says, develop a system that goes as far as possible in remedying—with programmed foresight and as it were automatically—the inequities and irregularities in the imposition of the death penalty. In that way, between *Furman* and *Gregg*, and then beyond all the way to *Callins*, *Baze*, and *Glossip*, the machinery of death gets invented precisely as machinery, in a way that was not the case before. It is a machine that will require constant tinkering, and whose technicians or mechanics attempt and ultimately fail, according to Blackmun, to keep it in working order.

But that machinery, which is called on to provide consistency, and avoid the arbitrariness identified in *Furman*, remains in tension with the competing requirement of individualized consideration of each case. "The consistency promised in *Furman*," Blackmun writes, "and the fairness to the individual demanded in *Lockett* are not only inversely related, but irreconcilable in the context of capital punishment" (*Callins*, 1155), referring to *Lockett*, which found in 1978 that the death penalty could not be automatically imposed without consideration of mitigating circumstances.[18] The consistency machine is therefore in tension, according to Blackmun, with recognition of what the plurality in *Woodson*—deciding against automatic sentencing on July 2, 1976, the same day that *Gregg* reinstated the death penalty—called the "diverse frailties of humankind."[19]

For Blackmun, for whom the Court, between 1971 and 1972, blinked long enough for a judicial machine to be installed, the twenty or so ensuing years of new and improved models will not have improved anything. The courts indeed installed a certain automatism in the process of capital trials and sentencing, erecting "procedural devices from which fair, equitable, and reliable outcomes are presumed to flow" (*Callins*, 1144–45), the very devices that, in *McGautha*, Harlan found desirable but impossible. Those wheels are still turning in 1994, as Blackmun sees it, but he finds subsequent upgrades to have proven "futile." As a result, the Court "now is retreating not only from the *Furman* promise of consistency and rationality, but from the requirement of individualized sentencing as well. . . . [It] has chosen to deregulate the entire enterprise . . . abdicating its statutorily and constitutionally imposed duty to provide meaningful judicial oversight to the administration of death by the States" (*Callins*, 1145). Like every machine, the justice system requires human maintenance and oversight, or regular servicing, but in the twenty-two years between *Furman* and *Callins*, Blackmun is saying, such regular and regulatory servicing has been absent.

However—this is the conclusion I am working toward—it is not certain that the arbitrariness that seems to have crept back into the system by 1994, or which was perhaps never obviated, is any longer a human arbitrariness in contrast with a technological certainty. Remember that in

Furman, the extreme formulation of that arbitrariness was provided by Justice Potter Stewart's concurring opinion: "These death sentences are cruel and unusual in the same way that being struck by lightning is cruel and unusual. . . . I simply conclude that the Eighth and Fourteenth Amendments cannot tolerate the infliction of a sentence of death under legal systems that permit this unique penalty to be so wantonly and so freakishly imposed" (*Furman*, 309, 310). A lightning strike is a natural arbitrariness, perhaps even a "freakish" perversion of nature, which nevertheless functions as a type of deus ex machina; it certainly has nothing human about it. Therefore, following Blackmun's logic, and inasmuch as arbitrariness is the consistent object of his criticism, the humanity of twenty years before—capricious on one hand, but capable of good judgment and mercy on the other—will have given way to a choice between two machines: the machine of technological reliability and the machine of a type of automatized arbitrariness: "death will continue to be meted out in this country arbitrarily and discriminatorily . . . the proper course when faced with irreconcilable constitutional commands is not to ignore one or the other, nor to pretend that the dilemma does not exist, but to admit the futility of the effort to harmonize them. This means accepting the fact that the death penalty cannot be administered in accord with our Constitution" (*Callins*, 1157).

We can therefore understand the rapid change of heart experienced by the Court between *McGautha* in 1971 and *Furman* in 1972—which, at the time of *Furman*, Blackmun refused to accept—as a change of temporal order. By embracing the need for consistency against arbitrariness, the *Furman* majority led death penalty jurisprudence as if unwittingly into the order, or expectation of mechanically or automatically applied standards that would provide justice in the form of a programmable immediacy. In 1994, that machinery is found by Blackmun to be far from perfect, in spite of attempts to improve its performance; it continues to be marked by arbitrariness. Indeed, in his view it was as if that arbitrariness were so consistently arbitrary as to display, itself, all the features of a machine; and furthermore, regulation of that machine would have been outsourced— the entire enterprise "deregulated"—such that the expectation of a human, and humane justice, had become a broken cause.

Or, to interpret things from a converse point of view, as it were the flip side of the same logic: The imperfect machinery of consistency is unable to resist the implacability of humanly manufactured arbitrariness, for even more consistent than mechanically designed consistency is the reliability of human fallibility, our refusal to behave according to the rationality that

by presuming it, in 1791, as has been repeated numerous times since? How can he not "see" reason? Therefore, Thomas seems to think, only if I am able to confront the public with the naked cruelty of the criminal acts I so vividly, so visually describe, will the Court stop, as he hopes in his concluding sentence, "making up Eighth Amendment claims in its ceaseless quest to end the death penalty through undemocratic means" (Thomas concurring, 10).

Now, the vivid description of crimes is necessarily part of the judicial process, and the distinction between "cold hard facts" and graphic hyperbole is susceptible to abuse by prosecution and defense alike. Those descriptions rely in general terms on the rhetoric of narrative, and indeed, the importance of "telling a story" that a jury will find plausible is a time-honored courtroom strategy on both sides.[5] But as I wish to argue in this chapter, the descriptions that figure in accounts of gruesome crimes such as those provided by Thomas and Scalia are designed to function as particularly *photo*graphic images. They present to our imagination, in realist visual terms, acts and events that we precisely could not or should not bare to look at. But beyond that, photographic realism in turn relies on the reduction of time to an appropriable instant, on the ability to capture the very instant of reality that is depicted. It therefore mirrors the quest for an instantaneous death penalty that was examined in the previous chapter, and, as we shall see in subsequent discussions, operates sometimes in concert with, sometimes in contrast to other discursive effects relating to the death penalty. The logic at work here is as follows: One expects death penalty justice to be seen to be done both through the idea that the punishment fits the crime, and by the efficiency and efficacy of the execution itself. On one side there would be an egregious criminal act, on the other an impartial and dispassionate justice system that puts the criminal to death; jurists are therefore led to contrast the bloody cruelty of the criminal act with the painless instant of execution. When that contrast seems no longer operative—for example when the dissenting opinions in *Glossip* argue that Oklahoma's lethal injection protocol is, in spite of all appearances and expectations, cruel enough to be unconstitutional, implying by extension that an execution might be causing the criminal to suffer as the victim(s) did—it is as if visual proof is required, leading a Scalia or Thomas to show it like it really is by producing even more graphic images. In my view, if the graphic force of those images is able to succeed it is only because our culture subscribes to a visuality that is essentially photographic, determined in turn by photography's conception of instantaneity. As I seek to show in what follows, the evolution of the modern practice of the death penalty as an evolution toward a rapid, and supposedly humane taking of human life, comes therefore to be interwoven with the development of photographic visuality.

The death penalty's first modern moment of mechanical instantaneity arrives with the introduction of the trap door gallows, even if the precise date of that innovation remains imprecise. In his comprehensive history of capital punishment in the United States, Stuart Banner records that "Boston had such a device as early as 1694," seeming to predate the use of the trap door scaffold in England by several decades, London's Newgate Prison having performed the first executions on its famous "New Drop" gallows in 1783.[6] But whatever the precise chronology of that technological evolution, it is clear that by the end of the eighteenth century the trap door had come to be a part of the generalized application of the gallows as the preferred form of capital punishment in the Anglo-American world.

Banner describes the steps in that evolution of technological innovation in respect of hanging. First performed from the branch of a tree, then, as of sometime before 1650 in Boston, by means of a form of scaffold, the practice nevertheless had to contend with numerous botches:

> A hanging required some method of dropping the condemned prisoner from a height. In the seventeenth century the drop was commonly achieved by means of a ladder placed against the tree or the gallows. The prisoner, with a rope tied around his neck and his hands tied, would climb the ladder. When all was ready, the executioner would simply turn the ladder away, depriving the prisoner of support. A person hanged in this manner was said to be "turned off."[7]

The method was not without its shortcomings: Dorothy Talbye swung back and caught the ladder with her legs; Cotton Mather records how Mary Martin swung long enough to twice acknowledge her attempted infanticide and "was turned off the Ladder *Twice*, before she Dyed."[8] The ladder was later replaced by a horse-drawn cart that was driven off at the appropriate moment, and then by a fixed scaffold with a trap door that opened under the victim. Henceforth, this technological innovation—as always, essentially that of speed—allowed the condemned, rather than being turned off, to be "launched into Eternity."[9] Nevertheless, the botches continued, and prisoners who were supposed to die from an instantaneous fracturing of the vertebrae and severing of the spinal cord were instead left swinging until they asphyxiated some minutes later, or in some cases, if the drop was too great, were decapitated.

The introduction of the trap door is thus a pivotal or hinge moment in the history of the death penalty, a pivotal moment in its automatic mechanization. But the introduction of the trap door also serves as a hinge moment connecting different regimes of visibility within the practice of capital punishment. In *Discipline and Punish*, Michel Foucault offers a gripping spectacle of orgiastic cruelty that marked the execution, for the attempted regicide of Louis XV, of Robert-François Damiens in the Place de Grève in Paris in 1757. A large crowd gathered for the event, including Casanova, who had arrived in Paris the day of the assassination attempt. He rented a ringside window and allowed his friend to make something of a seduction party of the execution, as he recounts in his memoirs.[10]

The official sentence provided for Damiens's punishment was as follows:

> on a scaffold that will be erected there, the flesh will be torn from his breasts, arms, thighs and calves with red-hot pincers, his right hand, holding the knife with which he committed the said parricide, burnt with sulphur, and, on those places where the flesh will be torn away, poured molten lead, boiling oil, burning resin, wax and sulphur melted together and then his body drawn and quartered by four horses and body consumed by fire.[11]

But that description of Damiens's sentence sounds almost anodyne when compared with the monumental botching of the execution itself—particularly the quartering—such as Foucault documents, from the record, in the opening pages of *Discipline and Punish*.[12] For it had been almost 150 years since the previous such execution, carried out on the assassin of Henri IV, François Ravaillac, in 1610. Ravaillac died in an orgy of perhaps greater excess than Damiens by supposedly having his body torn to pieces for onlookers' souvenirs, portions of it perhaps having been eaten. That specter of a cannibalistic theatrical ritual returns in certain royalist accounts, no doubt exaggerated, of the execution of Louis XVI in 1793, which portends the resilience of forms of ritualistic spectacle in the modern period of the death penalty.[13]

As we have already seen, the 1791 Bill of Rights, and in particular the Eighth Amendment of the American Constitution, determined precisely—as did the French Revolution, however perverse the excesses of the Terror—that the death penalty should be performed in such a way as not to inflict such extreme suffering; in no way should it amount to torture. However, the tradition of spectacle had, since colonial times, brought thousands, perhaps tens of thousands of onlookers to witness executions. In 1774,

Banner reports, the execution of "Daniel Wilson, a Providence rapist, drew more than twelve thousand . . . nearly three times the population of Providence."[14] Those spectacles would continue into the nineteenth century and in certain states public executions lasted well into the twentieth century. The last such event in the United States was the execution of Roscoe Jackson in 1937, witnessed by several hundred people who crowded into the small town of Galena, Missouri. Those able to pay the admission fee were allowed into the stockade surrounding the gallows; others crowded outside. It is reported that a number of spectators left the scene with a souvenir piece of the rope used for the hanging. A year earlier, Rainey Bethea, a black man, was hanged (judicially, for we must not forget the whole other history of lynching, as discussed in Chapter 5) for the rape of a white woman, before an audience of perhaps 20,000 in Owensboro, Kentucky.[15] But already in the first half of the nineteenth century movement began toward a less public death penalty such that, according to Banner, "between 1830 and 1860 every northern state moved hangings from the public square into the jail yard."[16]

It would be difficult to determine the exact correlation between a death penalty that was performed more efficiently thanks to technological innovations like the trap door, and a death penalty that was increasingly removed from public view, if never altogether from sight. The requirement of any judicial death penalty is that it be somehow visible, seen by more witnesses than simply the executioner. Nevertheless, one can surmise that attempts to rationalize and "anesthetize," and especially to expedite the fact and act itself of putting to death, led the public, and the judiciary, to concentrate on speed and efficacy according to the rationale that continues to the present day. From at least the end of the eighteenth century we have come increasingly to expect and seek an ever more certain and rapid death for the criminal sentenced to die. Hence the idea developed of a better-oiled killing machine in parallel with a desire for a less cruel spectacle, and eventually that led to the desire that there be no public spectacle at all, at least not in the form of a leisure activity and spectator sport that, at its height, would draw thousands, even tens of thousands of onlookers.[17]

Another historical and technological evolution, however, overlaps within that same time frame of the first half of the nineteenth century, making the trap door moment something of a "shutter" moment. That evolution began with Niépce's efforts at heliography in about 1816, culminating in what is now recognized as the first photograph about ten years later, followed by the development of the daguerreotype, which led to widespread photographic practices starting in the mid-1830s (until photographic plates were revolutionized in turn by Eastman's film in 1888–89). Photographic innovation progressively becomes, and more and more explicitly so, a matter of controlling the instant, and thanks to its capture of a single moment in time a particular visual concept of the instant enters the cultural consciousness. Thus, although the *modernist, technologized*, or mechanized death penalty begins with the invention of the trap door—not that the death penalty was ever other than technologized—it is rather the guillotine, with its more definitive and operationally effective "shutter," that will, beginning in 1792, assume control of the instant of execution, reinforcing it as an instant of technologized visuality.

Before coming to that moment I wish to draw attention to a particular prephotographic demonstration by example from Puritan times, namely the execution sermon. It provides an uncanny reverse image of contemporary attempts, for example by Clarence Thomas, to reinforce with almost *photographic* vividness the criminal malfeasance of the worst of the worst. The execution sermon insists, by means of a different but comparable equation, and by means of a different medium, that the punishment fits the crime. As Benjamin reminds us in his seminal text, the mechanical reproducibility of the image does not begin with the photograph in the nineteenth century; photography is rather a radical transformative moment within a structure that might be called that of originary technological iterability: "Graphic art," he writes, "was first made technologically reproducible by the woodcut."[18] As one might expect then, woodcuts, illustrated broadsheets, and drawn depictions of executions were relatively common throughout the eighteenth and into the earlier nineteenth century. But it was the combined illustrative and instructive power of the execution sermon that—in the Western country that preserves a postmodern death penalty—provided a special discursive context for those visual reproductions during the period of premodernist or pre-Enlightenment cruelty and spectacle. Examples of such sermons are recorded in America from 1638 to the late eighteenth century: "Printed versions of the sermons, confessions, and other gallows ephemera, which sold as pamphlets and broadsides on execution day and often contained woodcuts of the hanging scene, helped disseminate the message of the hanging through the crowd and across the region."[19] More than one such sermon might be delivered, either from the church pulpit—perhaps on the Sunday before the execution, and with the condemned person in attendance—or from the scaffold itself. They were, according to Ronald A. Bosco, "one of the principal examples of jeremiad form,"[20] extending the moral example of the condemned person to a general warning about the declension of the Puritan polity. Bosco begins his essay with a detailed account of *The Cry of Sodom Enquired Into*, given by Reverend Samuel Danforth in the presence of Benjamin Goad, condemned for the "prodigious villany [*sic*]" of sodomy (punished as a capital crime for the last time in the United States in 1785),[21] a crime narrativized by Danforth as follows (I abridge considerably):

> He gave himself to Selfpollution [*sic*], and other Sodomitical wicked-
> ness. He often attempted Buggery with several Beasts, before God left
> him to commit it. . . . Being at length, by the good hand of God,
> brought under the Yoke of Government . . . he violently broke
> away . . . and shook off that Yoke of God, calling reproach and
> disgrace upon his Master. Having now obtained a licentious liberty, he
> grew so impudent . . . as to commit his horrid Villany in the sight of
> the Sun, and in the open field, even at Noonday.[22]

The execution sermon became the televangelical platform for dia-tribes on the wages of sin of which the execution itself was the stark il-lustration: listen here (to my warnings against an impure life); then look there (at the fatal punishment to which such a life leads). The jeremiad attracted a congregation that increased exponentially the number of souls that might attend any given Sunday church service. No less a figure than Cotton Mather thanked "a very strange Providence" for creating the cir-cumstances for his preaching a sermon "whereat one of the greatest Assemblies, ever known in these parts of the World, was come together."[23] But the vast social networking potential of the execution spectatorship also favored a contagious discursive drift whereby the sermon expanded beyond the particulars of the crime being punished to encompass warn-ings against every imaginable evil, as in Thomas Foxcroft's 1733 *Lessons of Caution to Young Sinners*: everything from ignorance and error, ungodly principles, profanity and irreligion, sensuality and vice, disobedience to parents, sins of pride, lying, rash anger, envy, malice, a spirit of revenge, self-murder, covetousness, a worldly mind, lasciviousness, uncleanness— "ye know that no whoremonger nor unclean person (whether fornicator, or adulterer, or effeminate, and abusers of themselves) have any inheri-tance in the Kingdom of God"—intemperance, gluttony and drunken-ness, idleness, evil fellowship, carnal security, to hypocrisy.[24] The proliferating illustrative potential of the sermon thus extended well be-yond the visual specificity of the execution scene that it accompanied, which suggests its potential independence from the scene that the listen-ers were about to witness. On the one hand, they were being told not to commit the sins of the condemned person so as to avoid the punishment that was about to be meted out; on the other, their presence as a captive audience not likely to leave before the grand finale gave preachers ample opportunity to sermonize at will, to digress considerably from the simple allegorical reality of the scene of judgment. And that divergence of discourses mirrored a divergence of regimes of visibility, for what could be seen by a multitude swelling to thousands or tens of thousands was not, except for those in close proximity to the scaffold, illustrative in any direct sense. Indeed, those closer to the fringes would, literally or figuratively, be required to turn their backs on the spectacle of the execution itself, and, increasingly, find their entertainment in the generalized carnivalesque ambience, in diverse activities such as the very drunkenness and lesser or greater forms of debauchery that were typical objects of a sermon's scathing diatribe. Casanova's account of what took place in the crowded window space he had rented in 1757 has its echoes in various reports of hanging-day crowds in the United States into the nineteenth century—indeed all the way to the 1930s—by which time the paradoxes of the capital punishment carnival had become more evident.

Banner thus begins his chapter on the move away from public executions by giving two contrasting accounts by witnesses to a hanging in North Carolina in 1852. The first witness, a female farmer, tells of a town overflowing with people, how she pushed to the front of the crowd to secure a place near the gallows from where she heard the sermon—as well as back and forth shouting between the condemned man and witnesses who had testified against him—before seeing the execution itself. The second account is from a lawyer who writes to the woman he is courting, and tells disapprovingly of five thousand people gathered, half of whom were women; but he stays only to be edified by the sermon and leaves before the hanging itself. The farmer is swept up in the spectacle and participates in a discursive framework that retains as its centerpiece the visual event of the execution; the lawyer finds himself mingling with a crowd given over to various passions and much more in need of admonitions from a pulpit than the visual demonstration of the hanging itself, whose lesson tended to be lost in the general conviviality and its decidedly less structured discursive context. To the extent that the cohesiveness of hanging day was maintained by a strict allegorical adjacency between execution and sermon, and attended by a rapt audience, the spectacle functioned as intended. But once that cohesiveness began to be loosened, thanks on one hand to a sermon that digressed seemingly at will, on the other to a crowd that frayed and dissipated into various forms of intemperance, then the hanging no longer provided either the visual focus it presumed, or the concentrated instant of moral example that it similarly relied on. The death penalty seemed thus to lose its power of visual demonstration.

Foucault records a similar mechanism in his analysis of the birth of the prison, especially in describing the shift, from torture or torment (*supplice*) to punishment, to which I earlier referred. That shift is for Foucault a disappearance: "the disappearance of the tortured, dismembered, amputated body, symbolically branded on face or shoulder, exposed alive or dead to public view. The body as the major target of penal repression disappeared."[25] As a result, throughout the first half of the nineteenth century "punishment had gradually ceased to be a spectacle. And whatever theatrical elements it still retained were henceforth seen in a negative light."[26] That shift in the visibility of punishment, its public enactment upon the body of the condemned person, in favor of what Foucault will trace as technologies of disciplining, was motivated in the first place by a juridico-political move away from considering crime as an injury inflicted on the sovereign body itself. The spectacle of public torture and execution had provided ritual confirmation of the king's invincibility in response to such an offense against his person:

> The punishment is carried out in such as a way as to give a spectacle not of measure, but of imbalance and excess; in this liturgy of punishment, there must be an emphatic affirmation of power . . . of the physical strength of the sovereign beating down upon the body of his adversary and mastering it: by breaking the law, the offender has touched the very person of the prince; and it is the prince—or at least those to whom he has delegated his force—who seizes upon the body of the condemned man and displays it marked, beaten, broken. The ceremony of punishment, then, is an exercise of "terror."[27]

The "technical mutation" that Foucault describes as a "transition from torture, with its spectacular rituals, its art mingled with the ceremony of pain, to the penalties of prisons,"[28] thus signaled the disappearance of that form of sovereignty.

In the second place, though, as with every public ceremony, the ritual "liturgy" of capital punishment carried with it the possibility of excess on the side of the spectators themselves, such as we have just seen in the colonial American context. Executions risked becoming "momentary saturnalia,"[29] including "a whole aspect of the carnival, in which rules were inverted, authority mocked and criminals transformed into heroes."[30] From that point of view the very sovereign power that was on display, reimposing its sheer physical strength by crushing the body of the condemned person,

with my machine I can have your heads off in the twinkling of an eye and you will not feel the slightest pain," he maintained.[38] If the condemned person does feel something, it will be "no more than a slight sensation of coolness at the back of the neck [*sur le cou . . . une légère fraîcheur*]."[39] One can presume that his simple mechanical solution facilitated adoption of the 1791 penal code in October of that year, and within a period of six months the design of the guillotine will have been perfected, thanks principally to the efforts of another doctor, Antoine Louis. As if extending the humanitarian mission of the apparatus, it will be a piano and harpsichord maker, Tobias Schmidt, who earns the right to construct the first prototype, having undercut by some 500 percent the estimate tendered by the official state carpenter. "I profess the art of the mechanical construction of pianofortes," Schmidt writes in a letter to the Convention following the Terror, "but I sometimes abandon that art to dedicate myself to mechanical discoveries useful to humanity," going on to mention inventions such as a rudimentary submarine, an improved plow, and an extendable ladder, but neglecting to mention his guillotine.[40] Though he cut some corners in constructing a prototype—wood rather than copper for the grooves in which the blade would slide, blade of inferior steel—he subsequently made the necessary improvements and the machine was ready for testing in April 1792.

At that point the medical community took over, with Antoine Louis writing to the chief surgeon of the Bicêtre Hospital, Michel Cullerier, asking for space and a series of cadavers to enable the momentous experiment. Cullerier was only too happy to oblige:

> You'll find at Bicêtre all the facilities that you desire to try out a machine that humanity cannot look at without quivering, but that justice and the social good have made necessary. I'll hold on to the corpses of the unfortunates who perish between today and Monday. I'll have the amphitheatre arranged in a suitable manner, or if, as I presume, the height of the ceiling doesn't accommodate the machine, I can put at your disposal a small isolated courtyard situated next to the amphitheatre. The preference you have shown the Bicêtre Hospital is a very nice gift that you offer me, and it would be all the more so if you were to accept a simple and frugal dinner such as a young man can provide. . . . I await your favorable response, flattered in expectation [*avec une flatteuse espérance*].[41]

Among the dignitaries present at 10:00 a.m. on Tuesday, April 17, were the Drs. Guillotin and Louis, Schmidt the builder, and Sanson the state executioner; but also in attendance were the philosopher and physiologist Pierre-Jean-Georges Cabanis, who had been Mirabeau's private physician, and Professor Philippe Pinel, founder of "moral therapy" for the mentally ill and renowned for his role in the unshackling of the insane. The corpses provided by Cullerier were those of two prisoners and a prostitute whose heads, according to Cabanis, were separated from the trunk with "the speed of a glance," their "bones sliced through cleanly."[42] Events thereafter conspired to the point where the convicted mugger Nicolas Jacques Pelletier was ready to be introduced to the national razor for its inaugural drop on April 25, 1792.

As the new revolutionary law required, usage of the guillotine lay to rest the desire that punishment be cruel, or that confessions be obtained by forms of torture, practices that the government of Louis XVI had already begun progressively to call into question, especially in the years immediately preceding the Revolution. But, beyond that, the new machine democratized the death penalty by being used in all cases, and introduced "the simple deprivation of life" by means of a decapitation that leaves no margin—especially no temporal margin—for the possibility of torture to be entertained. Foucault quotes an account from 1825 that emphasizes the presumed correlation between a pure mechanicity and an almost imperceptible death, adding: "The guillotine takes life almost without touching the body, just as prison deprives of liberty or a fine reduces wealth."[43] In this way guillotining amounts to a mechanism of instantanization as anesthetization, a death so rapid that it cannot be felt, such as will have inspired and structured the operation of judicial executions in the West ever since.

However, even at the moment of the guillotine's invention and implementation in the last decade of the eighteenth century, serious doubts were raised concerning its efficacy. Dr. Louis thought, based on his mechanist conception of "the human body as a system of interlocking parts," that even the common fear of death could be assuaged once it was understood that that body would be rendered instantly inoperative by an even more trustworthy cutting mechanism, one with a guaranteed instantaneous effect. Arguing before the National Assembly in March 1792, for the advantage of a slanted convex blade, Louis declared that

> considering the structure of the neck, with the spinal column as
> its centre composed of several bones whose connections overlap . . .
> one cannot be assured of a prompt and perfect separation by entrusting it to an *agent whose accuracy might vary* because of moral and

physical reasons. It is necessary, if the procedure is to take place with
certainty, to depend on *invariable mechanical means.* . . . It is easy to
have such a machine constructed, whose effect is infallible.[44]

But that mechanist assurance came into conflict—once the guillotine began to be used regularly, and perhaps abetted by the very fact and spectacle of the Terror's exponentially increased bloodletting—with new medical
opinions regarding consciousness.

Without going back as far as Saint Denis's legendary six-kilometer trek,
in the third century, with his head in his hands, common mythology held
that Mary Stuart's severed head spoke in 1587; and similarly, that the cheeks
of Jean-Paul Marat's assassin, Charlotte Corday, blushed at the indignity
of being slapped by the executioner who held up her severed head for the
spectators. But the question was given more serious consideration by the
German physician Samuel Thomas von Sömmerring, the journalist Kon-
rad Engelbert Oelsner, and, among the French, the surgeon Jean-Joseph
Sue and Cabanis. As Grégoire Chamayou makes clear in his comprehensive review of those opinions, and the ideas that supported them, the debate extended into broader questions of the irritability versus sensibility
of what lives, and the concept, and localizability, of a (conscious) self as
distinct (or not) from the Aristotelian notion of a living soul.[45] In observ-
ing supposed signs of life in a severed head, science was first asking, "What
survives in the head? Does only irritability survive or do sensibility and
consciousness also survive?"[46] But those questions, and by extension
the question of how or where death occurs, could not be separated from
research into whether life was located in a centralized brain (for example,
Descartes's pineal gland), or diffused throughout a more broadly animated
body.[47] In the case of the positions advanced by Sue on one side and Cabanis on the other, the differences were focused on Sue's somewhat paradoxical assertion "that the persistence [in a severed head] of sensibility without
perception was the same as the presence of an unconscious sensible life,
entitled as such to respect and consideration, [whereas] Cabanis rephrases
the question as: the only pertinent death here is that of the individual, the
self or subject."[48]

In a more specific sense, the debate over where person, soul, or life resides within a body necessarily raises the question of where to locate the
legal subject whose life the death penalty is precisely entrusted with ending. Given the difficulty of "finding the legal subject in the flesh of the
body with the aid of a scalpel," Chamayou demonstrates that the debate

initiated by Charlotte Corday's red cheeks uncovers "a constitutive aporia of the modern anthropological knowledge that was being established at the end of the eighteenth century, in which Man was born discursively from this impossible 'pinning down' of the transcendental subject onto the somatic subject."[49]

Clearly, then, the guillotine blade did not slice into a living body without also wading into a complex set of epistemological questions. If, as Arasse reports, death was considered, from the time of the *Encyclopedia*, to be double—both incomplete and absolute—the "plurality of deaths in death" to which debate concerning the guillotine gave rise led to a more difficult quandary.[50] As Chamayou poses it:

> There is a plurality of deaths in death just as there is a multiplicity of lives in life but these various deaths that are usually merged in the apparent unity of an event here became spectacularly desynchronized by this new execution technique. The guillotine produced a phenom- enon of imperfect death, posing the question of which death is the death of the self, which biological death is the death of the person.[51]

The effect—and it cannot be circumscribed as a side-effect—of the guil- lotine was that it both called for and provided for research into that quan- dary by means of experimentation on the human body: "this new mechanism gave rise to new death-related phenomena linked to a new method of producing cadavers that could be used immediately in research in experimental medicine."[52] Not that medicine had not seized on the avail- ability of cadavers for its research in the past, but the Terror provided an emerging science with samples on a grand scale, transforming its savants into veritable thanatopoliticians:

> With Guillotin and Louis, doctors became technicians of death. The unprecedented and scandalous nature of this new positioning of medical knowledge has been emphasized. It was unprecedented because it broke with the traditional mission of medicine. Even in cases where a doctor supervised torture, he remained nonetheless in charge of making sure the patient did not die, whereas here it was no longer a question of avoiding death in order to make suffering endure but of giving absolute acceleration to death in order to avoid all suffering. And it was scandalous because this new role flouted the historical mission of medicine: to treat illness, to preserve health, and above all, according to the Hippocratic Oath, not to harm. . . . Not

only did medicine attain a new position of expertise but also, and above all, in the late eighteenth century it entered into the service of what Foucault called *thanatopolitics*, the reverse side of biopolitics whose purpose is death.[53]

The other, perhaps converse way to interpret the guillotine as new death-dealing machine or automated execution mechanism, would be, consistent with my position throughout this book, that the invention and widespread implementation of this late eighteenth-century apparatus produced an innovative conception of the prosthesis that has always regulated relations between the human and the technological. The other side of the question about where life begins and ends, and in what part(s) of the body, is a similarly epistemological—as much as medical—question about how living flesh relates to the inanimate, how much interference by the inanimate within the living human is desirable or permissible, how much inanimate a body can assimilate. At what precise knife-edge point, or up to what precise instant can human life be said still to resist, or conversely to concede to its inanimate other? The blade of the guillotine was presumed to adjudicate those questions—which remain the subject of debate to the present day—as precisely the appeal for a decision, or the trenchancy of a necessary delineation, between life and death.

Consequently, though the precise terms of that interpretation of the guillotine's effect may have escaped him, Cabanis's reaction to the first testing of the apparatus effectively relies on it. Granted, on one level he seems simply to remain within the mechanist tradition of La Mettrie, or Descartes, presuming that the improvements to the mechanics of the guillotine decided upon by the surgeon Louis—giving the blade "an oblique shape [*disposition*], so that it cuts as it falls in the manner of a saw, which, as everyone knows, causes the severing to occur easily and more promptly"[54]— corresponded satisfactorily to the mechanics of an animal body. For Cabanis, such a body no longer has any sensation of what is going on once "one suspends the correspondence between a part and the whole. . . . A simple shock to the cerebellum or to the spinal cord, a violent blow to the occiput is enough to cause death."[55] He thus refutes the idea, represented by Sue, that "sensibility can exist in an organ, independently of any communication with the major nerve centers."[56] Yet, on another level, he is staking a claim concerning the *prosthetization* of the human. He is ceding to the inevitability of technological viability, and reliability—call it faith in the machine—that had essentially trumped any humanist qualms from the beginning. For, on the one hand, the human has always been negotiating with an inanimate, as it were inside and outside itself, an inanimate that it does not necessarily perceive as foreign; and, on the other hand, technology is by definition, from the moment of the most rudimentary tool, a means to assist the human, either to perform by more economic means what the human is nevertheless capable of, or precisely to outperform humans up to the point of superseding them. From that perspective the debate, and seeming impasse, concerning the desired level of prosthetic attachment or replacement, concerning the optimal human-machine *interfaciality*, a debate that resurfaces still over issues such as life support, euthanasia, or cloning, as much as over different methods of execution, will have in effect been resolved at the end of the eighteenth century by the mechanized death introduced by the guillotine. For not only did the guillotine introduce an unprecedented level of mechanically automated death but also, in a very novel way, it tethered the human to a machine on the extreme edge of its existence.

Cabanis was satisfied that "when a man is guillotined, it is all over in a minute. The head disappears, and the body is immediately put in a basket."[57] Out of sight, out of mind. Moreover, though the scientist and hospital administrator in him were content to observe the first dry run of the machine, he never witnessed the execution of Charlotte Corday or anyone else, being unable to "tolerate that spectacle."[58] After all, presuming that it can be separated from the preceding questions, the visuality of the guillotine remains complex. Arasse describes how an *invisibility* deriving from the speed of an execution motivated initial objections: either that very rapidity made it appalling by definition, or, conversely, "the very speed of the operation attenuated the exemplary value of capital punishment."[59] The impression such a machine gives of a justice that is swift and implacable does nothing to reduce the violence of the act of decapitation, and reinforces a finality of judgment and irrevocability of punishment that still recalls something of the absolute sovereignty of the monarch. Of course there is no justice that is not decisive, and no death penalty once administered that is not irrevocable, but the scene of guillotining in fact retains from earlier practices the spectacle of bloodshed, and perhaps even emphasizes it. Thus, in another formula attributed to Guillotin during his discourse before the Constituent Assembly the advantages of his machine were vaunted in a way that Cabanis's mechanist faith would repeat following the end of the Terror. According to Guillotin in late 1789: "The mechanism falls like lightning, the head flies off, blood spurts out, the man is no more [*La mécanique tombe comme la foudre, la tête vole, le sang jaillit, l'homme n'est plus*]."[60] Even as Guillotin promotes his machine from the point of view of its instantaneity, therefore, he allows for a spectacle that will endure throughout the instant of its operation, throughout the time it takes for however much blood will spurt out to spurt until the man is no more. And that spectacle is necessarily visual. The image that Guillotin depicts so vividly by means of what Derrida will call "a four-stroke verbal machine" (*DP I*, 222) is the image of a graphic instant: a flash, a flight, a gush, a termination. Thanks to its light, its truncation, its profusion of color, and its limit, we might call it a photographic instant. It has three successive phases—the fall of the blade, the decapitation itself, and the bloody effusion—that amount to a single image of a man becoming no more. Each of those successive subdivisions of a single moment has its own visual force: the industrialized efficiency of the accelerating descent of knife-edged steel; the scientific precision of an ablation and automatic disposal of the human rational nucleus; and the reflex physiological reassertion of a gushing, wasted vitality. But it is the blood spurting out that fills the image with its vividness, as it were reaching out to be "in the face" of a viewer, as if the previous phases were preludes to the main visual act, adjusting the lighting and clicking the shutter to capture what really remains to be seen in all its unstoppable scarlet effusion. As historian of the guillotine Daniel Arasse avers, there was no avoiding the fact that however much the "inhuman spectacle of public execution" were reduced by the machine, it could not sublimate "the sudden spurt of blood [*une brutale effusion de sang*]."[61]

It is in that way that the guillotine becomes a photographic instant, the moment seized in the heat of its intensity, and in the intensity of its color. But it is not just the effusion of blood, the blood itself that produces a crisis of visibility—something intolerable to see yet fascinating in its intolerability—it is also the crisis of exposing to view the critical tipping point between life and death. Thus, for all that was presumed about the relation between the speed of the machine and invisibility, there came to be concentrated at its focal point—variously called the *lunette* or window— what Arasse calls "the *blind spot* around which there crystallizes a terrible *visibility*."[62] He continues: "It is not that there was nothing to see; but what was seen was something other than the operation of the guillotine. . . . Within the frame in which the blade falls, something does indeed happen, something intolerable."[63]

It is perhaps then no surprise, for reasons as apt as they are macabre, that an executioner's assistant in France came, as the technology of the image developed in the nineteenth century, to be called the "photographer." The so-called photographer's task was to position the condemned person's body once it swung into place on the trestle, and, as the top half of the yoke was fixed in place, to pull the head firmly toward him, holding it by the hair or behind the ears. Thus, hoping neither to be bitten nor lose his own fingers or hands as the blade dropped, he was expected to offer a nicely exposed nape in marriage to the blade. Once the blade had fallen he would quickly remove the severed head, trying to avoid being showered with blood, and place it in the basket. It was clearly the analogous idea of a peephole into abjection that gave rise to photography as a figure for guillotining: the yoke or *lunette* as lens, the blade as shutter, the activator as photographer. As explained by Fernand Meyssonier, who claimed to have served in such a capacity, assisting his father in more than a hundred executions in Algeria between 1947 and 1961, first as voluntary then as official executioner:

> One designates by the term "photographer" the member of the team
> (generally the first assistant) who stands on the "head" side of the
> guillotine. He receives the "client" by passing his arms between the
> two uprights of the machine, an operation that is famously danger-
> ous. . . . From his position he sees the condemned person arrive
> through the "lens" constituted by the lunette, whence the denomina-
> tion "photographer."[64]

But the specific function "activated" by the photographer was the immobility of the instant—or at least an attempt at the same—an immobility
that was as important for a successful decapitation as it was for the clarity of
a photographic image (until progressive improvements in the operation
of the lens and control of the aperture reduced the problem of blurring or
overexposure). Thanks to the executioner's assistant known as the photographer, the client subject remained still for a brief moment, as it were outside of time, a time during which there would be nothing moving except
the blade, set falling by something like the click of a shutter. As it made
contact with the neck the guillotine simultaneously severed the head and
revealed the spectacle of blood flow. Picture-perfect; justice done.

In a discussion that details the extent to which the guillotine introduced
a series of esthetic preferences in the first hundred years of its use, preferences that were reflected in "painting, the art of makeup, wax figures," Patrick Wald Lasowski shows clearly how those literary and artistic fashions
culminated in the esthetic revolution brought about by photography. The
analogies between guillotining and photography abound: in the crowd's
scopophilic enchantment—"One can then imagine an instant of silence.
The pose is struck. Release of the guillotine, and the head cut off";[65]
in the fantasy of capturing that instant of decapitation on film; in the

headrest that portrait photographers will adapt from the guillotine to insure the subject's immobility:

> It is in this sense that the 19th century brings about the encounter, the
> superposition, the filiation between the guillotine and photogra-
> phy. . . . In fact, the guillotine announces and brings about the entry
> of the 19th century into modern times. . . . [It] imposes mechanization,
> anonymity, and the effects of speed and instantaneity.[66]

In his analysis of the guillotine Arasse will add a further vector to this modernist intersection of instantaneous capital punishment and photography,
namely the economics of industrialized automation: "The guillotine, that
product of the Enlightenment, was also one of the first machines considered in economic terms, the cost-effectiveness of its output being evalu-
ated according to the time taken."[67]

Indeed, common to both Dr. Guillotin's assurances to the Constituent
Assembly regarding the efficacy of his machine—decapitation performed
by a simple mechanism, your head off in the blink of an eye without your
feeling a thing—and the promises of photographic reproducibility, is a constant insistence on the progress of mechanical automatization. No longer
does the judicial system have to rely on the fallibility of the human. But,
as we have seen, what is for Guillotin a humanitarian advance will later
amount, for Blackmun, to an unacceptable level of dehumanization.
Indeed, Blackmun's suspicion of the impersonal machine some two centuries later finds an echo in the response to Guillotin's proposals to the 1789
Assembly, which were greeted with derision precisely because his compa-
triots could not reconcile themselves to "the mechanical instantaneousness
of death"[68] that he vaunted. As Arasse explains, "the guillotine was perceived from the first as barbaric, for it brought together two virtually in-
compatible characteristics: a cold technical precision, and the savagery of
physical mutilation."[69]

It is also the case that, if we are to give credence to the accounts of Fernand Meyssonnier, the role of the "photographer" renders Guillotin's
promise of an automatic machine rather less assured. Meyssonnier describes a function that was crucial to the success of an execution, and ascribes rather to a human temporal economy the management of the
"instant" of decapitation. For unless the photographer was able to ensure,
by his own sheer strength, that the condemned person did not instinctively
pull his head back toward the shoulders but instead exposed his neck, there
was a risk that the blade would not cut cleanly, slicing through the cra-
nium, or requiring the final decollation to be performed with a knife. And

it was up to him to direct the proceedings once the head was engaged in the lunette, for the chief executioner, situated on the other side of the machine, could not see when to choose his moment to let the blade fall. Both the machine itself, and the machine of time, therefore, operated thanks to a mechanized or prosthetized human element, as can be understood from the account I quote here at length:

In an execution it is the role of the first assistant, called the "photographer," that is the most skillful and dangerous. From a technical point of view the role of the "photographer" lasts less than five seconds. . . . If sometimes there are badly cut off heads, 95% of the time it is the fault of the "photographer". . . . That is why one has to act fast, and be especially precise, and not panic or rush in such a moment. If I don't pull the head quickly, the condemned person is likely to draw his head back into his shoulders. . . . [Depending on the diameter of the lunette] he might have his whole lower jaw inside the two halves of the lunette and there it'll be botched. Half of the head is torn off and, one time out of four, there are still some muscles attaching the head.

The most dangerous part is just before the upper half of the lunette is secured. When the condemned person seesaws down, I'm there to help. I help the chief executor because the condemned person might turn his head to the side, or pull his head back toward his shoulders. I help so that he doesn't grab on to the half-lunette. If I let him he might bite the half-lunette. And then it's like a vice. He won't let go. A human being knowing he is going to die has terrible strength, he no longer feels pain. So when the condemned person swings down I put my two arms through the uprights.

Yes, my two arms are between the uprights, in the middle of the guillotine. I even practically put my head between the uprights. At that point, watch out! If the chief executioner starts the blade falling . . . I lose my two arms. . . . Yes it's dangerous and risky being a "photographer." Watch out! One has to have confidence in the executioner. He mustn't let go too quickly, otherwise there's an accident, hands cut off. That's why it was me who would say to my father (the chief executioner): "OK, go!" Because the chief executioner, when he drops the upper half-lunette into place, can no longer see. He is on the body side. He can't see what is happening on the other side. He can't see whether I am holding the head steadily, whether the condemned person is in a good position. But I am on the other side. He can't see. And when I say to him "OK, go!," boom, he lets it go [*il déclenche*, also "presses the shutter"]. It is fast, it's really fast. Swinging

"photograph," condensed into the single frame of the lens or "lunette" of the guillotine, at the same time revealing the triumph of technology over the frailty of the human (the blade falling like lightning, a head flying off), and reasserting a naked human animality (blood spurting forth). Though late twentieth-century refinements of such an instant, for example lethal injection, no longer have as point of reference the graphic effusion of blood—except where it finds its equivalent in the sordid botchings that we continue to witness—I would argue that the same realist visual regime obtains.

Clarence Thomas's descriptions of the awful circumstances of the crimes perpetrated by criminals condemned to death, and who, in his view, plainly merit the kinder, gentler execution that we now accord them, bring us full circle from the hanging day scenes and sermons of the age of the trap door to a certain retentionist logic developed in the context of Supreme Court Eighth Amendment debates. Cotton Mather's ministrations, or those of others, were a descriptive prelude to—and often a prelusive description of—what a certain percentage of the crowd would see once the trap door was activated and the condemned one dropped out of sight, launched into eternity. But the whole community of those present would understand the gravity of the occasion and their role in the spectacle. By the time the guillotine came into use, the spectatorial community had lost much of its cohesion; however, the instant inherited from the trap door would then come to be refocused in a new form of graphic visuality reinforced by a new technological form of certainty. Now, with executions having receded into a form of clinical darkroom, Thomas's descriptions bring back to light the self-evidence of a depravity about which the electronic darkness or silence of current lethal injections should not allow us to split hairs: if I can just tell you or show you who these criminals are and what they did, he implies, any objections will be understood as totally obscurantist, and certainly null and void in the face of the Constitution.

Hence, it is no longer a matter of arguing that, should we for a moment let our Puritan guard down and open the door to impure thoughts, we will find ourselves on the road to perdition, in effect mounting the steps of the scaffold. That is not the allegorical or moral truth that is being propounded; rather, what is being communicated is an automatic, realist truth. That truth presumes the possibility of an incontrovertible, as it were photographic demonstration—whence the description of the crime that Thomas gives us—that the only people who suffer the death penalty in our day in the United States are the worst of the worst ("in my decades on the Court,

I have not seen a capital crime that could not be considered sufficiently 'blameworthy' to merit a death sentence"). We are supposed to see for ourselves in the horrors he depicts that it is only the most egregious criminal acts that lead to a sentence of death, just as we are supposed, by means of arguments he advances in the same context, to see or imagine in the clean clinical execution chambers of various state institutions the extents to which we go to insure that those worst of the worst die the least painful of deaths. It is less a moral contrast that he establishes between crime and punishment—although it can easily be exploited in that way—than a photographic convergence, such that two moments continue to be seen, as if superposed in the same graphic space, as was the case with the guillotine: in the latter case, incontrovertible death-dealing and bloodletting (at the scene of execution) superimposed over implacable mechanical automaticity and technological certainty; in contemporary times, intolerable cruelty (at the scene of the crime) superimposed over the same implacable mechanical automaticity of the lethal injection apparatus.

Of course, my reconstitution of that logic appears to involve a flaw: The realist image cannot in fact be a superposition of two images, for that would detract from its clarity. But we can understand such a flaw to exist in any realist ideology that presumes to function on the basis of an unmediated technological automatism such as the operation of a camera. The image cannot in fact appear in all its clarity unless it is "accompanied," however implicitly, by the extensive support system that produces it: the supposed automatically produced photograph in fact relies on an inversion of the real in a dark room, the same dark room (*camera obscura*) that names the apparatus, just as it relies on a chemistry of development and reproduction, not to mention its reception within a specific cultural and ideological field. We would have to understand all those mediations as subsuming the simple reproduction of the real that a Bazin supposes.

Or else, to interpret the superposition of two images in terms that are more specific to our interest here: the existence within the same visual space and temporal instant—that of realist revelation—of an egalitarian, even humanitarian, and technologically refined execution apparatus on the one hand, and, on the other, a well framed and focused photograph, suggests that the instant is not single and indivisible, that it is a constructed rather than an automatic and naturally occurring instant, that it has no absolute status, and of course no absolutely irreducible duration: no pure *instancy*. Against the evolution from Niépce's eight-hour exposure, through Daguerre's fifteen minutes, to the Kodak Brownie's 1/50th second at the dawn of the twentieth century one could no doubt match the

instantanizations of various methods of execution from guillotine to lethal injection, without for all that arriving at anything other than an idealized conception of a still divisible instant.

There is no degree zero instant. An innovation such as the guillotine,
supposedly invisible by virtue of its lightning speed, stages the very paradox of the instant. Citing a commentary on the guillotine that dates from
the Terror, according to which "from the first point of contact to the last
there is no distance; there is only an indivisible point: the axe falls and the
victim has died," Arasse draws this conclusion: "there lies the frightening
paradox of the guillotine; this 'zero distance' defining an indivisible point
in time is, *in spatial terms*, a height of fourteen feet. Raised to the top of the
uprights, the blade defines a space which provides a figure for the instant,
which is a *spatial figure of the instant*."[77] The guillotine gives an instant that
measures fourteen feet: fourteen times one foot, seven times two feet, and
so on, an obviously divisible instant; merely a figure of or for the instant.
Similarly, lethal injection, in its three-drug protocol form, has nothing
purely instantaneous about it; it is an instant divided into the moment of
sodium thiopental or midazolam, the moment of pancuronium bromide,
and the moment of potassium chloride. Like Guillotin's falling blade,
projected head, and spurting blood, it represents the divided time of successive instants. For that reason, beginning with the trap door gallows
and all the way to lethal injection, what we call the instant of execution,
what we call upon to function as an instant, will never be anything other
than the definition and management of a noninstantaneous instant.

Photography will have taught us, contra Bazin, that the management of
the instant is also the structure of control or manipulation of the instant.
He was ready to concede that "the personality of the photographer enters
into the proceedings . . . in his selection of the object to be photographed
and by way of the purpose he has in mind," but presumed that to be a benign and limited intervention (it is the single word "only" that my ellipsis
drops out of the quotation).[78] Bazin omits to say here, for example, that
the photographer must also regulate the amount of light that will enter the
camera by adjusting speed and aperture settings, on the basis of which the
depth of field—the extent to which foreground, center and background will
all be in focus—will be determined. Indeed, given his extensive promo-
tion, in other writings, of a style of filmmaking that prefers deep focus and
long takes, and often highly choreographed movement by the actors, over
multiple shots that must then be subjected to a more complex editing process, those technical choices are very important and the production of the

photographic image immediately becomes less "automatic" than he imagines. There is no degree zero of intervention when it comes to photography, but rather a set of possible interventions that go from pointing the apparatus all the way to highly codified aesthetic choices, and including everything in between (field of vision, angle, lighting, focus, type of camera, type of film, developing and printing processes; and in the case of moving pictures, what we call editing or montage).

I would argue that the analogy I have been developing between the instant of the image and the instant of an execution carries over into a comparable set of choices. One can argue that current methods of execution in the United States manage the instant in a nonmanipulative, benign, even progressive manner, and do so within a regime of visibility that excludes, as much as possible, any effects of spectacle. In contrast to international practices among nation states—hanging in India and Japan, firing squad in Taiwan and Indonesia, and beheading in Saudi Arabia[79]—that argument would appear to have weight. And indeed, beyond those examples, another contrast warrants being drawn. In the period during which I wrote this book, everyone, from a Cotton Mather to a Clarence Thomas and well beyond, had been outranked, in all respects, by the entity that calls itself the Islamic State: outranked in terms of the graphic spectacle of an execution, from burning to drowning to beheading or worse,[80] outranked in terms of the cautionary discourse, spoken or written, that accompanies it, and outranked in terms of the visual surplus value of mediatic dissemination, of the publicity and telephenomenality of the event. We would seem to have been reduced to rank amateurs, bashful virgins, prurient titillaters in the domain of the image, in the purveyance of moral education, and in the management of the instant of an execution.

Islamic State's cruel and morbid exploitation of a crude machinery of death, whether it be the sword, the drowning cage, or the firebombed cell, is a calculated manipulation of the machinery of the instant of death designed for maximum spectacular effect. It aspires to universal exposure by means of the Internet. It defies every measure of judicial conventionality, and in a sense one should not dignify it with inclusion in discussion of the death penalty, consigning it instead to the category of murder. Unfortunately, however, the executions perpetrated by the Islamic State mime and mock in every way the possibilities that are created by the most judicial of death penalties. By opening a space that it must then try to control by recourse to criteria having no relation to the automatism that defines it, the most faithful reproduction of the real allows for every faithless distortion of the real; so the congruence Clarence Thomas wants to establish between

a heinous crime and an impassive judicial death penalty allows for a hei-
nously murderous or criminal death penalty.

It is, after all, difficult to read Thomas's presentation of his argument
in *Glossip* without interpreting in it some sort of advocacy for a vengeful
retributive justice, the same vengeful retributive justice that the Islamic
State exploits to the hilt. By means of his shock image reality check he implies, at least, that the worst criminals deserve worse than their punishment,
that the retribution the contemporary state visits upon them is unjust retribution given the egregiousness of their crimes. Once one accepts the
retributive permissibility of the death penalty, one risks going down the
slope of arguing for more and more punitive pain: "each of these crimes,"
Thomas insists, "was egregious enough to merit the severest condemnation that society has to offer." That would be the same argument and
same logic that was advanced by our Puritan forebears, by the eighteenth-
century French monarchy, and by Islamic State, however much those different judicial systems would disagree over the elements within that logic:
"crime," "egregious," and "severest."

It is also difficult to read Thomas's vivid descriptions without suspect-
ing that they contain an iota of scopophilia, even prurience; not that he
takes pleasure in *what* he describes, but that he takes a certain pleasure in
the very describing, in offering such a graphic visuality. Yet even if one
rejects my suspicions, or uncharitable ascriptions of impure motive, it remains that his argument obeys a rhetorical logic that by definition cannot
be neutral. Once again, it is a rhetorical logic that is *structurally* no different from the awful spectacular excesses of the images provided by the
Islamic State. In each case, there is an appropriation of the instant for
rhetorical purposes, even if on one side the case is being made that we are
as just as one can ever be, whereas on the other side it is first a matter of
celebrating cruelty in the act itself, and second in compounding that cruelty by means of the technological reproducibility of the Internet image,
by effectively forcing us to watch.

Every capital punishment henceforth turns around the appropriation of
the instant. That is so in the most straightforward sense because the rejection by the West in the seventeenth and eighteenth centuries of putting
to death by means of judicial and judicious torture means that the death
penalty is now defined as something other than that torment, as some form
of, or attempt at reducing the punishment—to return to the terms of the
four dissenting justices in *Resweber*—"as nearly as possible to no more than
that of death itself" (*Resweber*, 474). Torture as more or less prolonged physical punishment has become, from that point on, a separate category from

a death penalty understood as more or less instantaneous punishment. Thus, although both death by torture or torment such as Damiens suffered in 1757, and the modern death penalty involve managing the *time* of putting to death, only the second manages that time by means of a presumed *instantaneity*. Furthermore, despite the fact that execution practices around the world vary considerably, and in some cases, it might be argued, regress back across the line into torture, the adoption by successive international treaties gives to the eighteenth-century human rights rejection of torture universal recognition. And, as I have just contended, even the executions practiced by an Islamic State that explicitly rejects those very human rights values in favor of a premodern judicial apparatus, and that promotes precisely its outlaw status, cannot avoid addressing and thereby acknowledging the fact of the instant. At least when it comes to the executions—whether drowning, firebombing or beheading—that it wants the rest of the world to see, there is a sadistic exploitation not of forms of torture but of forms of more or less instantaneous execution.

As long as one is in the logic of the death penalty, one is necessarily in the business of the technological management of the instant, and faced with the impossibility of any absolute circumscription of that instant. An execution henceforth can be only relatively slow and painful—or, conversely, relatively fast and painless—but beyond a certain point of slowness, however difficult it be to determine that point, we are no longer talking about the death penalty. Supposedly, for Thomas, the American death penalty has now managed to reduce the pain of punishment to an unassailably acceptable extent, in spite of the fact that some executions in the United States continue to paint a much less pretty picture than others, and most would accept that the forty-odd minutes Clayton Lockett spent writhing and gasping for breath in April 2014, which set in motion revisions of the fatal cocktail in Oklahoma, was far from pretty, unacceptably so. But the only way to avoid—absolutely—both the intractable Eighth Amendment debates such as dominate *Glossip* and previous cases, as well as invidious comparisons that go all the way to the bloody excesses of the Islamic State, is not to perform capital punishment. Whatever physiological and psychological, juridical and political, ethical and moral distinctions can be made, and however stark those distinctions be, between an execution undertaken by the U.S. system of justice and the Islamic State system of justice, *both share the structural space of capital punishment and negotiate or appropriate its instant.* Any structural distinction drawn by the death penalty operates not between one form of it and another, but between retentionist states or entities such as those just mentioned, and abolitionist states.

As long as one is in the death penalty, therefore, inhabiting a position that accepts it as a (e.g., constitutional) practice, one is automatically in the business of arguing the merits of this or that form or speed or efficacy of an execution. Some are preferable to others. Perhaps sodium thiopental plus pancuronium bromide plus potassium chloride is preferable to pentobarbital plus pancuronium bromide plus potassium chloride, or midazolam plus hydromorphone. As I read it, it is frustration with having to decide within those parameters that leads Breyer in *Glossip*, after twenty years or so of presuming the death penalty to be constitutional, to argue, finally, that it isn't working, and therefore to challenge its legality. It may well be a similar frustration that leads Thomas to plead for giving up on the hairsplitting; to suggest that we are talking after all about more or less painless forms of death for the worst of the worst, who inflicted painful or torturous death on their victims.

If, conversely, one is outside the death penalty, in the sense of refusing its permissibility, understanding it to be inhumane as a matter of principle, in all instances, then there can be no comparing sodium thiopental plus pancuronium bromide plus potassium chloride to pentobarbital plus pancuronium bromide plus potassium chloride, or midazolam plus hydromorphone, just as there can be no comparing beheading to burning to drowning; one form of execution is as unacceptable as another. From that place beyond the death penalty, the door to it off its hinges, the scaffold, guillotine and gurney dismantled, from that point on, though it by no means signify the end or bottom of the abyss of the spectacle of terror, torture, suffering—that of humans to begin with, but not necessarily to end with—something in the instant will have been transformed. From that point on the instant we call snuffing, the extinguishing of the candle of life, will have lost something of its imagistic force and violence. Something will have changed in the concept of the instant of death, and hence in the concept of human time, or at least human judicial time.

CHAPTER 3

The Future Anterior of Blood

There will have been blood:

> When the blade cuts through the neck of the condemned one, three
> unequal jets spurt out forcefully: the two cariotids project blood in
> powerful jets that can exceed two meters; in the center there is a lesser
> whitish jet extending 30 centimeters, namely the cephalorachidian
> fluid that, brutally compressed, spurts from the severed vertebral
> column. The recipient that the head falls into has an external wall high
> enough to stop these spurts of blood. But there is some splashing,
> clumsiness. One inconvenience of the job of the executioner is that his
> clothes are soiled. Sanson was already complaining about that.[1]

In France, the country that instituted the Declaration of the Rights of Man
and introduced what was conceived of as a humane, instantaneous death
penalty in 1792, there will nevertheless have been that blood. And by re-
taining the guillotine as method of execution up to the moment of abolition, France will have insured that such state-sponsored bloodletting
remained in the Western imaginary until 1977.

So there will have been blood, but according to the tense and temporality of the formulation, by the time we get to the present moment, the
moment in question, there will be no more; no more blood. Blood will
be over; after *having been all over*, it will *all be over*. It is tempting to imagine that: no more blood, blood no more. It is tempting to take the time to
imagine that: no more blood for all. For there will also have been time,
flowing like blood, and coming up against the particular programmed
interruption of mortal time that is the death penalty. Time for the condemned one will have run out; for a convict who is executed, the state
will have announced the event of no more time. He or she will have lived,
will have had time, up to the moment when he or she has no more; he will
have had blood flowing until the moment when his blood flows no more.

The French call what *will have happened* a future anterior; in English we
call it a "future perfect." In the French language the future anterior refers
to a future in the past that is nevertheless anterior to, that precedes another explicit or implied event that could be either in the future or the
past. It figures in a diversity of constructions going well beyond possible
English examples such as "by the time the DNA evidence becomes available you will have already been executed" or "the Supreme Court will have
made its decision by this time tomorrow." In French it is also used in the
following invented formulations (transliterations of the French usage appearing in brackets): "as soon as the drugs [will] have been found on the
black market, the execution can proceed"; "the public defender missed
that important detail as he fell [will have fallen] asleep"; "in 2005, in *Roper*,
Scalia was [will have been] scandalized by the idea that American jurisprudence might be inflected by international opinion or conventions when it
comes to executing juveniles." The choice of the French classification for
my chapter title is intended to emphasize a difference between what is done,
perfected, achieved in time, and what still seeks to determine the anterior-
ity or posteriority of the thing; how in this quirk of language there is a type
of intersection between future and past such that what appeared to be happening within the perspective of its own future gets preempted by the past.
For according to my argument in this chapter, that is what happens when
the death penalty presumes to abandon the shedding of blood: the more
capital punishment claims to move beyond the cruelty such bloodshed
represents, the more it appears that blood *will still have been* a necessary
element in its operation; and that is because, according to the hypothesis
that I will develop here in detail, blood is a function of time.

My first sentence also serves to imagine some time in the future, a point
at which the death penalty will have been practiced in the United States

but is no more; imagining also the time it will (or would) have taken, less for the current death penalty to be abolished, than for the casuistry of calculating the permissible quantity of pain and suffering to appear as the absurdity or obscenity that it is. I'd like, and this book would like to imagine a time when that calculation is held to be similar to, and as unconscionably incoherent as determining how to define a slave as a fraction of a whole person: three fifths, as we remember, in 1787, thirty years after Damiens was divided into quarters. Perhaps by 2057 or 2087 we will be able to smile at the manifestly ludicrous seriousness with which Supreme Court justices must currently determine how much it has to hurt to hurt too much as the state puts someone to death, how much more pain there is in a cocktail of midazolam (to render you unconscious), vecuronium or pancuronium bromide (to stop your breathing), and potassium chloride (to stop the heart), than, say, in a single dose of pentobarbital; or how long a condemned person has to writhe on the gurney to demonstrate that their constitution cannot withstand permissible constitutional pain: whether the correct dosage of time is eleven minutes, as it was for Scott Dawn Carpenter in Oklahoma in 1997; or twenty-four minutes, as it was for Raymond Landry in Texas in 1988; or twenty-five minutes for Dennis McGuire in Ohio in 2014; or thirty-four minutes for Angel Diaz in Florida in 2006; or forty-three minutes for Clayton D. Lockett in Oklahoma in 2014.[2] Perhaps by 2057 or 2087 those good-faith Supreme Court deliberations will seem as offensively quaint as Kant's lucid sense of how to apply the *ius talionis* in the cases of rape, pederasty, and bestiality (castration, quite clearly, in the first two cases, permanent expulsion from civil society in the third, obviously).[3] In the meantime, however, while there is still the death penalty, that moment will manifestly not have arrived.

In the Anglo-American world, the generalized institution of hanging as preferred form of capital punishment until late into the nineteenth century either answers to, or satisfies by fiat, a desire for a death penalty that avoids the blood-soaked practices of the guillotine, and those of previous times. In 1769, William Blackstone's *Commentaries of the Law of England* was able to offer this self-congratulatory observation: "It will afford pleasure to an English reader and do honor to the English law, to compare [the catalogue of English forms of death penalty] with that shocking apparatus of death and torment to be met with in the criminal codes of almost every other nation in Europe." And as recently as 1999, in *Provenzano v. Moore*, when the Florida Supreme Court weighed, and confirmed the Eighth Amendment constitutionality of the electric chair following the botched execution of Allen Lee Davis, dissenting Justice Leander Shaw saw fit to compare Davis's "bloody execution" with France's use of the guillotine:

> As conceded by the State in the present proceeding, the guillotine as used in the French Revolution is a prime example of a method that would fail in this regard [a method of execution must entail no undue violence, mutilation, or disgrace], for while beheading results in a quick, relatively painless death, it entails frank violence (i.e., gross laceration and bloodletting) and mutilation (i.e., decapitation) and disgrace (i.e., public spectacle) and thus is facially cruel.[4]

The frank violence and mutilation of the guillotine makes it prima facie cruel; it cannot avoid gross laceration and bloodletting. For blood is itself cruel: the Latin *cruor* refers primarily to blood that "flows from a wound, a stream of blood," in contrast to the less restrictive *sanguis*, which designates both blood "circulating in bodies and that shed by wounding."[5] Externally streaming blood, the effusion produced by a mechanism like the guillotine, points to a conjoined history of cruelty and blood, as Derrida notes beginning in the third session of the first year of his death penalty seminar: "What is the *meaning* of cruelty? Is it *blood*, a history of blood, as the etymology seems to indicate (*cruor* is red blood, blood that flows)?"[6] But he follows up those two questions with a third, asking whether "one put[s] an end to cruelty on the day that one no longer makes blood flow?" (*DP I*, 96). That question, which led Derrida to understand differently from Foucault the transformation of punishment in the second half of the eighteenth century, preferring to call it a "de-spectacularization" (*DP I*, 43), is reposed in the ninth session of the second year, and explicitly related to "the move from decapitation . . . to lethal injection, or even to the gas chamber, which no longer causes bleeding" (*DP II*, 220). Thus, a first element of the complicated set of ideas that I will try to analyze here is the question of whether, or how, blood flows in a visibly bloodless death penalty.

Derrida begins his seminar series by invoking four paradigmatic executions: those of Socrates, Jesus, Al-Hallaj, and Joan of Arc (*DP I*, 21–22). Among those examples, only Al-Hallaj dies a really bloody death—by some combination of torture, crucifixion, and dismemberment reminiscent of Ravaillac and Damiens—in contrast to Socrates's hemlock, Joan of Arc's burning, and Jesus's crucifixion. Blood is already occulted even in Jesus' case, although the subsequent iconography has often wallowed in it.[7] For although Jesus was whipped and crowned with thorns, the Gospel of John, the sole gospel to record the fact, states that it was only after he died that a soldier pierced his side so that out flowed blood and water (John 19:34). One might therefore suppose that more primitive technologies of execution, but also contemporary forms, play on a judicious application of pain that works precisely by controlling blood flow, which also involves a play on visibility and, in complicated ways that we have seen, on spectacle. Blood loss is economized in order to prolong the torture in the cases of flaying and crucifixion, and it is as it were bypassed in the case of hanging; blood is purified with elemental fire in the case of burning and infected in order to confound death with anesthesia in cases from Socrates's hemlock to lethal injection.

We have also seen in some detail how the post-Enlightenment period appeared to transpose or deflect the question of blood, and relations between blood and cruelty, by concentrating on mechanisms of an instantaneous capital punishment, by eliminating the duration that is conceptually consonant with sensibility, and therefore with pain. But Shaw's dissent in *Provenzano* again combines the idea of cruelty deriving from the duration of an execution with that due to a presence of blood.[8] That is because blood, as a function of cruelty, is necessarily articulated through time: how much flows or for how long. Bloodshed belies the instant; a bloodless execution, it is presumed, enables it, but as we analyzed, identifying the instant proves elusive. My overarching presumption in this chapter will be that the flow of blood and the passage of time are indeed inseparable, and that it is once again the death penalty that enables us to interrogate particulars of the strangely prosthetic relation that obtains between the human and its forms of temporality: Time is the fulcrum where blood meets cruelty beyond any etymology, and via the instant of putting to death the supposed naturality of blood comes to be doubled by an uncanny mechanicity.

Derrida's question about the cruelty or noncruelty of a bloodless death penalty is put into relation with two broader ideas. First, blood is for Derrida the site of a homo-hematological nexus whereby "the cultural history of blood, and also the imaginary, symbolic, phantasmatic, techno-scientific history of blood . . . ultimately merges with the history of what is called man" (ibid.). And that nexus extends through the history of "what one conceives as blood, blood conceived [*le sang conçu*], a history of the treatment of blood, a history of bloodletting, of the blood one sees flow, of the blood one lets flow, of the blood one causes to flow, of the blood that one does or doesn't staunch" (ibid.). In terms of what I have just stated, the merging of the history of blood with the history of humanity derives from the fact that blood marks *the time of the human*. Blood is the temporal measure of life, specifically human (or mammalian) life.[9] It is therefore a crucial question for the death penalty as interruption of that measure; and conversely it makes the death penalty a crucial question not just for those who suffer it, but as well for the human in general: Capital punishment disrupts life as bloodflow of time.

Derrida's second broader idea is implied in the formulation "what one conceives as blood." He expresses it in these stark terms at the beginning of the session:

> The concept and blood.
>   How to *conceive*, how to conceive of it, the relation between the concept and blood?
>   How to conceive of blood? Can blood be conceived? And how might a concept bleed, how might it, this concept, lead to an effusion [*épanchement*] of blood? (*DP II*, 214)

In this clear reference to Hegel, as canonical conceiver of the concept and of speculative dialectics in the Western tradition, Derrida draws on ideas published in *Glas* some twenty-five years earlier. He returns to the importance given, in Hegel's development of the concept and of absolute knowledge, not just to Christianity as the supreme moment of revealed religion, but to blood as that which, in that moment, is shed without for all that being lost: "we have had to conclude, since Hegel, that the blood that Christ lost on the cross, he didn't lose, it wasn't lost. The concept, the history of spirit, the history of truth or the history of God will in a certain way have staunched its flow. The absolute concept will have staunched the blood by giving it meaning" (215). As Derrida reads Hegel, Christ's blood managed to flow as a result of his cruel execution, yet at the same time be sublated and invisibilized by the concept. Blood gives the concept its sense; blood underwrites the concept, and a primary sublation would be a type of transfusion: the sublation of blood by the concept: "A first philosophical and Hegelian, dialectical response to the question of the relations between the concept and blood is that the concept, well, the concept is the end of blood" (ibid.). The concept therefore succeeds, in Hegel's thinking, at the price of blood.

The discussion to follow will culminate in an analysis of how Hegel's dialectics causes blood to flow uncannily both inside and outside the body. What his concept thus introduces, contemporaneous with the despectacularization of a cruel death penalty, is effectively an artificial blood flowing like an external prosthesis to the human, a prosthesis whose name will again be time. My examination of the conceptual nexus of blood, time, and the death penalty begins, however, with Socrates. His capital crime, as we know, was that of perverting the youth of Athens by teaching them, among other things, to make of life a preparation for death. Many centuries later, Heidegger will have revised Socrates's version of a life spent in expectation of death by means of a very different conception of human time on the basis of which we might resist our static capture within the drudgery of the present. Heidegger's *ex-static* time challenges the presumption that time consists of a succession of "nows," a presumption that, he believes, has persisted since Aristotle and continued through Hegel. However, as I have suggested, time in Hegel is more complex, the particular complexity of interest to me being time's relation to blood.

Socrates is the obligatory philosophical or historical antecedent for any discussion of the conjunction between human temporality and the practice of capital punishment. His death penalty, recounted in the *Apology*, *Crito*, and *Phaedo*, was carried out in as anesthetic a manner as was available in 399 BCE, by means of a death penalty that approximated current practices of lethal injection. His death by lethal ingestion resembled a forced suicide—if that is not an oxymoron—rather than the violence that continues to plague even the most contemporary practices of execution. Yet, for all that, it was an execution whose timing appeared wholly determined by the clock, even if the ticking of that clock had to deal with elements of chance, in particular with a reprieve provided by meteorological whim.

We are told that almost a month elapsed between Socrates's being sentenced to death and the carrying out of that sentence. On the day before the sentence the Athenian state had sent a ship to Delos for the ritual commemoration of the safe return from Crete of Theseus's seven youths and maidens, and custom required that nothing like an execution be allowed to disturb the social and religious balance before the ship returned safely. As Phaedo recounts: "They have a law that as soon as this mission begins the city must be kept pure, and no public executions may take place until the ship has reached Delos and returned again, which sometimes takes a long time, if the winds happen to hold it back."[10] The eventual arrival of the ship is narrated in Crito's dialogue: "It hasn't actually come in yet, but I expect that it will be here today, judging from the report of some people who have just arrived from Sunium and left it there. It's quite clear from their account that it will be here today, and so by tomorrow, Socrates, you will have to . . . to end your life."[11]

It becomes clear, on the one hand, that the timing of Socrates's execution involves a complicated set of aleatory effects, which are as if programmed into it: how many days will it take to sail to Delos and back; how much time will elapse between the moment the ship is sighted from Cape Sounion and the moment when it docks in Athens; presuming it stops first on the peninsula, when precisely will it arrive in Piraeus; how strictly will "what the authorities say" concerning Socrates's having to "die on the day after the boat arrives" be interpreted?[12] And indeed, what if the ship were to be wrecked at sea, never to return?

On the other hand, in the ancient Greek context, those seeming chance effects would in fact be controlled by the Fates. Indeed, in Socrates's case, the commemoration that gives him a reprieve is that of a tragic fatality, the ritual trip to Delos being made to honor Apollo in thanks for, and in memory of Theseus's victory over the Minotaur. But prior to that victory, seven youths and maidens had to be sacrificed on a regular basis by being sent to appease King Minos of Crete, where they were either consumed by the Minotaur or lost in the Labyrinth. The voyage to Delos was therefore a memorial to the fateful and fatal sacrifice of Athens' innocents; it was the city's autoimmune death sentence, a regular inoculation that continued until Theseus decided to settle things with the Minotaur by taking it upon himself to sail with the victims. Thanks to Daedalus's advice and Ariadne's thread, he was able to kill the beast and exit the Labyrinth safely. Thereafter Athens would be able to avoid the slaughter of its innocents, but not without another tragic fatality, the needless sacrifice not of the youngest and finest but of the revered monarch himself: state infanticide thus became regicide. For Theseus, having told his father, King Aegeus, that he would rig a white sail to signify victory over the Minotaur and a black sail to signify failure, omitted to hoist the correct sail (perhaps because of his indecent haste to abandon Ariadne on Naxos). As a result, the sighting of his ship from Cape Sounion brought about a self-imposed sentence of death for King Aegeus, who, seeing the black sail and presuming his son was dead, threw himself into the sea.

The apparent clockwork of Socrates's death penalty does not, therefore, function within a mortal temporality conceived of in the way that we Moderns understand it. The mythology and ontology of ancient Greece prescribes a time that functions outside any human reckoning, and what the state imposed on Socrates may be called less a death sentence than a mortality sentence regulated by fate. With or without that sentence, however, Socrates famously inaugurated a negotiation of the fate of mortality that we continue to understand in terms of "preparing [oneself] for dying and death," following the example of "true philosophers" who spurn the body and instead "make dying their profession."[13] Within that logic, which has of course been revived by any number of thinkers throughout the

Western tradition, the chronometric interruption of mortality constituted by capital punishment is tempered, even transcended by forms of philosophical serenity in the face of death. As Socrates argues in the *Apology*, "to be afraid of death . . . is to think that one knows what one does not know. No one knows with regard to death whether it is not really the greatest blessing that can happen to a man, but people dread it as though they were certain that it is the greatest evil."[14] Preparing for death, making death one's profession means in that respect renouncing the whole clockwork of mortality; Socrates's preparation for death takes place as it were outside of life, at least outside of a life measured by mortal time. That allows him both to reproach his judges for their worthless and hence wasteful economy of time—"for the sake of a very small gain in time you are going to earn the reputation . . . of having put Socrates to death . . . [whereas] if you had waited just a little while, you would have had your way in the course of nature"[15]—and to reject Crito's invitation, at the end, to stave off the inevitable, by insisting that there is "no need to hurry." Socrates replies: "I believe that I should gain nothing by drinking the poison a little later—I should only make myself ridiculous in my own eyes if I clung to life and hugged it when it has no more to offer."[16] The example taught by Socrates's death penalty would be an acceptance of one's fate such as judicial logic presumes and encourages to this day—assume the crime, make amends to the victim, consent to the punishment—in exchange for an execution without violence or suffering. And indeed, as we noted, his execution would seem to be in accord with all the norms of a humanitarian post-Enlightenment death penalty whose evolution we have discussed at length. In Albert Camus's famous abolitionist text "Reflections on the Guillotine" (1957), the French writer makes reference to the Greeks who, "after all, were more humane with their hemlock" and the "relative freedom" they afforded their condemned.[17] Camus ends his text by arguing that if France is unable to abolish the death penalty, the execution should at least be carried out by means of "an anesthetic that would allow the condemned man to slip from sleep to death (which would be left within his reach for at least a day so that he could use it freely and would be administered to him in another form if he were unwilling or weak of will)," thereby putting "a little decency into what is at present but a sordid and obscene exhibition."[18] Above all, Camus is insisting, his country needs to move beyond the "revolting butchery" of truncation with its "spurts of blood dat[ing] from a barbarous period,"[19] namely the period when execution was inseparable from torture and when blood shed was the sign of a suffering body, a body suspended in the passive time of its torment.

Socrates's bloodless, anesthetic death is therefore alleviated further by his preparation for it, by his renouncing the temporality of mortality that regulates the span of life for the greater part of humanity. Much closer to us, Heidegger undertook a thorough recasting of the relation to time of the "being [*Seiende*], which we ourselves in each case are and which includes inquiry among the possibilities of its being," namely Dasein.[20] Heidegger's recasting, of course, took place by means of an investigation of how Dasein finds itself thrown into a world of other beings in which it has to "take care."[21] That is something it may do inauthentically, by falling prey to the everydayness of the world, being "tranquilized," "lost in the publicness of the they," or "tangled up [*verfängt*] in itself" (*BT* 169–71). Or it may do so authentically, which does not mean achieving some superior, uncorrupted version of the inauthentic but consists rather in "a modified grasp of everydayness" (172).

Now, as Heidegger comes to conclude Division One of his analysis (*Being and Time* will complete only two of six projected divisions), he returns to the question of care as if to displace the sense of how Dasein phenomenologically *is*. He seeks to move from the inevitable, or seeming, *spatial* connotations of being-in-the-world toward the *temporality* that is, for him, its primordial sense. Falling prey to everydayness means, most importantly for Heidegger, falling prey to a particular version of the present, one that neither provides existential enjoyment of the moment, nor frees Dasein from the stasis of the present, understood more precisely as the stasis of the instant as objectifiable unit of time. As we have seen, it would be that very conception of the instant—the condemned person's institutionally imposed, codified, and implemented instant of death—that is appropriated by capital punishment.

The lever for Heidegger's shift into temporality is the uncanniness produced by an "anxiety" that "fetches Dasein back out of its entangled absorption in the 'world'" (182). Thanks to anxiety Dasein recognizes that it has fled from itself (in the they), and comes to understand a potentiality of its being-in-the-world that orients it instead toward the future. Dasein's manner of being-in-the-world, defined as care, thus leads it not only to understand its situation vis-à-vis other beings but also to realize its own unrealized potential: "As long as Dasein is, something is always still outstanding: what it can and will be" (224). By means of that argument Heidegger will have effectively rejoined being to time: by simply being, by simply being in the world, by simply taking care of what is thereby encountered, Dasein is futurally invested in what it can become in relation to that world. Dasein therefore comes into time, its being becomes temporal: *What it takes care of above all else is time.*

It is also on that basis that Heidegger will define the specific temporality of Dasein as being-toward-death. The idea of Dasein's potentiality as something "always still outstanding" cannot avoid the implication of an end signified by death: "the 'end' itself belongs to what is outstanding [and] the 'end' of being-in-the-world is death" (224). So the ultimate uncanniness of being-in-the-world derives not from some nonspecific anxiety but rather from being thrown into a relation with death; as soon as Dasein is, it is ahead of itself, but we understand that what lies ultimately ahead, is death: "Death is a way to be that Dasein takes over as soon as it is" (236). As soon as it is, Dasein is involved in caring, it has no choice in that; being involved in caring, its understands its potential, for example the potential to care otherwise but also the potential simply to exist from one day to the next; but in realizing those potentials, let's say as passively or as actively as it wishes, as authentically or inauthentically as it cares, it is at the same time potentializing itself toward, and in death. That logic functions less, however, in the sense of being afraid of one's demise, than as an unsettling existential mood that, at the same time, works as an extreme challenge. For there is no stepping out of that existential situation, no handing it over for someone else or something else to deal with. Death—when it actually comes, as well as in the way it clouds life—has to be dealt with all alone: "Insofar as it 'is,' death is always essentially my own" (231).

From that perspective, Heidegger's ontology produces a way of being for Dasein that resembles Socrates's insistence on making a profession of dying. Although death counteracts, logically speaking, the dynamic potential that was presumed as soon as Dasein came to be in the world, it will nevertheless constitute the finite terminus of that potential, hence its fulfillment; there will, after all, be no Dasein beyond it. Death is the term and endpoint of a mortal's time. Once one understands that "with death, Dasein stands before itself in its *ownmost* potentiality of being," once being-in-the world becomes "the possibility of no-longer-being-able-to-be-there" (241), then everything lived goes into the effort of dealing with that potentiality. As we shall see further in Chapter 4, that potentiality means this paradox: Dasein's most extreme possibility also represents its "absolute impossibility" (ibid.). Not only, then, must Dasein face the fact that life and all the effort one puts into living comes to an end in death, but it must also prepare for something that it cannot know or experience in advance. In turn, one can make all that the pretext for various forms of avoidance, for example an "everydayness" that modifies one's empirical certainty (yes, I will die) with another (I am still alive, so I'm not dying just yet); or an everydayness that simply allows supposedly more pressing, immediate concerns to get in the way: "Everyday taking care of things makes definite for itself the indefiniteness of certain death by interposing before it those manageable urgencies . . . nearest to us" (248).

If Dasein were to hold death before itself as its most "eminent possibility" (250), it would be able to relate to it as a form of actualization and so attain authentic existence, transforming the mood-defined everyday into a life of "unshakable joy [*gerüstete Freude*]" (296). Death will not as a result be overcome, nor will one find a way of experiencing it before the fact, nor will one be able simply to treat it as an expectation (or conversely, convince oneself it will never happen). Heidegger instead asks us to prepare for death by means of a combination of resoluteness and anticipation, to transform being-toward-death into what he calls, by means of a double typographical emphasis, "*passionate, anxious* **freedom toward death**" (255).[22] Furthermore, in a move that returns us more closely to the terms of reference given in Socrates, such a freedom is related to "fate." On the one hand, of course, the certainty that Dasein will die necessary makes death its destiny or fate. On the other hand, by referring to fate, Heidegger is putting a seemingly modern concept of freedom, that of freedom toward death, into a paradoxical relationship with a fate that—from that modern point of view—it is difficult not to conceive of as deterministic: "Only being free *for* death gives Dasein its absolute goal. . . . The finitude of existence thus seized upon tears one back out of [the] endless multiplicity of closest possibilities offering themselves—those of comfort, shirking and taking things easy— and brings Dasein to the simplicity of its *fate* [*Shicksals*]" (365).[23]

In fact, though, Heidegger wants to make the simplicity of Dasein's fate a function of its freedom, which is what he presumes to do by radically rewriting the concept of temporality. However much death be inevitable or fated, freedom for death is a liberation, out of the "now" of a classical concept of time, into ecstatic temporality, allowing Dasein as it were to stretch along the span of time while at the same time living—double emphasis again—"***in the Moment*** *for 'its time'*" (366). It is as if Dasein, in its authentic possibility, were living along a parallel axis to the operations of fate, or indeed, by running ahead toward its destined death, were able to bring that predicted future to bear on the moment. Whereas we would normally understand fate as the events of our lives preordained beyond our control, written in stone in some supernatural register, a freed Dasein goes ahead of itself to meet the inevitability of its death, and in so doing undoes the obstructionist pall that death casts over life. At the same time, it imports that type of preemptive strike against death into everyday existence, as though *fating* itself in all its moments: "We call fate the anticipatory handing oneself down to the there of the Moment that lies in resoluteness" (368).

In *Being and Time*, therefore, death is promoted from being the mark of human finitude to become the motor for a thorough reinterpretation of temporality. Starting from a seemingly naïve analysis of how beings attend, by means of "care," to what is within immediate reach in everyday life, the argument has progressed to dealing with what is outside of reach—the death that is the presumed external limit of living—bringing that back in, both to unsettle the everyday and encourage a more authentic experience of it. Through that argument, Heidegger has not just disturbed the presumptive habits of moment-to-moment existence but also jolted what we call the present moment out of its supposed security. Once Dasein is being-toward-death it can no more revert to living through, or along, something it naively interprets as a "succession of nows" (314); it *is*, in time, otherwise.

As I recalled earlier, an objectively identifiable instant, a "now," is precisely what the death penalty requires. The appropriation of the instant of the "now" is both capital punishment's general condition of possibility and the fantasmatic investment of post-Enlightenment practices of it. In the first place, capital punishment imposes upon the flux of human life a "now" like no other: here is the now of your death; in such and such an instant your life will be terminated; we will choose and give you that instant; your nows will have no succession beyond the instant that we determine. Against the question, posed by every mortal, of how to economize time—"what am I going to do, what must I do to optimize or maximize or intensify the time I have left to live," as Derrida puts it (*DP II*, 151)—the death penalty calculates the time of an execution as an idealized instant. In the second place, therefore, from the time the death penalty came to be distinguished from torture, and juridical authorities began to lessen the duration of suffering associated with it, capital punishment presumed to control the now of an execution, to isolate and delimit it. That means defining and comprehending, in absolute terms, the instant of the now as the instant that separates life from death. But the converse effect of that tendency is to *infect* the time of life with the now of death. As if in grotesque parody of Heidegger's freedom for death, sentencing to death and thereby determining the precise "now" of the end of life means that the lived nows of the condemned person's everyday existence no longer function as moments in which death is possible, and which *potentialize* being. Instead, those lived nows come to constitute "dead" instants, instants of nonbeing that restrict or imprison a condemned person in a time devoid of, vacated by life.

For once "unnatural" death is practiced in the precise form of the death penalty, the present now comes to be staged as instant of death. That was something recognized by Arasse in his analysis of the guillotine as simultaneously instant-making and death-dealing machine, one that, "by its instantaneous action . . . sets before our eyes the invisibility of death at the very instant of its occurrence."[24] For him:

> The guillotine is perhaps the only machine thus to exhibit in plain view the essentially destructive, rending, agonizing potential of very instant. This formidable configuration takes us back to the etymology of the word: *instans*, that which stands over, that which threatens. The image of the machine is the more frightening in that its very reliability suggests but a single instant of time, that of death in its unerring stroke, a mechanized and more "productive" version of the immortal reaper's scythe.[25]

What impresses Arasse is precisely the idea that life is placed on the knife-edge of the guillotine blade and violently severed from itself by death. It is therefore as if death were endowed with a new form of technological precision that then comes to define, as it were to retrofit life, producing the "blinding immediacy [of] what lies between the last quiver of life and the instantaneous and fatal 'afterwards' of truncation."[26]

Such an objectifiably instant "now," a "now" conceived of as minimal unit in a succession of such units, constitutes for Heidegger the "vulgar understanding of 'time'" (291), in the sense of the everyday presumption to isolate a present moment, to separate it from both past and future. We saw how he begins *Being and Time* by resisting the tradition within which Dasein, the being that raises the question of its being, is treated as something objectively present, separated from other similarly present objects that it observes existing around it, according to the duality of subject and world that has persistently dominated Western thinking. And we saw his subsequent shift from treating being-in-the-world as spatial to temporal. Thanks to its thrownness and resolute anticipation, the being called Dasein, as being *in* time, is not objectively present in a now, but is instead *ecstatic, outside* any *stasis* of a given instant: "the ecstatic unity of temporality—that is, the unity of the 'outside itself' . . . is the condition of the possibility that there can be a being that exists as its 'there'" (334). Dasein's ecstasies are plural. First, it is taken outside of stasis toward the future in being-toward-death; one removes oneself from the trap of the now by entertaining one's future possibility. But second, in running forward in that way Dasein necessarily relates back(ward) to what it has been. Indeed that relation to what has been is imposed on Dasein as if from the beginning, in its constitution, from the moment it found itself being-there [*da-sein*]. So third, Dasein starts out *in media res*, there in the world without having decided to be at all. If you wish, Dasein arrives on the scene with a past that is not of its making but that nevertheless puts it where it finds itself, and any movement it makes into the future depends on realizing how that involves leaving behind.[27]

Thanks to those ecstasies, the presentness of Dasein avoids being a simple "now." It is rather a temporalizing of temporality—"Temporality . . . is not, but rather temporalizes itself" (314)—an idea that is in stark contrast to the tradition inherited from the Greeks. Based on a *moment* that is in tension with and even in opposition to a *now*—"the phenomenon of the Moment can *in principle not* be clarified in terms of the *now*" (323)—it differs radically from how, in Aristotle's *Physics*, the sense of temporal continuity, but also discontinuity, derives from understanding time "as a kind of number" (219b), indeed "the number of continuous movement" (223a). For in the Aristotelian schema each number represents, or occurs precisely as a momentary "now." Time, therefore, "is both made continuous by the 'now' and divided at it" (220a).[28] Aristotle's emphasis on the static instant as a divisible unit epitomizes what is for Heidegger the vulgar understanding of time, and "all subsequent discussion of the concept of time fundamentally holds itself to the Aristotelian definition" (*BT* 400); time consists simply in counting the nows, accumulating them "as an endless, irreversible succession" (401).

Heidegger's intense interest in being-toward-death does not lead him to discuss the death penalty, which so clearly imposes on the condemned person a very different kind of ecstatic time.[29] Nor does he develop a relation between time and blood. The reason for my detailed representation of his ideas in this context is twofold. First, the ecstatic temporality of being-toward-death thoroughly revises the Socratic preparation for death, recasting it as a resistance to the singular appropriable instants of time that the death penalty trades on in presuming to designate and circumscribe one such instant as it terminates a life. Second, Heidegger's critique, in *Being and Time*, of Aristotle's vulgar "now" includes explicit reference to Hegel. In filling out Hegel's thinking on time in relation to Heidegger's somewhat reductive dismissal of it, we discover a temporality operating at the beginning of life itself, as if on the other side of it, as a prosthesis to it;

and we are in turn led back to blood, as uncannily internal and external flow of both life and time.

In a scant few pages in the penultimate section of his major work, Heidegger argues that whereas Hegel claimed to have produced a different conceptualization of time based on the point, and on his sense of negation, he does not in fact move beyond Aristotle. Indeed, Heidegger states, "we do not need any complicated discussion to make it clear that in his interpretation of time, Hegel is wholly moving in the direction of the vulgar understanding," falling back on a "primary orientation toward the now" (*BT* 409).[30] In an article from 1968, Derrida provides a different perspective from that given by Heidegger at the end of *Being and Time*. His overarching argument, which will form a basis of his lifelong development of what has come to be known as deconstruction, is this: The consistent recourse had by philosophy, from Aristotle to Hegel (indeed from Parmenides to Husserl), to a conception of time articulated through the present moment, or Now, points to an unavoidable necessity for Western thinking, that of privileging the present to the extent that "no thought seems possible outside its element."[31] If one wanted to get to the bottom of what is for Heidegger the vulgar concept of time, one would have somehow to undo that structure, and stricture of our thinking, somehow to undo "the tie between truth and presence."[32] So Derrida wonders to what extent Heidegger himself manages to move beyond the Aristotle-Hegel axis that he critiques; whether the "vulgarity" that Heidegger attributes to their conception of time is not in fact an inextricable function of a whole range of metaphysical concepts that continue to rely on the concept of presence, and that therefore render a nonvulgar, primordial, authentic temporality more elusive than Heidegger imagines.[33]

Hegel defines time, in contradistinction to space, in his *Philosophy of Nature*, part II of his *Encyclopedia of the Philosophical Sciences*, first published in 1817. Space consists of a continuity that would be interrupted, negated by the point, and it is therefore maintained only by what Hegel calls a "negative punctiformity."[34] "The point has meaning only in so far as it is spatial" (ibid.); it does not itself make space. We might imagine an infinite number of conjoined points stretching out across space, but space itself would be constituted not by those points but by the uninterrupted spatiality found as it were on the other, negative side of them; besides, one must also consider the spatial extensions existing above and below that "line" of space. When it comes to time, though, the point is accorded actuality. In the case of time, "difference has stepped out [*herausgetreten*] of space . . . it is for itself in all its unrest" (*Nature*, 34). That is to say that unlike space, a continuity deriving from negated points, time *instantiates* the point as a "*Now*, which, as singularity, is *exclusive* of the other moments" (37), which is precisely where Heidegger directs his critique. But, in accordance with Hegel's dialectical thinking, the Now that steps out in its difference and exclusivity to constitute the present point or moment instantiates itself in that way only to be better preceded by, superseded by or sublated into those other moments. As soon as the Now steps out, its exclusivity is negated, returning it to the temporal continuity. That makes time a "perpetual self-sublation" (34), the process whereby no sooner is it punctuated by a now than "this proudly exclusive Now dissolves, flows away and falls into dust" (36). It might therefore be said that whereas space *has* a negative, time *is* the negative, the "negation of the negation, the self-relating negation" (34). The flux of time derives from the continuous dialectical motion of point and dissolution of the point, a now that steps out only to be reabsorbed.

We can see how such an unresting time provides a fundamental figure for the perpetually self-sublating dialectical operation that constitutes thinking, represented in the *Phenomenology of Spirit* as the ability first to progress from sense-certainty and perception to self-consciousness, and, ultimately, to spirit and absolute knowledge. It is time itself that allows difference, produces becoming, and marks the spirit that knows itself as its own concept. That whole movement of self-overcoming that, for Hegel, makes everything happen, could not take place without the operation of time. But it is for the same reason that, at the end of the *Phenomenology*, upon arrival at absolute knowledge, the time that has, from the start, been becoming, comes to be no more. Time is annulled: "Spirit necessarily appears in Time, and it appears in Time just so long as it has not *grasped* its pure Notion, i.e., has not annulled Time."[35] As long as thinking is in motion—self-identifying, self-conceptualizing, self-reflecting, self-negating, self-sublating, self-extending—it functions in time; it is a matter of time. As long as thought is about the extension of itself beyond itself, it exists in "unity" with time. But once it has reached the point where it can no longer go beyond itself, where the very operation of extending has achieved an identity with itself, then time separates off from that unity. In a sense it is left spinning its wheels; it appears as difference where there is no longer any need for difference, "difference left to itself, *unresting and unhalting time*, [which] collapses rather within itself" (*Phenomenology*, 489, my emphasis).

According to Catherine Malabou, in *The Future of Hegel*, time's self-collapse has a whole other side to it that, for referring back to Aristotle, by no means repeats him in the way that Heidegger suggests. Malabou promotes a seemingly marginal notion in Hegel, "plasticity," in order to account for how time exceeds itself to make a future for itself, but at the same time gives itself the possibility of being surprised by that future.[36] For Malabou, if Hegel finds in Greek thinking "the foundational principle" of his philosophical system it is because that thinking allows him to develop the "idea of subjectivity as support of its own ontological history, that is, of its own temporal self-differentiation."[37] Hegel's dialectical self-consciousness would derive from that self-differentiation of time, which emerges in Aristotle's play between the passivity (*paschein*) and activity (*energeia*) of the intellect (*nous*): the intellect receives thought, as if passively, but that receiving can also be understood as an activity inasmuch as the mind is transformed, or rather transforms itself in the process. In Hegel's words the mind thereby "becomes what it has."[38] That self-*activation* of a passively receptive intellect is obviously not the result of a decision on its part. It obeys rather the functioning of *eksis* (habit), which functions in a time that is outside itself in a way that Heidegger appears to ignore. As Malabou explains,

> Habit is a mode of presence that cannot be reduced to the *present of the now*. . . . Habit is a memory which, like all memory, has lost the memory of its origin. We never know exactly when habit began or when it actually ceases to exist. . . . In a certain sense the notion of *eksis* defines a time within time, as if time [could] . . . exhibit a strange ability to double itself. For *eksis*, as second nature, involves a *second nature of time that does not belong to nature*.[39]

Once one understands time in Hegel as temporalized in that way, then the end, annulling or collapse of time that comes with absolute knowledge correspondingly follows a different logic. Malabou will argue that when Hegel appears to propose "the final banishment of all temporality and the advent of spirit's unchanging and indifferent present,"[40] he is in fact restricting himself to the linear time within which he has been outlining the philosophical history of consciousness through reason, spirit and religion to absolute knowing. But what also operates there, as if in a subterranean way, is the return of time's second nature, the other time within a time of successive Nows, a type of originating force such as was identified in Aristotle, which means that what *is*, at a supposed given point in time, never could simply *be*, because it is informed by past habit that is not past in the sense of having no origin, and because it anticipates a future that it will nevertheless be unable to foresee.

Derrida extends Malabou's argument in a long review article written on *The Future of Hegel* in 1998. There he emphasizes how the plasticity of a temporal self-differentiation, such as we have just seen determining the history and operations of subjectivity in Hegel, similarly informed the latter's conception of the concept:

> The concept gives itself or receives from itself its own sensuous
> figures, its own rational imagination, its own intellectual intuition,
> etc. This giving and receiving, this giving to itself to receive, which is
> the very process of plasticity, the very movement of being as
> becoming-plastic, this would be the speculative and reflexive power of
> the Hegelian concept.[41]

More important for my discussion, Derrida underscores how the dialectical transformation by which Hegel's concept moves thinking toward a future, doesn't structure organic operations only, but introduces a plasticity that is ultimately a prosthesis of natural and technological that would be found at the beginning of life. Malabou seems to have opened that possibility in her chapter on "Habit and Organic Life," where she shows that although, as Hegel follows Aristotle in assuming, inorganic bodies cannot self-differentiate and therefore "lack the power to contract habit," the living organism nevertheless synthesizes the inorganic in a manner that amounts to "contracting all that comes before it [*ce dont il procède*]."[42] In other words, the inorganic participates *in the process of* contraction; the organism is, as it were, always already automatic contraction of the noncontractable inorganic that somehow constitutes it: "What results from such a contraction is, literally, *habitus*, at once the internal disposition and the general constitution of the organism."[43]

In that respect, plasticity is more "fundamental" than the self-differentiation that renders possible subjectivation and hence conceptualization; it would, in Derrida's words, "begin with life itself, within its very first contraction and with the first idealization of animal *habitus*. With the very appearance of life . . ."[44] As the originary temporalization whereby the organism habitually contracts, as the hardwired programming that *contrives* in what lives an automatic capacity to self-differentiate and become other than what it is, plastic is, in a way that Hegel no doubt will not have foreseen, at once natural and technological. In Derrida's words:

> A continual transformation and radical interruption, a process and an
> explosion, plasticity and gelignite [*la plastique et le plastic*]. But also
> *physis* and *techné*, nature and culture, nature and the technological,

nature and art, if you like: on the one hand, the natural or organic transformation of living forms, their plasticity, *and* on the other, plastic art, and the artificial or synthetic, indeed prosthetic technology of "plastic matter."[45]

We have there a concept of time that is far from the succession of nows that Heidegger set out to critique. Already reconceived by him as a temporality that stretches out from an inescapable past to an inevitable death, it is further understood here as a self-starting motor or type of artificial intelligence that enables every transformational development of the animal organism from the most elementary self-adaptation all the way through consciousness and conceptualization to self-generated obsolescence. But that is also to say that—structurally similar to, but different from Heidegger's stretching from thrownness toward death, closer perhaps to Freud's concept of the drives[46]—time is a machinic impulse functioning from beginning to end, of life and of itself. If, as Malabou suggests, we are to read the collapse of time in Hegel's absolute knowing not as its end but as yet another enfolding, then we might similarly imagine a self-differentiation that sublates all the way from an initial contraction of the inorganic to an ultimate transition into death, another plastic transformation, albeit back into the inorganic. Rather than give death back its traditional sense of a transition to an afterlife, however, that would suggest a plasticity of life up to and including death, or a plastic death within life. It also points, as we are progressively noting, to two questions: first, regarding the presumption that an instant separates life from death, the very presumptive instant from which, as I argued earlier, the death penalty derives, and on the basis of which it maintains its power; and second, regarding the prosthetic operation by means of which a machine is attached to the human body in order to bring about its death.

Hegel's time, then, is the engine of difference and becoming, "unresting and unhalting," until coming to be annulled by Spirit. As a function of habit, though, it operates as a type of automatism beyond any linearity that might lead to its being annulled, revealing instead what Malabou calls a second nature "that does not belong to nature."[47] And as we saw Derrida argue, its self-differentiating drive is also that of the concept. At a key point in *The Phenomenology of Consciousness*, Hegel writes, as if in passing, that the absolute concept "may be called the simple essence of life, the soul of the world, *the universal blood [das allgemeine Blut]*" (100, my emphasis). That passing reference to blood comes at a critical moment. It appears during discussion of the emergence of self-consciousness, toward the end of the chapter regarding force and understanding, which is the third "level" of consciousness following sense-certainty and perception. This is also one of the places in Hegel's argument where speculative dialectics receives a particularly explicit elucidation, as he moves from explaining opposite forces by means of physical examples, such as electricity and magnetism, to thinking "pure change or . . . *antithesis within the antithesis itself* . . . inner difference or difference in its own self" (99). That idea of a world wherein same and difference both subsist (99–100), a world that "is itself and its opposite in one unity," is called by Hegel "difference as an *infinity*" (99), and he chooses to give it fluid form. Here is the passage in full:

> This simple infinity, or the absolute concept, may be called the simple essence of life, the soul of the world, the universal blood, whose omnipresence is neither disturbed nor interrupted by any difference, but rather is itself every difference, as also their supersession [*Aufgehobensein*]; it pulsates within itself but does not move, inwardly vibrates, yet is at rest. (100)

Blood is here a fluid infinity, a universal formlessness that nevertheless carries difference within itself: no difference, every difference; inward vibration, rest. The idea of flow, flux and fluidity as the figure for "a difference into which the many antitheses have been resolved . . . an absolute universal difference that is absolutely at rest and remains selfsame" (90) is in fact a constant in Hegel's *Phenomenology*, and it is emphasized repeatedly in the chapter—on The Truth of Self-Certainty as a function of self-consciousness (104–11)—that follows the passage having recourse to the figure of blood.

For the fluid infinity of "absolute universal difference" is in fact that of the dialectical process itself, and also the process of life itself:

> Life in the universal fluid medium, a *passive* separating-out of the shapes [independent objects] becomes, just by so doing, a movement of those shapes or becomes Life as a *process*. The simple universal fluid medium is the *in-itself*, and the difference of the shapes is the *other*. But this fluid medium itself becomes the *other* through this difference; for now it is *for the difference* which exists in and for itself, and consequently is the ceaseless movement by which this passive medium is consumed: Life is a *living thing*. (107)

In fluid life there is both "every difference" and a "*general dissolution*" (108) of differences; fluidity is both form and medium of "infinity as the supersession of all distinctions . . . its self-repose being an absolutely restless

infinity . . . flux, as a self-identical independence . . . simple fluid substance of pure movement" (106–7).

But if blood makes an appearance, in the *Phenomenology*, as a figure for
the "simple infinity" of a generalized, universal fluidity, it seems, there at
least, not to be the blood that circulates in a finite body. For that, one turns
to the *Philosophy of Nature*, where, in contrast to an immobile pulsation of
consciousness on the way to spirit, real animal blood is under discussion.
Somewhat predictably, perhaps, by the end of the *Philosophy of Nature*, Hegel
returns to a fluidity that clearly recalls the *Phenomenology*, understanding
how, with the death of the individual, "from this dead husk, proceeds a
more beautiful Nature, spirit" (*Nature*, 443). In concluding the text, Hegel
explains that death means the sublation of the opposition between the singularity of an individual nature and the universality of spirit. Thus, when
an individual animal dies, "the last *self-externality* of Nature has been sublated and the Concept, which in Nature is present only *in principle* (*an sich
seiende Begriff*), has become *for itself*. With this, Nature has passed over into
its truth, into the subjectivity of the Concept . . . and this is spirit" (443).
The Zusatz notes to that same section put it this way: "Herewith the Idea
exists in the self-subsistent subject, for which, as organ of the Concept,
everything is ideal and fluid" (443–44). It would not be exaggerating, in
my opinion, to read the "organ" mentioned there as the blood that was uni-
versalized in the *Phenomenology*; the self-subsistent, self-conscious fluid
subject has once again become the blood whose sublation produces the concept. Indeed, in following the thread, or stream, of blood on one side and
concept on the other, one finds in the *Philosophy of Nature* a persistent comparison between restless blood and a restless time, which is ultimately the
pulsating motionlessness or vibrating rest of the absolute concept.

Animal blood, we are first told, is characterized by irritability, which,
along with sensibility and reproduction is one of the three properties that
define the organic (*Nature*, 357): irritability is "inward activity, pulsation,
living self-movement, the material of which can be only a fluid, the living
blood, and which itself can only be circulation" (360). Conversely, blood is
the "irritable concentration of everything into the interior unity" (368).
Even plants live thanks to irritability, and indeed have their own blood circulation, thanks to the sap that "circulates through the entire plant. This
quivering of vitality within itself belongs to the plant because it is alive—
restless Time. That is the blood circulation in plants" (329). However, the
sap of a plant is not sufficient to transcend the vegetal dehiscence into two
independent elements: A plant divides to produce a bud and does not re-
unite. The life of the animal, though, attains the "highest point of Nature

[as the] absolute idealism of possessing within itself the determinateness of its bodily nature *in a perfectly fluid form*" (352, my emphasis). Animal blood, then, is not just the universal essence of life, the soul of the world, but also "the individual life itself" (368). Life achieves its ideal form in the perfect fluidity of the blood.

Now, Hegel's simple fluid movement is never in fact simple but complicated by an ambiguity between fluidity and mechanicity. The universal blood of the *Phenomenology* was said to "pulsate" (*Phenomenology*, 100), and the "restless infinity" of "universal flux" was also "the pure movement of axial rotation" (106). That ambiguity returns in *The Philosophy of Nature*, where a perfectly fluid mammalian blood nevertheless retains enough mechanicity to be called a "fluid magnet" (*Nature*, 355). Blood flows through interruptions, however modulated, of that flow, such that its circulation is recognized to be an "*oscillatory* circulation" (370). But such a modulation of blood flow does not, as one might expect, derive from the heart as mechanical pump that regulates, and produces blood circulation. The heart is described less as a sluice that controls blood circulation than the seat of pulsation, as it were the repository of vital irritability: "No nerves are found in the heart, but what pulsates is the pure vitality of irritability present as muscle in the centre" (369). We are told twice in the space of half a page of the *Philosophy of Nature* that any attempt to explain the physiology of the blood and the heart in terms of mechanical operations is misplaced, for it ignores the fact that "the blood must be regarded as itself the principle of [its] movement" (ibid.). The irritability of blood is thus to be understood as a "*self-movement*" on the basis of which we can conceive "the universal, the ground, the simple, which is the unity of opposites and consequently the immovable which yet moves" (ibid.). Indeed, blood is finally "absolute motion, the natural living self, process itself"; it is "not moved but *is* motion" (ibid.).

The circulation of blood within the animal organism described in *The Philosophy of Nature* thus returns to the idealism of universal blood as absolute concept that was posited in the *Phenomenology*. Blood is a fluidity that remains unfazed by any mechanist interruption, a flowing that manages also to be a stepping, a liquid that is able to separate itself into opposing parts. It very much resembles the time that we saw earlier, "stepping out" of space to be "for itself in all its unrest" (*Nature*, 34). In the chapter on the animal organism that concludes *The Philosophy of Nature*, blood is said to be "the ground and the movement itself. But also, it steps to one side [*es tritt . . . auf die Seite*] as *one* moment, for it is the distinguishing of itself from itself. The movement is precisely this stepping aside of itself . . . and the supersession [*das Aufheben*] of its standing aside, so that it overlaps itself and its opposite" (369). Blood, like time, indeed like the concept on the way to Spirit, produces and sublates mechanist difference; in circulating, animal blood becomes "this endless, unbroken unrest of welling forth" (368).

Somewhat strangely, however, the grand advantage of blood as a figure for dialectical sublation in the concept is a type of visibility that it affords. In welling forth, blood becomes all but visible: "The endless process of division and this suppression of division which leads to another division, all this is the immediate expression of the Concept which is, so to speak, *here visible to the eye*" (368, my emphasis). By "looking" at blood, one is able to see the operation of the Concept, the uninterrupted fluidity that is nevertheless "every difference [and] their supersession" as the *Phenomenology* had it, both inward vibration and restfulness.

But of course blood that was visible to the eye would not be blood flowing and circulating—except in a couple of liminal cases, as we shall see—but blood being shed; it is "visible to the eye" only "so to speak," in a nonliteral sense. How then does it gain its sense of visibility and its figurative force? Precisely from the idea that blood does in fact participate in a system of externalization, in a type of *visibilization*: It steps not just to one side, but outside, as it were, where it transforms the air. Blood circulation operates both internally, and, by means of pulmonary action, externally; it functions in a more literal sphere of visibility by sublating air: "The blood in the pulmonary circulation, having its own movement, is this purely negative immaterial life for which Nature is air and which has here the sheer victory over it" (367). In the dialectic between blood and air, blood effectively steps *outside*; though the air has been sucked inside, it is as if the blood had gone out to meet it. As a result we can finally "see" the fluid overcoming of mechanical interruption that we could previously only intuit, when blood was stepping *aside* of itself to become both difference and the dissolving of difference in general.

To reformulate and summarize: Blood is presumed to suffer some internal interruption of its circulation, caused if not by the heart, then at least by muscular movement: "muscular movement is the elastic irritability which . . . posits a peculiar, self-dividing movement which arrests the circulatory flow" (366). But, on the inside, such interruptions are overcome by the pure force of fluidity itself; blood "steps to one side" of such an arrest of its flow, it detours around such an "inert persistence," as Hegel calls it, and that "stepping aside of itself" is understood as an "overlapping" of itself and its opposite. In that way blood remains united in spite of its self-division; it is "the organism which through its own interior process returns into itself" (366). That overcoming of its interruptions, the smoothing over of interrupted fluidity, has its own paradoxicality smoothed over by the pulmonary operation: the "dissolution of this [arresting, inert] persistence is the pulmonary system, the true, ideal process with the outer world of inorganic Nature, with the Element of air" (366). By interacting with air, blood achieves a whole other level of stepping aside and returning to itself, and that idealizing sublation carries through into any other opposition between fluid and structural mechanics. Quite simply: "The self of the organism is the unity of its blood or pure process, and of its structure . . . [which is] completely sublated in the fluidity of the blood. . . . The organism is thus raised into pure ideality, perfectly transparent universality" (381).

However, the apotheosis that blood achieves by sublating air and rendering the concept visible has another side to it. On the one hand, blood's sublation of air, of nature's negative, consists of a "sheer victory" (*Nature*, 367) over immaterial, *inorganic* life. And thanks to the same operation the constant and more general problem of an articulation between the living organism and an inassimilable external nature is resolved back into the body. For that has been the general problematic for the organism from the beginning: it becomes a living organism by contracting the inorganic, and that struggle seems never to be over, permanently defining "the organism [as] that which preserves itself in the face of the outer world" (381). The organism is involved in a constant operation of assimilation that requires it to "posit what is external as subjective, appropriate it, and identify it with itself" (ibid.). Yet that assimilation is also a *fluidization*: "the organism is in a state of tension with its nonorganic nature, negates it and makes it identical with itself. In this immediate relation of the organic to the nonorganic, the former is, as it were, the direct *melting* of the nonorganic into organic *fluidity*" (397, my emphasis).

On the other hand, therefore, the sheer victory that blood achieves over air is but one front in the constant state of tension that obtains between the organism and nonorganic nature; in its continuous contracting of the inorganic an organic body is always externalizing itself. Blood is held up as the paradigm for that externalizing process because it appears to be the ideal assimilator. It is represented as almost vampiric in its thirst for achieving "being-for-itself through negativity of its otherness" (392), functioning as a sort of insatiable sublation machine: "Now why is the blood connected with this ideal assimilation of the abstract Element [by means of the respiratory process]? The blood is this *absolute thirst*, its unrest within itself and against itself. *The blood craves* . . . to be differentiated" (ibid., my emphasis).

A blood that craves to be differentiated, one surmises, must expose its differentiations as much while circulating inside the body as it does once it comes outside to assimilate inorganic nature. In fact, the unresting blood, self-dividing only to better sublate into a new unity, competes for paradigmatic status with a generalized organism that melts the inorganic into organic fluidity. Whereas in the first case differentiation remains invisible, in the second case that differentiation is a radical opposition. When it comes to the air we breathe, the organism has to deal with a differentiation that is different enough to represent *the inorganic exterior to organic life in general*. In negotiating or transacting with air by means of its blood, the organism steps more problematically to the side of itself, indeed *outside* itself. For what begins with air as inorganic nature extends all the way into the space of artificial mechanicity.

It is the heart that is called upon to figure that problematic. Logically speaking, the heart produces an internal articulation or mechanical interruption of blood flow, whereas it seems not to be recognized as interruptive by Hegel. But, to paraphrase Shakespeare, the heart *will out*. The radical step out into otherness that is performed in the transaction between blood and external air gives rise to versions of the heart on, or near the outside, and the heart, whose operation "inside" the blood seemed barely significant, is seen operating to maximum effect on the organic surface.

That occurs in general terms as circulation through different organs produces a heart said to be "everywhere," such that "each part of the organism is only the specialized force of the heart itself" (*Nature*, 371). But it happens more clearly in the specific case of the sex organs. According to Hegel, what makes the male the active and the female the receptive principle is a difference in their organs that keeps the ovaries enclosed and prevented from emerging "into opposition" and from developing "on [their] own into active brain" (413). Similarly:

> the clitoris is inactive feeling in general. In the male, on the other hand, we have instead active feeling, *the swelling heart, the effusion of blood* into the *corpora cavernosa* and the meshes of the spongy tissue of the urethra. . . . In this way, the reception (*Empfangen*) by the uterus, as a simple retention, is, in the male, split into the productive brain and *the external heart*. (413, my emphasis)

Putting aside Hegel's obviously phallocratic conception of human sexuality, one can see the following logic operating here. Given that the real interruption between the organism and its other is constituted by inorganic externality, then the heart cannot avoid being externalized, as it were in spite of itself. If the blood goes outside to conquer inorganic nature the heart will have to accompany it, swelling like a penis, becoming an external heart. It will have to circulate its force "everywhere," and especially into those extremities—the penis, and sexual activity—where the animal organism enters into relations with an external difference that it is unable to sublate. In the penis the heart swells toward externality, going out to meet the outer world of inorganic nature, ready to sublate and assimilate it; but it is unable to do so. Instead, this external heart turns the organism inside out. As the penis swells and its blood effuses, it tends toward producing a heart that beats, and, presumably, blood that circulates, on the outside.

But how could that not be, for not only are we told that the organism "preserves itself in the face of the outer world" (381) by assimilating that world, but also that "the nature of the organism is to produce itself as something external to itself" (404)? Indeed, "the self-subsistent being from which the animal distinguishes itself is posited *not merely as something external, but also as identical with the animal*" (ibid., my emphasis). Accordingly, blood, as animal internality itself, will necessarily also be produced in externality. *Blood flowing* would thus articulate with *blood shed* as a function of organic unity.[48]

The idea or figure of a pulsating yet unperturbed "universal blood" as simple infinity, or absolute concept, central to the development of the speculative dialectic in the *Phenomenology*, cannot in fact permit inassimilable difference. The paradigm prioritized in *The Philosophy of Nature* is therefore intact blood circulation, operating in conjunction with a nonmechanical or minimally mechanical heart:

> The heart moves the blood, and the movement of the blood is, in turn, what moves the heart. But this is a circle, a *perpetuum mobile*, which would necessarily at once come to a standstill because the forces are in equilibrium. But, on the contrary, this is precisely why the blood must itself be regarded as itself the principle of its movement. (369)

The importance of the blood—as well as blood circulation and the blood's articulation with exteriority—clearly answers to Hegel's sense of a teleology that also manages to be circular. But it is in the same terms that his blood as autokinetic perpetual motion becomes time: "The blood as axially rotating, self-pursuing movement, this absolute interior vibration, is the individual life of the whole in which there is no distinction—animal time" (366). Even plants, as we saw, to the extent that they have blood, live thanks to the "quivering vitality [of] restless time" (329). Hegel's definition of time, in the opening section of the *Philosophy of Nature*, as a difference that "is for itself in all its unrest," the difference that "step[s] out of space" (34), that cures itself of paralysis, can thus be said to derive from the circulation of blood. The same, bloodlike, restless time will reach its apotheosis as "difference left to itself, unresting and unhalting time, [which] collapses rather within itself" (489), as it were spinning its wheels, at the end of the *Phenomenology*.

When Derrida asks about the relation between the concept and blood in his final two death penalty seminars, he first evokes attempts at what one might call conceptual *staunching*,[49] supposed to prevent opposite terms that have been discussed in previous sessions—for example, cruelty and noncruelty, hetero- and autopunishment, Kant's *poena forensis* and *poena naturalis*—from bleeding into each other (*DP II*, 217–8). But the discussion then comes into focus in this explicit form: "Is there a future for blood?" (219). That is to wonder, in the first place, whether we might not be witnessing a shift away from the seemingly universal cultural force of blood, what he calls its "imaginary, symbolic, phantasmatic, techno-scientific history" (220), something that he finds folded into the history of humanity as a form of *homo-hematocentrism* referred to at the beginning of this chapter. He will not exclude the possibility that such a hematocentric basis for thinking the human is coming to an end, that "what is happening today presents itself [as] a transformation of our experience, etc., in relation to blood in all of its registers: culture, religion, but also medicine, genetics . . . our perception of blood is changing" (245). But he is also asking, in the second place, whether the death penalty can survive once it is no longer a function of the bloody sacrifice from which, in its ontotheological roots, it appears to derive: "when it came to question of the death penalty and execution, we also registered something that looked like a disappearance of blood, of the effusion of blood, of the flowing of blood" (ibid.).

That blood is a totemic element of human culture would hardly be in dispute. That it has been inscribed in cultures of the Abrahamic tradition—Judaism, Islam, Christianity—via the story of Cain and Abel is similarly commonplace. It is such a nexus, and the subsequent divine injunction against murder—"the voice of your brother's blood is crying out to me from the ground" (Genesis 4:10)—that leads Derrida to link capital punishment to the question of sacrifice, precisely bloody sacrifice. Punishment more generally, as *castigation* or *chastisement*, is etymologically a function of purification or rendering *chaste*, hence tied to sacrifice as a means of protection or indemnification, making safe.[50]

The anthropological/mythological analysis of that nexus is of course developed by Freud in such works as "The Taboo of Virginity," *Totem and Taboo*, and *Moses and Monotheism*, and Derrida discusses the first of those writings at some length in session 9 of the second Death Penalty volume. Recently, a comprehensive analysis of *hematology* in the Western tradition has been undertaken by Gil Anidjar, whose *Blood: A Critique of Christianity* deals with "multiple iterations of blood—medical and anthropological, juridical and theological, political and economic, rhetorical and philosophical."[51] Like Derrida, Anidjar raises the possibility that "blood is a thing of the past," and argues that blood is a figure for "that which politics transcends, manages or excludes; what it should at any rate exclude: the archaism of blood feuds, the threat of cruel and unusual punishment— or of menstruation—and the pertinacity of kinship, of tribalism, and finally of race."[52] Conversely, however, he finds blood to be "through and through political," requiring that Western politics, and in particular Christian politics, "be rethought in its hematological registers."[53] As his subtitle announces, Anidjar concentrates on ontotheological concerns that are similar to those that orient much of Derrida's seminar, and his critique parallels the relation Derrida develops between Christianity and blood in the particular case of Hegel.[54]

Abel's blood crying out to God from the ground is a perversion of the role of blood as the seat of life: blood belongs in the body, *sanguis* rather than *cruor*. We retrace the circulation of blood throughout the body as the conductor of human life to William Harvey's *De motu cordis* in 1628, even though Islamic science, culminating in the discoveries of Ibn al-Nafis in the thirteenth century, had established certain principles of pulmonary transit three hundred years prior to the European medical renaissance.[55] If Europeans prior to Harvey did not understand the principle of blood circulation, they well understood blood shedding. It was what stopped life, and staunching the flow of blood meant preserving life. In 1552, the soon-to-be king's surgeon, Ambroise Paré, learns from firsthand experience at the siege of Metz that the practice of staunching bleeding, caused by amputation of a member, by cauterizing the wound could be more effectively superseded by ligature of the arteries.[56]

Another three decades would pass before Galileo correlated his pulse with the swing of a pendulum, and only following the latter's discovery of isochronism in 1602 did Sanctorio Sanctorio develop the pulsilogium on the way to Harvey's groundbreaking discovery some twenty years after that. Harvey not only detailed the operations of cardiac and pulmonary circulation but also determined that *only* blood flowed in the arteries, that it was not in fact doubled by vital heat or *pneuma*; blood itself was henceforth life. One might therefore characterize—albeit arbitrarily—the seventy-five-year period from Paré to Harvey as that of the *externalization* of the time of blood, according to this logical succession: Blood within the body is the sign of life, bleeding outside of the body is a countdown to death; yet the pulsation of blood functions as the body's self-chronometrization, and, because it operates on the surface, it can be synchronized with an artificial machine of measurement. Chronometrical time will therefore develop, in that version at least, as an externalized, artificial, mechanical version of the *pulse* of life.

But the motor for such a rotating time is of course its very self-division, the principle of self-differentiation that might be said to produce it.[57] By downplaying the mechanical necessity of self-division in favor of a self-dividing, self-reconstituting, and self-perpetuating fluidity, Hegel would seem to preserve the idea of an organic, animal, even human time. In many respects Heidegger appears still to reason within that same concept of it.[58] But, as Galileo already surmised in relating his pulse to a pendulum, time is the necessarily externalizable self-differentiation machine; always already some form of clock, some type of technology. It begins in the habit that Malabou identified as originary temporalization, some impulse whose clock is already ticking in the first contractions by the organic of the inorganic that it proceeds from. The human has that habitual *pulse* or *impulse* built in to its system, we might say in its blood: "Human beings are those who, in order to be, must observe that *speculative clock* which is habit."[59] But Hegel also emphasizes, as we have seen—and irrespective of whether he recognizes it in these terms or not—that the overarching concern for the organism is its "state of tension with its nonorganic nature," and that the blood itself, in order to achieve its victory over that nature, must assimilate the air; it must therefore externalize itself and externalize its time along with it. Its pulse tends toward that externalization, by means of a heart that beats everywhere, by means of a penis that is a swelling, effusive, external heart. Any victory over, or sublation of the nonorganic air will consequently be achieved at the cost of the technological imposition of time. From then on, *time will be that blood pulsating on the outside*.

From Galileo to Guillotin, then, or, in another zone, from Socrates to Heidegger, time has been the exteriorized and technologized temporality of the human. And its chronometric obsession has become: how to appropriate the instant. The working out of that obsession through the juridical, medical and mechanical aspects of the death penalty does not just imply a seemingly endless refining of the definition of the instant; it also *constitutes*, in a precise way, the specific technologization of human temporality that consists in delimiting it. As I explained in the Introduction, once there is capital punishment we know not just that human life is finite, not just that it can be terminated by artificial means, but we also know that its finitude can be counted, its ending timed. By deciding a particular instant for the end of a life the death penalty determines and measures the duration of the temporal "instant" constituting that life. As a result, whether or not blood is shed in a given execution, blood is nevertheless flowing and pulsating outside, mechanically and metronomically; it is *chronometronomically* technologized outside the body in the way that this chapter has attempted to explain.

By extension or analogy, whether blood is shed outside the body in the manner of the death penalty in its "classic" age of cruelty, or anesthetized and poisoned inside the body by means of lethal injection, it continues to be chronometronomically technologized in the same way. In engineering, and continuing to refine the most explicitly brutal confrontations between animate and inanimate, between the human body and rope, iron or pharmaceutical prostheses, capital punishment will have always negotiated with that more or less technologized, and temporalized blood. Indeed, lethal injection works by *parasitizing* blood flow in order to infect and arrest the circulatory system; it introduces into the blood a foreign and artificial temporal order to control, by countermanding it, the human pulse. It breaks the time of the blood.

Now, within a traditional logic, employing an artificial mechanistic means to end life would contradict the sense of a prosthesis that is attached to the human body to enhance or prolong it: the death penalty would therefore constitute an antiprosthesis. However, as my Introduction explained, that is not the way I conceive of prosthesis. Every animal body is, from its beginnings or in its constitution, prosthetic, in the sense of being always already involved in negotiating relations with what is external to it, including with the inorganic or inanimate. That originary prosthetic function allows both extensions to the body that enhance or prolong life, and incursions on the body that terminate it. The same originary prosthetic function also allows time to be superadded to human existence, as a result of which the mortals that we know ourselves to be count or account for the flow of our existence, secure in the knowledge that life will end, but in the nonknowledge of precisely when it will end. That is what I have been calling here mortal temporality. We are as if born with time, but of course we know that time is not ours to own, no more than is the language we speak; it is an artificial apparatus that our bodies bear.

Every mortal is technologized by time in that way. But something different occurs once life's term and terminus come to be programmed by the death penalty. Once one is under sentence of death, mortal temporality is interrupted and one's temporal technology is reconfigured. A condemned person no longer navigates within the same flow as the rest of us; his or her temporality functions in a different mode, determined by the brutal prospect of the programmed death penalty. He or she is differently prosthetized than are other mortals; his or her temporal technology is no longer that shared by the rest of us. It is as if the everyday mortal prosthetic condition were doubly reversed by the death sentence: first by a time machine that has fallen out of joint to become a shaky contraption, then later by a supposedly infallible execution machine that takes over to end lifetime.

As long as we conceive of time as a pulse of life regulated by blood circulation, as Hegel appeared on the one hand to do, execution by lethal injection will be able to represent itself as a type of organic death penalty, its chemicals dissolved in and sublated by the blood. But once, on the other hand, we syncopate Hegelian dialectics in the way this chapter has attempted, time comes to be seen as a prosthesis *in the blood*, beating, pulsating, and flowing on the outside. Then there is no bloodless death penalty. Once time is understood as blood circulating on the outside, then stopping the heart and immobilizing the blood effectively means shedding that blood. Once the state concocts, constructs, and sets in motion a machine of death whose basic component is the interruption of mortal time, then it matters little whether an execution takes place by means of decapitation or lethal injection: vis-à-vis the time of blood, both are equally bloody, and, one might argue, equally cruel. The death-dealing prosthesis to the human that is the death penalty, whatever its precise technological mechanism, ruptures human time; it therefore amounts to a cruel bloodletting whether or not the spectacle of blood accompanies a given execution. On one side the uncertainty of not knowing when one will die is what preserves the modality of mortal time; on the other side, interrupting that modality is an act of extreme violence; it means shedding *mortal bloodtime*.

CHAPTER 4

Spirit Wind

"He'd fly through the air with the greatest of ease, that daring young man on the flying trapeze." But then he'd fall. It could be an accident, or the mechanism could fail; or he could be pushed. Or he could jump. "The Daring Young Man on the Flying Trapeze" was a popular song in 1867, written about trapeze artist Jules Léotard. Its popularity returned with recordings by Walter O'Keefe and Don Redman and His Orchestra and a film with W. C. Fields, in the mid-1930s, around the time that the last public hanging was taking place in the United States, as Roscoe Jackson was "launched into eternity" from an outdoor trap door gallows, condemned to a flight ruled by gravity and without a safety net.

As we have understood, the gallows had long been considered, in the Anglo-American world, a more or less instantaneous and bloodless state killing machine; and we have also seen how Utah's firing squad (1879) and New York's electric chair (1890) introduced the first of what would represent the twentieth-century refinements of that instantaneity, coming progressively to replace the gallows across the United States and eventually evolving to lethal injection as preferred method of execution. Hanging remains on the books, although it has effectively fallen into disuse, in

Delaware, New Hampshire, and Washington. Since *Kemmler*, then, the instant has been sought elsewhere, although the presumption stated in that case, that execution "must result in instantaneous, and consequently in painless death" (*Kemmler*, 443–44), has continued to inform debate concerning capital punishment. Indeed, one might say, appropriation of such an instantaneous instant remains the dominant consideration of American death penalty jurisprudence.

At the end of volume I of *The Death Penalty*, Derrida reaches back to Michel de Montaigne for a premodern take on capital punishment, referring to the sixteenth-century writer as one who did not—essentially could not—envisage its abolition to the extent that the judicial practice or principle of putting to death was not yet posed as a question or problem.[1] Montaigne seems indifferent to how death arrives, including by one's own hand, writing that "wherever the thread breaks, that's all there is to it, it's the end of the skein [*Le filet se rompe, il y est tout, c'est le bout de la fusée*]."[2] In his commentary on that passage, Derrida plays on Montaigne's use of the word *filet*, which now more commonly means "net," to make life a sort of high trapeze and the fall into eternity or oblivion a case of a broken safety net:

> I imagine a trapeze artist who spends his life throwing himself like a madman from one trapeze to another while relying on a net, whether real or not, on a phantasm of a net in which he has the strength or the weakness to believe. . . . He believes in this net, and he dies on the day the net breaks, and then it's a fall without a net, willed death, the beautiful death that Montaigne then speaks of. This death would be thus that of a trapeze artist who decides himself to put an end to the net. (*DP I*, 275)

And, following Montaigne, Derrida opens, or reopens the question that he has raised at a number of points during previous seminars, concerning the extent to which the death penalty is coextensive with suicide.

As Montaigne's translator assumes, the essay writer was probably not thinking of any high trapeze but rather imagining the unreeling of a skein wound around a loom spindle, a simple to-and-fro progressive unraveling of life's thread as it is woven into the fabric or tapestry of existence up to the very end: no more thread, sudden tension, snap. But in the essay where the passage occurs, "A Custom on the Isle of Cea," Montaigne was clearly expounding on that fatality in the context of whether man "gives himself his death or suffers it":

It all comes to the same thing whether man gives himself his death or suffers it, whether he runs to meet his day or awaits it; wherever it comes from, it is still his; wherever the thread breaks, it is all there, that's the end of the skein.

The most voluntary death is the fairest.

Life depends on the will of others; death, on our own.

In nothing should we suit our own humor as much as in this.

Reputation is not concerned in such an enterprise; it is folly to consider it.

Life is slavery if the freedom to die is wanting.[3]

Indeed, by the end of the essay, when Montaigne finally comes to what is customary on the Isle of Cea (modern-day Kos), it is only after parading before us a seemingly endless line of historical characters who preferred to end their own days, and often those of wives and children, or citizens for whom they were responsible, rather than surrender or be captured. "History is chock full of those who in a thousand ways have changed a painful life for death," Montaigne writes, but the peaceful end of the ninety-year-old woman of quality on Kos, in a very happy state both of body and mind, who invited Sextus Pompeius to witness her suicide, is a rarity in contrast to example after example that Montaigne draws upon of violent, and more or less coerced, self-inflicted deaths. Among such examples are cases where an Antinous, Theodotus, or Jacques du Chastel threw himself at the enemy knowing he would have to die but hoping to kill as many of his foes as possible by means of that death.[4]

Given that focus, Montaigne might be reinterpreted as imagining or envisaging the extreme other end of death by suicide, his *bout de la fusée* referring not only to the trajectory of a trapeze artist who swings higher or farther than he should dare, but also to the end of a missile, a gravity's rainbow screaming across the sky to the end of its parabolic lift, the zenith of its arc, as its tip reaches its own tipping point, before the fall that is a mighty explosive crash. In that sense the high trapeze act would be the gesture of a warrior who becomes a weapon, one who, like the historical figures described by Montaigne, opts for a suicide that is simultaneous with the slaying of one's enemies. The high trapezist to be imagined here is a kamikaze or suicide bomber, and I propose him (or her) as performing not just at the extreme end of suicide where it doubles with murder but also, according to a logic that this chapter will develop, at an extreme outer edge of the death penalty, where the perpetrator of a capital crime simultaneously enacts his or her execution.

In Japanese, *kamikaze* means "divine wind," perhaps "spirit wind," and it was used to refer to the divine deliverance in the form of a typhoon that destroyed the ships of Kublai Khan as Mongol and Korean armies invaded Japan in 1281.[5] That original *kamikaze*, the spirit wind of a nature gone all wild and technological, nature superseded by itself to become weapon of shock and awe, would of course be structurally comparable to the suicide attacks by Japanese bombers on Allied ships in the closing stages of the war in the Pacific. In those attacks of 1944–45, it was instead a case of humans gone all wildly technological, sacrificing themselves in a desperate attempt to harm the enemy in a new, organized version of cannon fodder. And such a structure would be repeated, among more recent instances, by the Hezbollah campaign to drive Israeli, U.S., and French troops from Lebanon beginning in 1983, and the war waged by the Tamil Tigers in Sri Lanka starting in 1987. But it would find its most notorious enactment—and inaugurate the current instance from which, from our present disadvantage point, we can see no early deliverance—in the hijacking of civilian planes for the September 11, 2001, attacks in New York and Washington. By means of suicide bombing, the human body is prosthetized in the specific form of becoming projectile, as a means to effect a divine-like intervention into an asymmetrical conflict. The body becomes spirit via a more or less spectacularly technologized mortification of its own flesh, taking place simultaneously with the murder of those it targets. It is therefore something of a trapeze act without a safety net, all forward propulsion until a point of suspension and a self-inflicted fatal fall.

Spiritization, or spiritualization of one form or another, by no means necessarily religious, is systematically attributed to violent suicide from the *seppuku* of the samurai *bushidō* code of conduct to contemporary bombing attacks, although one struggles to accept such a highly aestheticized transcendence in the case of young women, or young men, who have found themselves co-opted as bombers.[6] But presumptions concerning the spiritualizing wind that blows away a suicide bomber—the wind of the fanatic (from Latin *fanaticus*, an inspired enthusiast devoted to a temple, *fanum*) that blows all the way from Jewish Zealot actions against the Roman occupation of Judea to the current mythology of a Muslim martyr's promised seventy-two virgins—all such mythologizing spiritualizing presumptions detract from the simple military calculus that underwrites terrorism of every stripe: the desire to inflict maximal harm upon a given enemy.[7]

On March 13, 1881, in Russia, Narodnaya Volya or "People's Will" member Ignacy Hryniewiecki (Ignaty Grinevitsky) is standing against a fence when two comrades throw bombs, but fail to assassinate Tsar Alexander II. Hryniewiecki, however, has positioned himself close enough so that his bomb will have its desired effect, even though that means sacrificing his own life. He will expire at 10:30 that evening, surviving his royal victim by some six or seven hours.

More than forty-five years later—still within the reverberating context of the overthrow of the Romanov dynasty and its mutation into what was by then the Third Communist International or Comintern—at 10:30 p.m. on April 11, 1927, in Shanghai, stands another young man. Ch'en, as he is named, is waiting, flying high and simultaneously falling without a net. He is a fictional protagonist in the novel by André Malraux aptly entitled *La condition humaine* (awkwardly translated as *Man's Fate*), and he shares the same geographical space with historical figure Zhou Enlai. Both are communists intent on resisting the collaborative maneuvers of Chiang Kai-Shek's Guomindang, remote-controlled by Stalin, who was not yet ready to back the revolutionary aspirations of the Chinese Communist Party. That eventually allowed Chiang Kai-Shek and his Green Gang allies to massacre thousands of militants in Shanghai in 1927 and hundreds of thousands across China during the following year. Before the Shanghai massacre, the fictional Ch'en decides that direct action is required, and so the reader of the novel finds him seconds away from blowing up both himself and what he thinks is Chiang Kai-Shek's passing car, "in a blinding flash that would illuminate this hideous avenue for a second and cover a wall with a shower of blood."[8] He is alone, his action shrouded in the belief he expounds, that terrorism must become something mystical, propelled by an "ecstatic joy" (245). When he hits the earth the thread of his existence is, unfortunately, like Hryniewiecki's before him, seriously shredded but not entirely broken. He lies there with his shattered body become "nothing more than suffering" (ibid.), which means, as we have seen, nothing more than the passage of time. Seeking the transcendental self-sublating instant he has instead found pure duration, where "everything was turning, slowly and invincibly, along a very large circle—and yet nothing existed but pain" (246).

Readers of *La condition humaine* have been well prepared for the terrorist act perpetrated by Ch'en, which occurs almost three-quarters of the way through the novel; just as they have been prepared for the breeze of its spiritualization. We see him in discussion with Gisors, his mentor and intellectual inspiration for revolutionary action, now fallen into opium addiction, explaining his quest for a death "on the highest possible plane" by means of an intoxication similar to that of Gisors's drug habit (60–61). We see him again, in discussion with the orthodox revolutionary Kyo, Gisors's son, still seeking the absolutist certainty that killing provides, fascinated by death, hoping again to find in it a thicker and deeper ecstasy than that delivered by opium (153–55). Finally, in debate with his two fellow conspirators following an earlier aborted attempt to kill Chiang Kai-Shek, Ch'en repeats the need for terrorism, less as religion than as the "meaning of life . . . complete possession of oneself" (192).

But more important, to my mind, than that form of mystical overlay, more pertinent than the transcendentalizing mytho-logic of sacrificial martyrdom, even if in no way distinct from it, is the precise temporality of the experience of death and killing that dominates Ch'en's quest: He seeks nothing less than a form of the absolute that can be "seized only in the instant" (155). That temporal dimension is evident from the opening pages of the novel, which is itself structured and chaptered (except for the epilogue) by reference to dates and times alone. On the first page, at thirty minutes past midnight on March 21, 1927, as he prepares to perform his first assassination in the service of the revolution, Ch'en finds himself in a "night in which time no longer existed" (3). Suspended in that atemporality, the time without time of hesitation before the act of murder that will inaugurate a transcendent time, he finds absolute immobility, utter motionlessness (6), his "convulsive heart the only moving thing in the room" (ibid.). At the end of the novel, that immobility will find its converse echo in Gisors's grief beside his dead son Kyo, the child who was his "submission to time" (329). "I am thrown outside of time," Gisors says, rejected into an immobility from which there was no return (*l'immobilité sans retour*) (742).[9]

That spiritualized immobility of space and time is contrasted with what is referred to as "the resistance of flesh" (4). Contemplating the sleeping body of the man he will kill—he must neutralize an arms merchant to procure the invoice that will allow the revolutionaries to hijack a shipment and launch their insurrection—Ch'en is led to wonder what that carnal resistance constitutes. He responds by acting out his question, inflicting on himself a flesh wound. That return to the flesh "releases" him briefly from his stasis and he is then able to perform the same gesture by stabbing his victim. For Ch'en, then, the suspension within immobility and atemporality that he experiences in the instant prior to his first murder, a desired yet intolerable instant that he must interrupt, will be the ideality that propels him from that first rupturing of the thread of life to his ultimate performance of it in his planned simultaneous assassination of Chiang Kai-Shek and of himself. He carries out that first political murder, then descends from his vantage point high up in a hotel of old Shanghai in or-der to return to the world of those who do not kill, but that is only so that he can find the means to again ascend, to climb once more on the wire, to swing with the force of an ecstatic forward propulsion to the point where everything is let go, to feel the bliss of an infinitesimal instant of aerial suspension that obliterates any difference from the fatal fall. So he runs with an ecstatic joy toward a car that he presumes is carrying Chiang Kai-Shek and throws himself and his bomb upon it, eyes shut (245), hoping to die not in the moment of impact with the earth but in an upward explosive momentum. How intolerable, then, by contrast, to fail to find that simul-taneity of murder inflicted and death self-inflicted, to be subjected instead to the fall itself? How insufferably paradoxical to return to consciousness a few seconds later and find himself barely existing in the nothing-but-time of nothing-but-suffering, to return to being pure flesh without release, obliged to end it all in the total banality of firing his gun into his mouth?

Ch'en's failed death and subsequent descent into the total suffering of his own flesh is of course a form of punishment, an almost ultimate pun-ishment or penalty, but one that is far from the ecstatic instant that he was seeking. For the logic of suicide bombing is that of a simultaneity of crime and capital punishment that it is possible to understand as a form of ideal death penalty. That logic is extremely complex. On the one hand, it will quickly be retorted that suicide bombers seek in their self-inflicted death the very escape from the punishment of an everyday mortal that their crime of murder merits. Their self-imposed "justice" is, from that perspective, purely poetic, or rhetorical; for the state is deprived of its power to exact a penalty for a crime, and the survivors are deprived of seeing justice done. It is precisely because justice is so thwarted, one might surmise, that post-Enlightenment democracies have recourse, in the case of suicide at-tacks, to forms of collective punishment that their jurisprudence would normally reject out of hand: demolition of houses belonging to the family of the bomber by Israel; invasion and decades-long pacification of Afghanistan by the United States and its allies following September 11, 2001; France's seemingly delirious stagger through its constitution, jurisprudence, and foreign policies in response to the November 15, 2015, attacks.[10]

On the other hand, in suggesting that the suicide attack be understood as a form of ideal death penalty, I am referring to the way that it provides what the death penalty seeks in its "essence," presuming there is such a thing: a type of visceral yet transcendent immediacy of retributive justice that would avoid delay, process, deliberation; a type of ideal talionic sym-metry and simultaneity, as if the judgment had been passed by a god and his sentence delivered like a thunderbolt. The pure instant of murder-suicide performs precisely such a desire for absolute justice as inspires, at some level, support for the death penalty. If, as I have consistently supposed, the death penalty puts mortal time out of joint, disjoins it from the rhythm of a life whose end point cannot under normal circumstances be predetermined, then the suicide attack would offer its ideal instance in the form of the reengineered mortality of a death that is absolutely own-most, the warrior's idealist choice, while remaining at the same time faithful to the ideology of a punishment that posits for itself a capital extreme or outside.

The suggestion of suicide lurks on the edges of the death penalty. The deterrent argument, for example, presumes that if potential criminals know that they will pay the ultimate penalty they will not commit a capital crime; conversely, therefore, criminals who commit such crimes are acting suicidally, obeying somewhere in their psyche a type of death wish. In "Reflections on the Guillotine," Camus supposes "that the desire to kill often coincides with the desire to die or annihilate oneself," adding in a footnote that "it is possible to read every week in the papers of criminals who originally hesitated between killing themselves and killing others." Hence, the murderous criminal kills "in a way . . . in order to die."[11] And indeed, we see especially how contemporary mass killings, whether politically motivated or not, often return, by precipitating armed police intervention or by culminating in suicide, to the logic of Antinous or Jacques du Chastel as recounted by Montaigne.

The idea of a "drive" to commit a crime whose consequence will be one's own death runs parallel to the belief in a criminal recklessness, and both are adduced as abolitionist arguments to dispute the deterrent effect of the death penalty. But the suicide structure of capital punishment extends beyond what is argued in that regard by Camus, as Derrida develops in his seminars. In the first place, as we saw so spectacularly in the case of American Puritan hanging days and the histrionics of the guillotine—not to mention the pageantry of torture—putting to death by the state always involved important elements of visual spectacle. That is what allows a writer such as Jean Genet to elaborate a whole fantasmatic ritual of the death penalty, and to relate it to the ritual sacrifices of Christianity. His novel *Our Lady of the Flowers* is a veritable hymn of passion for capital crime: "to love a murderer . . . . I want to sing murder, for I love murderers . . . . the murderer compels my respect. Not only because he has known a rare experience, but because he has suddenly set himself up as a god, on an altar."[12] The novel is framed by references to two such murderers, Maurice Pilorge, to whom it is dedicated, and who returns in the passage just quoted as saint and martyr—"More than of anyone else, I am thinking of Pilorge . . . . Pilorge, my little one, my friend, my liqueur, your lovely hypocritical head has flown off [*a sauté*]"[13]—and Weidmann, whose name opens the novel, constituting the appearance and apparition that Derrida analyzes: "Weidmann appeared before you in a five o'clock edition."[14] The iconic status of such criminals is reinforced by the images of them with which the narrator of Genet's novel adorns his cell wall; and, in the real life case of Weidmann, who was guillotined in France's last public execution, by the recent discovery of not just photos of his execution but also more than one amateur film.[15] As Derrida comments, without exaggeration:

> [Weidmann] is the first name on a list of famous condemned ones who are celebrated, sung, commemorated, one has to say *glorified* by the narrator, glorified because it is a matter of a certain "glory" (you are going to hear the word "glory" resonate, that is, the word of a certain luminous radiance, a lustrum, an aura, a halo, a Christlike light provided, above their head, by their execution, sometimes by their decapitation, by their very decollation). (*DP I*, 30–31)

As Genet describes them, the murderers he worships and desires clearly organize their crimes in the prospect of martyrdom, a self-sacrifice whose ritualistic structure calls capital punishment down upon the criminal and so defines the crime as a form of suicide.

As converse to that criminal recklessness, which of course diminishes the state's "satisfaction" vis-à-vis the ultimate reckoning, sanction or punishment, there is a much more important structural element in the death penalty that ties it inextricably to suicide, and indeed threatens the whole logical scaffolding of capital punishment. It will allow Derrida to argue that "execution is sui-cide. For the autonomy of juridical reason there is only auto-execution" (*DP II*, 67). The philosopher brings those ideas into focus more than a year after his discussion of Genet, in the Fourteenth Session of his seminars, this time developing the question in a reading of Kafka's *The Trial*. In Derrida's reading of the climax to that novel, when the two men produce a dagger and induce Joseph K. to believe that he should take the knife and stab himself, which he refuses to do, and again when the men perform the execution themselves, what invites analysis is K.'s overriding sentiment of shame. K. is first ashamed of being "denied the remnant of strength necessary" to perform his own execution, of not being able to "rise entirely to the occasion . . . [and] relieve the authorities of all their work"; then he is ashamed for dying "like a dog!"[16] Paradoxically, K.'s suicide would have appeased his shame, having him rise to the occasion of taking responsibility for his misdeeds as the law requires.

According to Derrida, that suicidal obligation structures every death penalty: "if the guilty party is responsible for an act committed with intent, then he must rationally approve his punishment and thus, in fact, impose it on himself" (*DP II*, 66). The requirement that whoever commits a crime acknowledge responsibility for that crime and, by extension, "approve" being punished for it, is fundamental to every system of justice that is defined by "crime" or "offense" and "punishment." And, to the extent that one approves of being punished—acquiescing to the idea of it even if one resists or resents it for being too harsh—one participates in whatever punishment is meted out. On that basis, first, the legal system demands recognition (and conversely, a refusal to validate the system or to recognize a court's authority is the strongest form of subversion of such a system); second, legal systems place heavy emphasis on an accused person's remorse, or lack thereof, in determining the punishment, which effectively assures the criminal's active complicity in the punishment by having him or her negotiate its severity; and third, when it comes to capital punishment, the system requires that the condemned person be conscious and of sound mind, in other words rationally capable of acknowledging their being put to death (even if contemporary anesthetic executions begin by injecting a sedative or barbiturate that is designed precisely to deprive the convict of that very consciousness).

As Derrida understands it, then, such complicity in one's own punishment gives to the death penalty a structure of suicide. That would be the logical consequence of Kant's idea of the "rationality of the death penalty" (*DP II*, 66) for a being who chooses the dignity of raising "himself above life (which beasts cannot do)" (*DP I*, 9). Derrida has been tracking that idea as the major philosophical challenge to any abolitionist argument throughout his seminar. If there is a point in the twenty-one sessions where he comes closest to deconstructing Kant's apparent authority—setting off what he calls "a real self-exploding bomb" (*DP II*, 69)—then it would consist in this undercutting of the force of the state's authority to kill, by having it understood as a state-assisted suicide:

> The logic of suicidal execution, of the truth of execution as suicide . . . even if the executioners lend a hand in this suicide, this suicidal truth of the death penalty is unavoidable, even if the one condemned does not believe it or does not resign himself to it; it is structurally implied by the logic of the verdict. Insofar as the latter claims to be grounded

in law, in reason, in a juridical rationality that is supposed to be universally shared, the guilty one—the one who is found guilty—must acknowledge his judges and thus his executioners to be in the right, and from the moment that he acknowledges the rationality of the law to be right, from the moment that he proves the judges, the executioner, and finally the president who refuses him clemency to be in the right, from the moment that reason gets the better of him [*que la raison a raison de lui*], it is as if he were committing suicide, as if he were executing himself. He approves the sentence; he acknowledges the rationality of the sentence [*il donne raison à la sentence*], and thus he condemns himself to death, and in order to follow this to its logical conclusion, he himself executes the sentence. (67)[17]

In that way, as if mirroring the logic of the state's imposition of the death penalty—you will be deprived of life at the instant of our choosing; we will refine that instant so that it remains both punctual and precise, and definitive—a converse logic develops. In the first place, there operates a form of resistance on the part of the suicidal criminal willing to risk her own skin either in the event of the crime itself or by acceding to capital punishment. It is as if she were to say, "I will appropriate for myself the instant of death that you presume is yours only to determine," adding, when she is a suicide bomber, "I will define it in my terms, as an absolute instant of my glory and your destruction"; or, in the case of Genet's characters, "I will define it in my terms, as a cult of my glory and your impotence." In the second place, however, the death penalty functions as a type of opening or invitation, if not to suicide bombing, then to what might be called a legalized *suicidality*, requiring the condemned person's participation in his or her own execution, his or her complicity in killing, otherwise considered to be an illegal act.

There is of course another specificity of suicide bombing in relation to the death penalty. It involves the form of engineering, understood as the particular mechanization or technologization of the human body, that its performance requires; a mechanization that is specifically a temporal technologization.

We have seen how the "classic" death penalty technologizes the human in an uncanny reversal of orthodox prosthetic practice. It relies on a machine to interrupt mortal time, to deprive someone of additional or future life instead of supplementing a "deficient" existence; and it presumes to operate against the human will of the one who is so prosthetized. The suicide

bomb and bomber are, by contrast, pure death-dealing machines: they execute more or less indiscriminately, mobilizing technology to murderous
effect. The body of the bomber is reduced to the instrumentality of a
vehicle, and, in the instant of the explosion, effectively becomes indistinguishable from the bomb itself. However perverse one or the other of those
death-dealing penalties be, neither a "classic" execution nor a suicide bombing has in fact altered the prosthetic structure that, according to my argument, always has and always will define the human. The human body has
always been reaching, as it were from inside itself, toward an inanimate
outside that it wants or needs to grasp and exploit. We saw that in Chapter 3, as the basic impulse of the organism in Hegel. But, in a way that
Hegel's sublation of the inorganic did not acknowledge, those elements of
the inanimate outside, which the human precisely animates and prosthe-
tizes, exist outside mortal time and become the means by which the human
attempts to control and extend its mortality. In that way any technology—
the tool, memory—necessarily functions as a type of temporalization
wherein the mortal time of the human body comes to articulate with the
archival time of a technical object; and in that way time is a form of originary technologization. The suicide bomber refines that articulation, syn-
chronizing his particular prosthetico-technological relation with an
explosive device that will allow both body and machine to function in
coordination at the moment of combustion. But as we saw in the case of
Ch'en, he is caught between wanting to immortalize himself by becoming
part of the archive—a memorable event, a martyr—and negating all time
by means of a supreme mastery of the instant. Only by seizing the absolute in the instant, he believes, can he resolve those two contradictory
desires.

As military or militant tactic, suicide bombing masters the instant to
greatest advantage by means of shock and surprise. Its logic is that of a
commando raid, extending from strategic assassinations, or attacks on classical military targets, to wholesale operations against civilians outside a
recognized theater of war. It is predominantly when its victims are civilians that those tactics come to be called "terrorist," although the term is
commonly attributed to any form of guerilla warfare including resistance
to military occupation; and increasingly employed in cases where only
property is attacked.[18] As is too easily forgotten, the word "terrorist" issues from a particular historical moment, and a particular concentration
or radicalization of the historical that took place during the French Revolution, namely the (Reign of) Terror. The Terror refers to the period following the execution of Louis XVI, in particular from June 1793 to

July 1794. About halfway through those violent times, on February 5, 1794, Robespierre famously addressed the assembly and the people on the principles of political morality that must guide the National Convention in its interior administration of the Republic:

> One must stifle the interior and exterior enemies of the republic or perish with it. Now, in this situation, the first maxim of your politics must be that of leading the people with reason and the enemies of the people with terror.
>
> If the mainspring of popular government in peacetime is virtue, the mainspring of popular government in revolution is at once *virtue and terror*; virtue without which terror is fatal, terror without which virtue is impotent. Terror is nothing other than prompt, severe and inflexible justice. It emanates therefore from virtue; it is less a particular principle than a consequence of the general principle of democracy applied to the most pressing needs of the homeland [*patrie*].[19]

Terror is advocated by Robespierre as a weapon to be applied to internal enemies of the state, a weapon that will function in collaboration with virtue, applying a rapid and harsh democratic justice in defense of the homeland. We well know how that summary justice played out as a semi-official vigilante bloodletting called for by different political factions involved in the Revolution, how it came to be codified in a series of emergency powers that short-circuited judicial process, leading to the March 1794 formation of the Committee for Public Safety, all of that against the backdrop of very real threats to the nation both external (England, Austria) and internal (the Vendée rebellion). It is estimated that the Terror and associated repression claimed tens of thousands of victims, most of them, however, outside Paris—of 16,594 identified victims, only about 2,600 were judged and condemned in Paris. Most were shot or drowned in a long series of massacres throughout the country.[20] But the mythologized instrument of terror, the symbol of machinic efficacy in terms both of the swift application of a summary justice and the mechanical execution of an instantaneous death penalty, was, as we have seen, the guillotine.

For Robespierre and his allies the Terror became something of a trapeze act. They stood astride events at a monumental point of fracture within Western history. Robespierre shared that historical stage, or high wire, with an actor whose notoriety matched his own, but whose actions played out very differently: the Marquis de Sade. Robespierre and Sade intersect on the historical stage, though with very different stances, at the revolutionary moment that Blanchot analyzed in so confounding a manner in "Literature and the Right to Death." In Blanchot's view, as I shall shortly discuss, Robespierre and Sade cross paths not just in the revolutionary moment, but at the particular *instantanization* of that moment, in the absolutized instant that is defined by the Terror.

During one of the brief periods when Sade was out of prison—thanks to the Constituent Assembly's abolition of the infamous *lettres de cachet* (imprisonment by royal warrant) in April 1790—he advanced side by side with Robespierre. He was elected to the Convention in July 1790 as a representative of the same right-bank Parisian quarter, the Section des Piques, as Robespierre, and went on to become that section's President. Like Robespierre, Sade opposed the death penalty when the question was first discussed in May 1791, an opposition that is stridently maintained in the pamphlet that his fictional character Dolmancé reads into the record in *Philosophy in the Bedroom*.[21] Robespierre himself progressively abandoned his opposition to the death penalty following the flight and recapture of Louis XIV, and he became increasingly intolerant of Sade. But the latter was still a Jacobin stalwart at the end of September 1793, when he wrote a eulogy for the assassinated martyr Jean-Paul Marat. It was rather because of his anticlericalism that he ran afoul of the Terror, finally being reimprisoned a little over two months after delivering the Marat eulogy. In July 1794 he was condemned to death, and he likely escaped that fate thanks only to Robespierre's own downfall at the end of the same month, allowing him to remain free until being interned once more by Napoleon in 1801 (and living out the final thirteen years of his life in the Charenton asylum).

Within that complex network of fictional characters, political actors, and writers it is difficult to clearly distinguish the limits of political action, and indeed of what is called real life, especially vis-à-vis the actions called literature. It is in order to address that question at another fractured moment of Western history—the years following World War II—that Blanchot publishes his 1948 essay "Literature and the Right to Death," and, in order to understand that "right to death," looks not at the wholesale slaughter of the war just past, but rather back at what "the Reign of Terror and revolution—not war—have taught us."[22] Blanchot's initial concern is to analyze the numerous paradoxes that motivate and generate literary writing, and more specifically to lay the groundwork for what appears as his own intransigent revolutionary approach to writing, something that he will make explicit in the prefatory note to *The Infinite Conversation*: "Writing: the exigency of writing . . . an anonymous, distracted, deferred and dispersed way of being in relation, by which everything is brought into question—and first of all the idea of God, of the Self, of the Subject, then of Truth and the One, then finally the idea of the Book and the Work."[23] From this point of view, he concludes, "writing is the greatest violence, for it transgresses the Law, every law, and also its own."[24] Given that revolutionary intransigence, indeed its embrace of violence, it is perhaps not surprising that at the center of "Literature and the Right to Death" one finds Blanchot affirming that "literature contemplates itself in revolution, it finds its justification there, and if it has been called Terror, this is because its ideal is indeed that historical moment in which 'life bears death and maintains itself in death itself'" ("Right to Death," 311).

Blanchot arrives at that central point in his argument by means of an itinerary that is difficult to summarize or reduce to a single logical strand.[25] But his starting point is the presumption, laid out in his second paragraph, that literature begins "at the moment when literature becomes a question" (300), a question whose real sense—"this is the 'question' that seeks its fulfillment in literature, the 'question' that is its being" (322)—will be the self-contemplation and justification in revolution and the Terror, to which I have just referred. In the intervening pages he will have rehearsed possible approaches to literature as a matter of writing, and of reading, its aestheticism and its labor, and he will have discussed a series of "dangers" and "temptations" that are risked by the writer in the course of the literary enterprise. He will have addressed obvious and less obvious reproaches to that enterprise: Literature's "self-infatuation" (301), self-importance, self-indulgence; the nullity that nevertheless, in its pure state, represents its "extraordinary force, a marvelous force" (ibid.), its ability to exist as an everything that is simultaneously nothing (302). But the constant preoccupation that runs through these pages is with literature's relation to a supposed reality or history, and its function in what we call the world of action. First, he notes, literature necessarily emerges from something real, from something existing in time: "It begins at a certain moment in time and . . . that moment in time is part of the work" (305). Second, despite whatever the writer seeks or desires, the literary work necessarily comes to exist as a "public, alien reality, made and unmade by colliding with other realities" (306). The failure to recognize those links with the real is what leads certain writers to presume that their writing can coincide with some other cause, for example a political one, neglecting the fact that fidelity to that cause will have to be compromised by an unavoidable and primary fidelity to the cause of literature itself:

> It is easy to understand why men who have committed themselves to a
> party, who have taken sides, distrust writers who share their views;
> because these writers have also committed themselves to literature. . . .
> What is striking is that in literature, deceit and mystification not only
> are inevitable, but constitute the writer's honesty, whatever hope and
> truth are in him. (309–10)

Blanchot therefore rejects the idea that literature amounts to nothing, that
its fictional status renders it null and void, a "passive expression on the surface of the world" as opposed to "action, which is a concrete initiative in
the world" (313). On the contrary, the writer should instead be understood
as having a greater capacity for action than anyone else, for in acting in a
realm that recognizes no limits, by founding new laws and producing a new
creation the work of literature constitutes "a prodigious act, the greatest
and most important there is" (315). Rather than run the risk of floundering
in inaction, literature must deal with the opposite danger that derives from
its absolute power of action, and from a consequence of that power: "If the
writer acts in quite a real way as he produces this real thing which is called
a book, he is also discrediting all action by this action, because he is substituting for the world of determined things and defined work a world in
which *everything* is *instantly* [tout de suite] given" (316; *Part du feu*, 307).
Literature "ruins" action by producing a world where everything is
imagined, and by throwing down that absolute gauntlet to those who would
hope or presume to change the world into something they "imagine" to
be better. For in spite of the changes for the better wrought by those political actors, better still can always be imagined, and better still, and that
high stakes aspiration haunts every political action from casting a vote to
fomenting revolution.

From that point of view the work of literary imagining—gone to its
absolute extreme—reduces the achievements of what we call political action
to pale inaction; it raises the stakes of what can be done, and taunts so-
called real world actors as ineffectual and impotent. Thus literature might
think it has found its true political and revolutionary calling, either by
boldly presuming itself to be a work of pure imagination, forgetting that
it operates precisely in the gap between what it imagines and what is everyday reality, or else, conversely, by presuming itself to be action and a call
to action, forgetting that "the language of the writer, even if he is a revolutionary, is not the language of command. It does not command, it presents" (317). Blanchot refers to those seemingly revolutionary alternatives for

literature precisely as "dangers," and he then goes on to contrast them with the Hegelian series of "temptations" represented in *The Phenomenology of Spirit* by stoicism, skepticism, and unhappy consciousness.

However, literature is tried or tested by a further temptation, which brings us back to the Terror, to Robespierre and to Sade. Blanchot posits the Terror as both the outside or ultimate temptation for literature and the place for formulating, if not answering, its question. According to Blanchot's logic, terror will be something with which literature must, by definition, reckon, something with which literature intersects. Therefore, literature will, at the extreme, have something of a suicide bomb(ing) about it; or, conversely, the suicide bombing, as a function of terror, will not be something foreign to literature, something unknown to it or misrecognized by it.

Let us try to unpack that. Literature's absolute power of action functions as a form of negation that pushes the writer "toward a worldly life and a public existence in order to induce him to conceive how, even as he writes, he can become that very existence. It is at that point that he encounters those decisive moments in history when everything seems put in question, when law, faith, the state, the world above, the world of the past—everything sinks effortlessly, without work, into nothingness" (318). That is to say, because literature, with its absolute power to produce a world, mocks the impotence of supposed real action, it seduces the writer into an encounter with those moments in history where the real world of political action is in meltdown or in radical reconstruction, into "the time during which literature becomes history" (321). A writer might find those moments in the past, in a creative version of the present, or in an imagined future. In such moments, when the real world seems to have tilted toward or overturned into one that is more extreme, or stranger, than fiction, the writer conversely considers his own fantastical imaginings to be less of a fiction.

The name for such a moment is Revolution: "At this moment [*instant*], freedom aspires to be realized in the *immediate* form of *everything* is possible, everything can be done" (318; *Part du feu*, 309). The writer might have thought that it was only in fiction that everything could be instantly given but now he or she encounters that happening in reality. Blanchot is not developing here a simple analogical relation between the writer's ability to invent everything out of nothing and the revolutionary's inaugural or inventive legislative action (writing a new constitution, declaring the rights of man and of the citizen). Or rather, the relation is first an analogous one:

> Revolutionary action is in every respect analogous to action as
> embodied in literature: the passage from nothing to everything, the
> affirmation of the absolute as event, and of every event as absolute.
> Revolutionary action explodes with the same force and the same
> facility as the writer who has only to align a few words in order to
> change the world. (319)

But it goes beyond analogy in that both literary action and revolutionary
action are driven to the extreme point of that logic, toward an ideal appropriation, the "absolute event" of it. Both revolutionary action and writing have "the same demand for purity" and are similarly convinced that
everything they do "has absolute value" (319). That absolutism propels one
and the other toward a fatal coincidence of all and nothing—"nothing left
for anyone to do, because everything has been done" (ibid.)—and, more
especially, into the unencumbered instant of freedom that is the right to
death. For that is the instant in which Revolution tilts over into Terror. In
the Terror, the absolute capacity for action of both writer and revolutionary comes to be measured, ultimately, in the possibility of wagering life
itself, of staking the freedom of invention, living on the edge all the way
to the right to death. This is less the death to which the Terror condemns
others, its wholesale mobilization of the guillotine, the daily rattle of the
tumbril wheels on cobblestones, the grating and thud of rising and falling
blade, than *the placing of one's own life on the line, the right to have it and to
lose it*. With the Terror one is no longer in the simple business of changing
the world, of acting and working on a specific task or series of tasks designed to bring about such change. Once the Terror arrives, the citizen is
outside the normal time and rhythm of life, he or she accedes to the no-
time of absolute freedom, living "universal freedom, which knows neither
elsewhere nor tomorrow, neither work nor oeuvre. In such moments, there
is nothing left for anyone to do, because everything has been done" (319).
At that extreme edge beyond plans and programs, one's business in life and
of life has become death; one inhabits a space of freedom that opens onto
the freedom to die. In the reign of Terror death becomes less something to
be condemned to—even if that is happening on an industrial scale—than
an essential right; it is less the punishment of the seditious than the unavoidable fatality [*échéance*] of all, the deadline for all, "in some sense the
desired lot of everyone" (319; *Part du feu*, 310). By the time Robespierre is
himself condemned and executed, his much vaunted virtue (the same virtue that, as we heard him declare, is "the mainspring of popular government in peacetime . . . virtue without which terror is fatal, terror without

which virtue is impotent") will be reduced to that of his "existence already suppressed" (ibid.). The virtue that is supposed to have guided his life will coincide with the abnegation of his life. He will be simultaneously the master and victim of *his* Terror: "the Terror that they [Robespierre and Saint-Just] embody comes not from the death they inflict on others but from the death they inflict on themselves [*pas de la mort qu'ils donnent, mais de la mort qu'ils se donnent*]" (320; *Part du feu*, 310). It is that same simultaneity, that same coincident instant that terrorism requires, the capacity to act in an absolutized instant, to enact the simultaneous instant of murder and suicide, the ultimate freedom of killing and of being killed. That terrorist freedom is the paradox of pure concentrated individual action (I am supreme master of what happens; I have the freedom to act out to the absolute limit), and at the same time an uncanny impersonalization or depersonalization of action and of what happens (I am in control to the point where everything is out of control; I enact everything to the point where a pure impersonal action takes over and things simply occur, everything, the death of others but also my own death):

> Terrorists are those who desire absolute freedom and are fully conscious that this constitutes a desire for their own death, they are conscious of the freedom they affirm, as they are conscious of their death, which they realize, and consequently they act during their lifetimes not as people living among other living people but as beings deprived of being, as universal thoughts, pure abstractions beyond history, judging and deciding in the name of all history. (320)

How then does the writer pursue that analogy beyond analogy, staking his or her own life in the same suicidal violence of absolute freedom? Blanchot appears to give two responses, the second of which is more explicit in "Literature and the Right to Death." The first would consist in taking seriously the Orphic challenge of writing that he develops elsewhere, in particular in *The Space of Literature* (where suicide is in many ways the principal question): the challenge of writing as self-abnegation and asociality that is also an intolerable narcissism, a rejection or reduction of both individual self and communal or social other to the point of annihilation; and the calling into question of self and subject and the "anonymous, distracted, deferred and dispersed way of being in relation" that he advocates in *The Infinite Conversation*.[26] The writer is called upon to go all the way down that unlit path, wagering his private life, health and sanity—more or less literally, depending on the writer—for the prize of invention, of writing what cannot be said otherwise.

The second response is something we also saw developed in *The Infinite Conversation* as the greatest violence of transgressing every law: it comes to be personified, back at the Terror, in the figure of Sade as writer of absolute freedom, chronicler of every fantasy and perversion including murder and self-immolation. It is Sade who, in 1793, Blanchot writes, "identifies himself completely with revolution and the Reign of Terror . . . because he understands that [freedom] is this moment when the most insane passions can turn into political reality, a time when they have the right to exist, and are the law" (321). If there were ever a writer who looked out from the bars of his prison cell and saw literature being made into history, who subsequently found in the Revolution and the Terror a world as madly perverse as the one in his head or the one he put so obsessively on paper, it is Sade.[27] We tend to associate him more with psychopathological sexual perversion and violence than with political extremes—and indeed with an aristocratic prerogative to perpetrate such violence—but that tendency overlooks the extent to which his campaign involves the destruction of every institution from family to church and to the state, and even how, in some places at least, it nevertheless sees itself in concert with causes such as the emancipation of woman or the abolition of the death penalty.[28] In the end, though, death is clearly his business:

> He is also the man for whom death is the greatest passion and the ultimate platitude, who cuts off people's heads the way you cut a head of cabbage, with such great indifference that nothing is more unreal than the death that he inflicts, and yet no one has been more acutely aware that sovereignty is found in death, that freedom is death. (ibid.)

Sade is on the political stage during the Terror itself, writing speeches, taking sides, making alliances, at least indirectly sending others to their death (although remaining stalwartly against capital punishment). But he is at the same time writing a literature that takes no prisoners, that takes scriptural and literary liberty to its ultimate limit, further than had anyone before, and further than has anyone since (at least in terms of what we call "content"). His is the terrible standard against which all literature comes to be measured. He builds the pressure of freedom within literature until it explodes and collapses upon itself, bringing the institution down, and him with it. In his writing nothing will stop him and he will stop at nothing: to this day his literature *resonates* as much as it *detonates*.

In the first volume of *The Death Penalty*, Derrida discusses Blanchot's "Literature and the Right to Death," suggesting that it can be read as a "terrifying document from a certain period of French literature, very

French literature," representing something of "the most equivocal political thinking of literature" (*DP I*, 111). He finds it necessary to understand Blanchot's text as the "obverse" of Victor Hugo's abolitionism, a right to death as the obverse of a right to life.[29] From the perspective of the death penalty, Blanchot repeats the very Kantian and Hegelian logic that Derrida is contesting. By situating in the literary enterprise the absolute stakes that we have just seen, by wagering death and the Terror as the limit of those stakes, he inscribes a "structural indissociability" between "the right to literature and the right to death, as right to the death penalty" (116). Literature's special calling, for Blanchot, derives what Kant calls "dignity" from raising itself above animality and biological life to the extent of putting life in play: "if one wants to sharpen the intention of Blanchot's text . . . one must clearly understand that the right to death signifies the right to accede to death . . . both by exposing oneself to losing it, or even by giving itself to oneself . . . and by giving it in putting to death or inflicting the death penalty" (ibid.).[30]

Blanchot's essay, Derrida notes, appears in the same year (1948) as the Universal Declaration of Human Rights, which itself comes some century and a half after the French revolution's own Declaration of the Rights of Man, both of which include as their first article a form of *right to life*: Men are born and remain free and equal in rights (1789); all human beings are born free and equal in dignity and rights (1948).[31] And it comes one hundred years after Hugo's impassioned plea for abolition made at another revolutionary moment, that of the 1848 Constituent Assembly for what will become France's Second Republic. If, conversely, the *right to death* has its corollary, it will be found in Articles 2 and 3 of the penal code finally adopted by the original revolutionary 1791 Constituent Assembly as discussed in Chapter 2, with its banal *guillotinist* logic: "The death penalty will consist in being simply deprived of life . . . every person condemned to death will be decapitated."

We saw how the motivating force behind those articles of the new penal code, was the desire, first, to bring an end to practices of judicial torture; second, to introduce a uniformity of justice; and third, to humanize, anesthetize, and *instantanize* the death penalty. But it is as if the very facility of capital punishment that was thereby instituted—simplified due process, a single penalty for all, a rapid, supposed painless death—allowed for its massive application under the Terror; as if the smooth functioning of the machine of capital punishment, both as judicial process and judicial execution, was what enabled it to run increasingly on automatic pilot from the moment of the guillotine's first blow in April 1792, through to the end of the Terror in late July 1794, and, at a different pace, until the machine's final use in France in 1977.

Added to that facility, in the light of "Literature and the Right to Death," is the freedom constituted by another type of instantaneity that also exists thanks to the Terror, thanks to its taking revolution beyond itself, raising the stakes to include life itself, revolutionizing life to the point of death: the simultaneous possibility of inflicting death on others and on oneself, the absolutization of an instant in which life is risked and given indifferently, mine, another's; the freedom, then, of being in the instant and possessing it absolutely, to the extent of being outside any mortal constraint, temporal or otherwise. That is the idealism of Ch'en's ecstasy of death on the highest possible plane, an absolute seized only in the instant; of Robespierre's chiasmus of virtue and terror; of Blanchot's Sade's lethal sovereign freedom; and of the guillotine's four-stroke temporal mechanism (falling like a bolt of lightning, head flying off, blood spurting out, the man no more), which is supposedly felt as nothing more than a slight coolness on the neck.

Where then has this logic of suicide—death dealt to one's self by means of dealing it to others, capital punishment occurring simultaneously with capital crime—brought us? First, concerning literature, if we follow Blanchot, literature will always be tempted by terrorism, by the terrorism of absolute mastery, the unimpinged, untrammeled freedom of producing whatever it wishes, with a snap of the pen, just like that; and it will be structurally tainted by the terrorism of freely following life to the knife edge that separates it from death, and that separates murder from suicide, the death of another from the death of oneself, presuming to refine that edge to the point and the moment where there is no separation. Literature will seek, and in certain cases find, that ecstatic indifference.

Second, concerning revolution, which, sufficiently refined, will make for instantaneous, indeed metamorphic transformation of the world and in the world; it will find the creative, inaugural, constituent instant of total change. Such immediate change is of the sort that, in human time, we can know only as the opposition—understood and, inevitably, ultimately experienced by all—between life on one side and death on the other, that supposed binary distinction between life and death. Only at the point of that distinction, in that instant, do we achieve our own ultimate revolutionary transformation. No change in life is more revolutionary—and in general more terrorizing—than death. At stake, therefore, is the idea of a revolution that, realizing that its force resides in the instant, co-opts, appropriates and abuses that instant, taking it to the limit where it exercises

its right to death. It is at that moment that the revolution comes to terror-
ize, by introducing the threat and practice of death into everyday life.

Terror defines the presumptive absolute freedom of possessing and governing the instant, the instant that decides that life will become death; it
is the capacity to manufacture such an instant as automatically as the guillotine manufactured the severed heads of 1793–94. Terror derives from
aligning itself with the instant in which death is dealt indiscriminately; it
derives from coinciding with, indeed becoming that instant. Further,
I would argue, the structure of instantaneity is precisely what produces
terror. I refer not that to the idea that, since we have to die, we would all
be happy to die in an instant, without forethought or suffering (second
only to dying outside of time, in our sleep). Different from any such desire
for sudden death, terror is knowing rather that we have ceded to another—
another mortal, another machine—the application of that instant, of knowing that some impersonal state mechanism is making the choice and
executing the instant: it derives from knowing the death-dealing, knife-
edge instant to be fully operational. In that sense terror is in the instant;
or else, terror is the instant and the instant is terror.

According to the logic of such a hypothesis, what follows is this: if the
appropriation and absolutization of the instant is what defines terror,
then the presumptive and presumptuous instantanization of the death
penalty—upon which the whole post-Enlightenment practice of capital
punishment has been wagered, and on the basis of which a certain human-
ization of it has been advocated—also amounts to its terrorization, its
terrorism. In searching for, presuming, and appropriating the instant, the
death penalty rejoins terrorism.

Montaigne's end of the line, accelerated spinning and snapped thread, in
"A Custom on the Isle of Cea," is included within the form of an essay.
Essai is of course his word, and he is trying it out, as though making it up
as he goes along. "If to philosophize is to doubt, as they say, then to play
the fool and follow my fancies, as I do, is all the more to doubt," is how he
opens "A Custom of the Isle of Cea."[32] At the time of writing that piece, a
lot of what Montaigne was doing still amounted to little more than com-
piling, as if practicing routines, not yet launching into the freer form of
later work, still relying on versions of the safety net. The word "essay"
comes from Latin *exagium*, and means a weighing in the balance: Let's
just see how this turns out, which way it tips; let it swing back and forth
for a while before deciding whether to leap. But such an essay, try out,
or attempt can of course end up being a much more serious *épreuve* or

ordalie, a trial by ordeal, of the sort that, still in Montaigne's time, could wager a person's guilt on the stakes of his or her buoyancy, her ability to sink or swim, or survive a fire.[33] Derrida turns to Montaigne, and his black-humorous, sanguine attitude toward death and what we now call the death penalty, in order to remind us that capital punishment, or at least the question of its retention or abolition, did not arise until the Enlightenment.

Blanchot underwent his own ordeal, as recounted in a complex admixture of first and third persons in *The Instant of My Death*. In that tiny text, written fifty years after the presumed event, the narrator speaks of remembering "a young man—a man still young—prevented from dying by death itself."[34] *The Instant of My Death* is the story of how that young man was taken from his house by the Nazis in 1944, as the Allies advanced and Resistance activity surged, and lined up before a firing squad.[35] When the Nazi lieutenant is distracted by fighting nearby, going off "to assess the situation" (*Instant*, 5), one of the members of the firing squad invites the young man to "disappear," which he does (ibid.). This "instant of death" is diametrically opposed to the terrorist instant of Blanchot's 1948 essay, and indeed amounts to an affirmative transformation of it. In this instant, within it, there is hollowed out a space cohabited by life as survival or, in Derrida's term, *survivance*, that makes for a type of absolute hospitality and accommodation of death in life.

In many ways, as Derrida makes clear in his long analysis of this narrative fragment, *The Instant of My Death* condenses the concerns of much of Blanchot's writing, restaging in particular the sibylline formulations of *The Writing of the Disaster* concerning "impossible necessary death."[36] The young man's instant of death will last through his sudden aging once he realizes his imminent fate—"already less young (one ages quickly)" (*Instant*, 5)—through the false steps of the event itself, and through the fifty ensuing years during which he reminds himself that he is alive, and it is as if a voice keeps replying "No, you are dead" (9). In the prolonged, expanded, multiform instant at which the narrator is expecting only to be shot, he experiences "a feeling of extraordinary lightness, a sort of beatitude" (ibid.) that is represented in various ways (and repeated three times in as many pages). In the first place, he reaches a point of indifference toward his fate, the feeling of resignation to it, or reconciliation with it that represents a type of "invincibility" (5). Following our discussion in the previous chapter, we might call that feeling Socratic, the type of acceptance we would wish for anyone faced with death. In the second place, he experiences a form of solidarity, "the feeling of compassion for suffering humanity" (ibid.). Third, we learn that "the feeling of lightness that I would not know how to translate" (7) must come to terms with the guilt of the survivor, for three innocent young men are killed, and the village is burned, whereas the narrator remains alive thanks to being considered a "Seigneur," and his family "Château" is spared the destruction (ibid.).

More important, though, the state he experiences is described as that of being "dead—immortal. Perhaps ecstasy" (5), and that seemingly paradoxical formulation opens the path to the affirmative transformation of the instant that I spoke of earlier. By means of it, death produces not an absolutized instant but rather an *infinitized* one, not its knife-edge concentration but its neutral suspension. Or rather, it will not have produced an instant at all as something supremely or absolutely present, something to be lived as a blaze of glory, the deadening instant of terror, something an exhilarated "I" appropriates in order to make it the cause of your death or my death. Being "dead-immortal" will instead be a new time stretched between imminence and abeyance.

Impossible necessary death is, as Blanchot states in *The Writing of the Disaster*, an "unexperienced experience [*expérience inéprouvée*]."[37] It is shared by those who have so-called near death experiences, and by those who, like Blanchot's young man, Myshkin's soldier in Dostoyevsky's *Idiot*,[38] and large numbers of death-row prisoners in the United States, are readied for execution—sometimes multiple times—before receiving a last-minute reprieve. But whereas those people have an extreme experience of unexperienced experience, the structure of it is common to all of us as mortals: we all live our lives haunted or overshadowed by the expectation of death; we all experience the necessity of death in one way or another—obsessing over it or repressing it or sublating it—while remaining unable to experience it; we all face it, therefore, as a necessary impossibility or an impossible necessity. Blanchot is exemplary among writers of the twentieth century in refusing to let that quandary rest, in trying to account for what defies analysis, the strangest and most intractable of phenomena that consists in an experience of death woven into life.[39] But *The Instant of My Death* brings him right up to the edge of that experience, and, at the same time, utterly disjoins the time of it. In the normal scheme of things, for this young man as for anyone else, old or young, the threat and promise of death is a fact of life; each of life's moments contain that threat and promise. But when that everyday fact of life becomes the fact of being about to be shot, there occurs what Blanchot's narrator characterizes as perhaps "the encounter of death with death" (5). As Derrida comments in *Demeure*:

What has arrived has arrived insofar as it announces itself as what must inescapably arrive. . . . The moment death encounters *itself*, going to the encounter with itself . . . at this instant lightness, elation, beatitude remain the only affects that can take measure of this event as an "unexperienced experience." . . . All living beings have an impossible relation to death; at this instant death, the impossible, will become possible as impossible. This is what, in defying analysis, also gives lightness. (65)

The sense of being "dead—immortal," like the "feeling of lightness," is echoed two more times in Blanchot's text. Once it is a type of direct speech exchange "I am alive. No, you are dead" (*Instant*, 9) whose speaker(s) is (are) unidentified. The second echo comes in the final words of the text, which close a type of postscript where we are told, "Later, having returned to Paris, he met Malraux" (11). The narrator is back in a familiar literary world, talking about manuscripts (we had heard previously that the Nazis had taken one from the Château), but whatever normal life returns continues to involve wrestling with unexperienced death: "What does it matter. All that remains is the feeling of lightness that is death itself or, to put it more precisely, the instant of my death henceforth always in abeyance [*l'instant de ma mort désormais toujours en instance*]" (11).

The *instant* of my death always *en instance*, an instant of death that is in abeyance or in imminence, can be understood precisely to represent the restoration of a mortal time that the death penalty will have interrupted. Following the ordeal of the firing squad, henceforth for the rest of his days, the young man feels the lightness that comes from knowing that his death is going to arrive at any moment, while also knowing, as he lives through the moment of that expectation, that, as far as this particular instant is concerned, he has been reprieved, his death has again been postponed. His instant, and his life, is given a future in the same moment as that future is put at risk. Derrida analyzes this instance of what will already have taken place, and its *time* of lightness, from various angles, but what he emphasizes in each case is precisely the extent to which it disrupts our "faith in a temporal order, in a certain commonsense ordering of time" (*Demeure*, 49).

This other time or time of lightness is presaged, or perhaps already instituted, by the young man's sudden aging in the face of death, referred to by Derrida as the "absolute anachrony of a time out of joint [*un temps disjoint*]" (*Demeure*, 61). After that everything is precipitated toward the coming fatal moment in an "acceleration of a time infinitely contracted into the point of an instant" (62), only to have that instant itself divide itself ("the same instant, but the tip [*pointe*] of the instant is divided here" [68]). Clearly this anachrony recalls Heidegger's ecstatic time as discussed in my previous chapter, a time reconfigured by Dasein as being-toward-death. Indeed, Blanchot's formulation "perhaps ecstasy" (5) could, in the light of other references, be read as invoking Heidegger, given his references elsewhere.[40] But we can read Blanchot's anachrony less as a matter of going ahead to meet one's death in order to challenge and modify the vulgar concept of time as a series of instants, than as a suspensive *extemporization*, and one can imagine precisely, via the everyday sense of "extemporizing," a time that is being adlibbed or improvised, a time of lightness where one is living floating, escaping the tether of each moment. Time is here deprived of its implacable sequentiality; it precisely *stands still*: "Such an instant does not follow in the temporal sequence of instants; this instant is another eternity, the stance or station of another present" (*Demeure*, 73).

The word *demeure* that Derrida picks up on and takes for his title, is used by Blanchot to mark the reprieve that is not yet one as far as the young man knows. When the Nazi lieutenant leaves to see who is attacking, the firing squad remains at the ready, "prepared to remain [*demeurer*] thus in an immobility that arrested time" (*Instant*, 5). Blanchot will use the same word again a few lines later, and, in differing senses, on three further occasions, notably in the last sentence of the narrative. The word *demeurer* will allow Derrida to recast the particular sense of survival that Blanchot provides in *The Instant of My Death* less as the *survivance* that Derrida analyzes in many other places, than as *demeurance* or *demourance*. *Demourance* undoes the simple sense of dying [*mourir*] while at the same time redefining the sense of the instant, affirmatively transforming its time and resisting its capacity for appropriation as a single *absolutizable* temporal entity, as I am suggesting here: "Demourance as anachrony. There is not a single time, and since there is not a single time, since one instant has no common measure with any other because of death . . . according to the cause of death there can be no chronology or chronometry. One cannot, even when one has recovered a sense of the real, measure time" (*Demeure*, 81).

Far removed from "Literature and the Right to Death," a literature that "contemplates itself in revolution" and "finds its justification there" and more particularly in the Terror as "historical moment in which 'life bears death and maintains itself in death itself'" ("Right to Death," 311), one finds in Blanchot's tiny 1994 narrative—or memoir, if that is what it is—a very different attachment to revolution. No longer the moment in which the writer collapses and sublates the "everything is possible" of fiction and the "everything is possible" of history into an ideal absolute instant, revolution is here a very different detonation of the instant, a collapsing of its edifice by means not of *absolutization* but *impossibilization*. This would be a revolution not *in* the instant but *of* the instant, countermanding its very possibility. It is first the overturning of one instant by another. In Blanchot's words, "At that instant [when the lieutenant was about to give the order to fire, the young man already experiencing his "extraordinary lightness"], an abrupt return to the world" (*Instant*, 5); in Derrida's, "the scene will turn or topple over in to the revolution of a single instant . . . . another instant will, in some sense, cause the world, existence, ecstasy itself to be overturned" (*Demeure*, 70). But when the order does not come, when impossible death has instead come to pass, it is for Derrida "as if the sudden interruption of an order were *nothing less than the interruption of time itself. Revolution*" (*Demeure*, 73, my emphasis). This new revolution is the interruption of *instantanized* time; beyond Hegel's circulating or revolving restless time, it is instead the means of unhinging the instant and removing any possible dream or fantasy of seizing it.

Blanchot's narrator's experience is indeed a capital ordeal, a type of rite of passage through the death penalty that brings an indifference comparable to that advocated by Montaigne: "whether he runs to meet his day or awaits it; wherever it comes from, it is still his; wherever the thread breaks, it is all there, that's the end of the skein." Montaigne would have come to that conclusion on the basis of his reading, his doubting, his playing the fool and following his fancies. The essays he thereby produces are relatively modest in comparison to the literary *temptations* that Blanchot lists in "Literature and the Right to Death," especially the temptation of absolute freedom that I have discussed at length. For temptation can, as we know, be lesser or greater. It is another venture, essay, try, or attempt to pull off balance, to have one lose one's center of (moral) gravity and eventually fall. The temptation of absolute freedom draws literature toward the abyss of terrorism, into a structural collaboration with it, into the greatest violence of a transgression and dissolution of all law including its own. According to the logic of Blanchot's analysis, whoever ventures into those stakes of literature, of literature as irresponsibilizing adventure of come what may, is bound, in remaining true to principle, to reach the point of indiscriminately desiring terror and death.

In those terms, the temptation, or risk run by literature, goes all the way from an experiment, test, or attempt (*essai, tentative*) to temptation (*tentation*), to the attack for which the word in French, since well before Montaigne, is *attentat*.[41] In French and other Romance languages the *attentat* (Italian *attentato*, Spanish *atentado*) is the attempt or enterprise that follows the temptation of criminality all the way into violence; hence, increasingly, the *attentat terroriste* such as that or those of November 2015 in Paris; it is the attempt, against custom and morality, or against life, that succeeds. It is the attempt, therefore, whose moment is fulfilled in a transcendent simultaneity of desire and act; the attempt that achieves its *ultimate instantiation* in an *absolute instantanization*, the pure moment of no-time, Ch'en's noncontradiction between complete possession of oneself and absence of flesh. It is also, finally, the indistinction of crime and punishment.

As I argued earlier, the relevance of suicide bombing to the death penalty is the fact of its performing an execution in the same instant as a crime that, for certain judiciaries, warrants capital punishment. Judicial process, however short or long, due or improper, is, to a central extent, robbed by suicide killings of its time, its judgment and its sentence; and it is robbed of its object. That does not mean, of course, that there can be no process, no inquiry, no evidence, no conspirators to be identified, and so on. But a certain impossibility logically ensues: that of the capital punishment of the criminal perpetrator, which represents a form of abolition or annulment of the death penalty, and means nullifying the crime by failing to punish it in an analogous way to how an unsolved case is closed when its perpetrator cannot be identified. Paradoxically, to the extent that he is advocating the indiscriminate death—murder and suicide—of the Terror, and of literary terrorism, Blanchot is also working to abolish the death penalty, which only compounds the intolerable scandal of his essay for morality, legality, and rationality of every stripe (even if one might argue that it advocates on the basis of morality, legality, and rationality). Against Derrida's claim—"even if it is unwarranted to conclude that Maurice Blanchot is *for* a literature in solidarity with the death penalty, the tone and movement of his text forbid concluding the contrary or saying that Blanchot is against the death penalty during this period" (*DP I*, 114)— one might instead argue that Blanchot's text is precisely abolitionist in a way that exceeds Victor Hugo's 1848 Constituent Assembly *"vote for the pure, simple, and definitive abolition of the death penalty."* That is, "Literature and the Right to Death," coming a century after Hugo's impassioned plea, can be read as the scandal of an abolition not just of capital punishment but also of crime, a suspension of judgment such as no state, no judiciary, no people could accept, a type of unconditional innocence that—further scandal—resides at, or is derived from the very heart, *in the very capital of the penalty of death.* As I read it, Blanchot's text can be interpreted in this way: in murder, and in what is presumed to be its reciprocal punishment, taken to the instance of its terroristic extreme, there is no longer any

crime, but not because the concept of crime is transcended by pure abolitionist goodness any more than by pure retributive evil. Rather, at a certain
point called "terror," death given or inflicted—on others, on oneself—
comes up against the instant of its own impossible death penalty. Once
every citizen has a right to death, Blanchot writes, death is no longer "a
sentence passed on him, it is his most essential right; he is not suppressed
as a guilty person—he needs death so that he can proclaim himself a citizen" ("Right to Death," 319). His freedom is born from "the disappearance of death" (ibid.) understood both as the citizen's disappearance by
being executed, and as the disappearance of death itself or at least, I contend, the disappearance in the sense of the abolition—to the extent of its
impossibility—of death as penalty.

Poles apart though it be from "Literature and the Right to Death," *The
Instant of My Death* can also be said to argue for abolishing or annulling
the death penalty, rendering it inoperative. But that is not because it describes a type of passivity in the face of death, a degree of acquiescence
before it, and not because it holds out the hope of a last second reprieve, a
justice—poetic or otherwise, resistance against or defeat of the oppressor—
that arrives in the end. Rather, if the violent imposition of death is overcome or replaced by a feeling of lightness, it will be because the instant
upon which such a violent imposition relies, the instant that can be defined, circumscribed, determined, assigned, and pressed into the service
of every machinery of death, is made to escape that grasp and those ap-
propriations of it.

Once one understands, as Montaigne already did, that it is preferable
to choose one's own death, then the thread or safety net of life stretches to
breaking: the possibility of suicide has as its other side the possibility of
murder. Try that, Montaigne suggests, in the way that his historical ex-
emplars did, be tempted by that pleasure, take that risk, string yourself
out, take the affirmation of life to the point where it includes a choice for
death, or at least for your choice of your own instant: "the most voluntary
death is the fairest. Life depends on the will of others; death, on our own."
Or else, as Blanchot suggests, allow the thread to spin out of control,
tempt yourself with the ultimate experiential experiment of the *attentat*,
the absolute freedom of revolution, launch yourself on the trapeze of the
right to seize an absolute instant wherein "'dying' is pure insignificance, an
event without concrete reality, one which has lost all value as a personal
and interior drama because there is no longer any interior. It is the moment when *I die* signifies to me as I die a banality which there is no way to
take into consideration . . . in these moments when freedom appears as

absolute, dying is unimportant and death has no depth" ("Right to Death," 320); swing way out there, all the way to a terror that—as we saw for Robespierre and Saint-Just—negates the particular reality of one's life, so that all that looms below is the explosive madness and chaos of indifferent indiscriminate killing. Or else, different again, in the terms of *The Instant of My Death*, swing out, further and further beyond all support, beyond even the support of the instant, of a controlled temporal entity whose nondurational parameters are guaranteed, swing out beyond any pure appropriable "now," let go of that, let go to be suspended instead in pure lightness, where there is nothing left but letting go, where you are self-propelled to the extent of leaving behind the apparatus itself, out there floating in the time of a stay without stays, no temporal strings attached and no chronological safety net, for only then might you begin to dismantle the whole *dispositif* of distinction between suicide and murder, death and death penalty, instant and death, life and death. Once one is flying out there, loom, spindle, the whole acrobatic caboodle is brought down, less however in destructive collapse than because where you are suspended, the instant itself disappears into the transformative desuetude of banal inconsequentiality. Then, in no time, it comes to a whole other end.

CHAPTER 5

Drone Penalty

I argued in the previous chapter that attempts to appropriate the instant by proponents and machineries of a supposed painless death penalty find an extreme outside in the absolute seized in the instant by the suicide bomber. In this chapter I will discuss what I view as a different version of that same appropriative gesture, and of the death penalty, namely killing by drone.[1] By means of that practice in its current form, the executive branch of the U.S. government extends the spatial reach of its military actions across oceans and continents in the split second of electronic time that it takes for an aircraft remote-controlled from Nevada or upstate New York to unleash its missile cargo on a chosen target in, say, Somalia or Yemen. The assassinating moment becomes the measure of the worldwide reach of American power, compressing global space into a single instant of decision and action. That repression of space—its conversion into tele-electronic time—has of course very different local effects: the target is destroyed in an instant but the blast reverberates across the impact zone to claim other than the intended victim or victims; and beyond that zone, it has the potential to reverberate all the way back to the United States, its allies, or its interests in the form of terrorist blowback.

In a provocative and insightful study, to which I will return, Grégoire Chamayou analyzes the logic of drone warfare as a mirror effect of the kamikaze attack:

> On one hand, the kamikaze or the suicide bomber, who crashes once and for all in a single explosion; on the other the drone, which fires its missiles repeatedly, as if nothing happened . . . . The kamikaze: *My body is a weapon.* The drone: *My weapon has no body.* Kamikazes are those for whom death is certain. Drone pilots are those for whom death is impossible. In this sense they represent two opposite poles on the spectrum of exposure to death.[2]

Chamayou's study is primarily interested in the technico-ethical transformations brought about by the drone, in what first emerges, in the theater of World War II, through an opposition between a Japanese sacrificial morality and American technical achievement. But those two sides are not only in competition; they also form a chiasmic relation whose vectors reappear in the case of the drone:

> The antagonism between the kamikaze and remote control reappears today: suicide bombings versus phantom bombings. . . . It sets those who have nothing but their bodies with which to fight in opposition to those who possess capital and technology. But these two regimes, the one tactical, the other material, also correspond to two different ethical regimes: the ethic of heroic sacrifice, on one hand, and the ethic of vital self-preservation, on the other. (86)

The extrajudicial killing that I will here refer to as the "drone penalty," has come to represent, in overwhelming statistical terms, the primary, if unspoken, instance of the American attachment to capital punishment. According to data provided by Reprieve, the Bureau of Investigative Journalism, and such American organizations as Code Pink and the Long War Journal, drone strikes performed during the period from 2002 to the present have performed something in the region of 4,136–6,203 executions of so-called combatants, and other men, women and children.[3] In contrast, a total of 1,483 judicial executions were performed in the United States from 1976 to this writing.[4]

My own analysis of the temporal technologies of the death penalty leads me to begin this chapter by following a very specific historical and geographical vector. For the way in which the present-day United States closes the geographical divide between its own territory and the putative enemies whom it executes abroad can be compared with a much slower and much more laborious negotiation of space. One can trace its line—a line of flux or flight—from a northern tributary beginning in Aden and its southern tributary in Mogadishu, until it converges in Zeila near the Somalian border with Djibouti, before skirting along the semidesert and steppes of the southern edge of the Sahara to track clear across Africa at one of its widest points, making stops in Khartoum (Sudan), Bilma and Agadez (Niger), Gao and Timbuktu (Mali). That track potentially or eventually passes through the lands of the ancient Ghana Empire to make a link with the West Coast of the continent. It would not be speaking figuratively to call such a line "positively medieval," for it traces one of the major trade routes of the Middle Ages along a dividing line, buttressed by the desert sands, between the Islamic east and north and the animist cultures of sub-Saharan Africa. And it would not be speaking figuratively to call that line *positively*, in the sense of *thoroughly* medieval, for it provided one of the paths for the development of the slave trade whose already existing African versions would come, following the European Renaissance, to be rationalized, supersized, and globalized to feed the insatiable appetite for coerced labor of the colonizing and capitalizing West. In that way the trans-Saharan supply lines converged on the western coast of Africa, only to leap seamlessly across the Atlantic and gush their human surplus on the shores of the New World. As Édouard Glissant notes in *Poetics of Relation*, "The slave Trade came through the cramped doorway of the slave ship, leaving a wake like that of crawling desert caravans. It might be drawn like this: ➤━━◄ African countries to the East; the lands of America to the West."[5]

Beginning in 2002, that line has tracked the relentless westward expansion of what might be called the transcontinental drone trade, as American Predators and Reapers faithfully follow the routes of medieval and modern human trafficking from Djibouti across to the latest bases in Niger, Cameroon, and perhaps Tunisia, for activities in Mali, and beyond.[6] Given that first George W. Bush, then Barack Obama, with particular relish, and now Donald Trump have increasingly embraced the targeted killing option over the pesky rules of war and vagaries of public opinion concerning American boots on the ground, we may not have to wait too long before this bloodied conduit pushes as far as the western coast of Africa. Perhaps it will extend into Mauritania, where slavery was abolished only in 1981 but is still widely practiced; or south into Senegal, where Barack and Michelle Obama were photographed in 2013, staring pensively and poignantly from a door of no return on Goree Island;[7] or into Guinea and Ghana and the familiar bastions of the European triage and relay of slavery that were established starting in the fifteenth century. Following that, perhaps it will come full circle, home to roost somewhere between the tobacco plantations remaindered for tourists in Jamestown, and the smoke-free and sterile very-much-open-for-business CIA operations rooms of Langley, Virginia. But that will not be because Rand Paul has proven the prescience of his March 2013 filibuster,[8] such that Hellfire missiles have begun to be unleashed on your local Starbucks. Rather, it will be because the history of capital punishment has always intersected, in the period following the Enlightenment, with the history of slavery.

My intention here is not to engage in a calculus that would mean weighing the ratio of Americans executed as against Somali, Yemeni, or Pakistani lives wasted; or to assess the racial and socioeconomic comparisons between the benighted of Africa and South Asia, and poor and black segments of the US population that are so shamefully overrepresented in capital punishment statistics; nor even to debate the necessary distinctions to be made between those that the law has decided to convict for capital crimes perpetrated against fellow citizens within the United States, and those living overseas who are determined by the U.S. government, with ever-widening interpretive liberality, to fall within the ambit of the September 2001 Congressional Authorization for Use of Military Force.[9] For a long time the only substantial public American policy document that existed concerning drones was a speech delivered by Obama at the National Defense University on May 23, 2013.[10] In that speech, the president based the legality of drone strikes on the September 2001 Authorization to Use Military Force while at the same time stating his intention "to engage Congress and the American people in efforts to refine, and ultimately repeal, the AUMF's mandate." The draft of a new AUMF, making reference to the Islamic State, was submitted to Congress in February 2015 but no legislation was enacted during the remainder of Obama's second term.[11] On July 1, 2016, an executive order was issued covering measures to address civilian casualties in U.S. operations involving the use of force, and on August 6, in response to an ACLU freedom of information lawsuit, Obama released a Presidential Policy Guidance document outlining the conditions regulating targeted killing.[12]

Obama's 2013 speech might be read as a response to the troubling questions raised by Philip Alston, the United Nations Special Rapporteur on extrajudicial, summary or arbitrary executions, whose 2010 report exposed in guarded but explicit terms the multifarious International Humanitarian Law implications of targeted killing such as is practiced by the United States. In particular, the report points to requirements of transparency and accountability under international law, noting that "no State has disclosed the full legal basis for targeted killings. . . . Nor has any State disclosed the procedural and other safeguards in place to ensure that killings are lawful and justified, and the accountability mechanisms that ensure wrongful killings are investigated, prosecuted and punished."[13] That finding echoes one of the introductory comments made in the report, namely that the failure of states adopting the practice to respect or consult "the policies and practice of the vast majority of States" correlates with the fact that "many of the justifications for targeted killings offered by one or other of the relevant States in particular current contexts would in all likelihood not gain their endorsement if they were to be used by other States in the future."[14]

Beyond that UN Report, there does exist the finding of a duly constituted judicial instance, the Peshawar High Court. The chief justice of that court, Dost Muhammad Khan, determined in the single case of Pakistan that drone strikes violate sovereignty and are illegal whether or not they have been consented to by the local government. According to his decision, a strike that takes place in an area, such as the Federally Administered Tribal Areas of Pakistan, where there is no armed conflict, is by definition inflicted against a civilian and constitutes a violation of international human rights law. It would seem possible in principle to extend that jurisprudence to Yemen, Somalia, or any other place where the West markets its technological prowess in confrontation with more or less bare lives.[15]

The correlation I made earlier between capital punishment and slavery compares the two rhythms of death penalty temporality that have been in play since the beginning of this discussion: on the one hand, a structure of suspension whose forms include remand, trial, testimony, cross-examination, deliberation, and incarceration and nonparole; on the other hand, the structure of the instant, of decision, sentence, and execution. Slavery—limited here to the New World enslavement of African peoples—is obviously a complex phenomenon with a particular historical duration; and it harbors within it all the forms of summary execution and quasi-genocidal negligence and murder that we know. In the context of this discussion, however, a comparison between what might be called the slow time of slavery and the structures of instantaneity of the death penalty also points to something that this study might otherwise seem to overlook, namely the myriad forms of biopolitical organization, from immigration restrictions to healthcare access, to selective incarceration and police violence, by means of which an otherwise liberal democracy economizes and monetizes the life of its people, or indeed, hastens their death.

On the one hand the death penalty is merely one among such "slower" forms of biopolitics; on the other hand, it produces the peculiar temporalities that have come into focus in my analysis of it.

Assassination by drone therefore presents itself as an object for study here not just because it functions on or over the edge of judiciality, or because it brings instantaneity into relation with intercontinental spatiality. As the comparison with slavery reveals, and as this chapter will develop further, drone warfare reinscribes the death penalty within the biopolitical nexus in a number of other ways. First, overseas drone attacks have domestic corollaries, less in Rand Paul's sense than because drones are increasingly used for domestic and border policing and surveillance; second, remote controlled assassination redefines personhood and corporality; and third, drones reconfigure sovereignty both in terms of how political authorities relate to their citizenry, and with regard to national sovereignty as a function of international law.

To return now to the relation between the death penalty and slavery emblematized by the flesh and blood meridian beginning between Aden and Mogadishu and ending in the Americas.[16] The contemporary U.S. death penalty recalls the biopolitics of slavery. It is frequently imposed in a number of southern, former slave-economy states that remain haunted by the *idea* of black violence, by the idea—more repressed than expressed— that violence cannot not result from the very real subjugation, economic or otherwise, of much of the African American population. The twisted logic of that idea is as follows: African Americans are condemned to death proportionately more frequently than whites because they are more violent; and indeed, how can they not become violent when we whites provoke them to it by various means of social and economic deprivation (in the same way that, as slaves, they had to be beaten into submission to protect slave-owners from what was feared as an imminent, because just, revolt).

Under slavery, capital crimes extended to all manner of offenses that could be construed as cases of *lèse-majesté*, and forms of execution perpetuated practices of excessive cruelty that American law, including of course the Eighth Amendment, sought to abolish. As Carol S. Steiker and Jordan M. Steiker recount in their recent comprehensive study of the actions of the Supreme Court vis-à-vis capital punishment, "As slaves began to outnumber whites in the South, white owners increasingly feared violence or insurrection. . . . Slaves convicted of murdering their owners or of plotting revolt often were subject not merely to ordinary death by hanging, but to even more terrifying and gruesome forms of execution. . . . The corpses of slaves executed for revolt might also be hung in chains or dismembered."[17]

Those types of unconstitutional cruelty come into focus in the specific extrajudicial killings that extended well beyond the end of slavery proper, namely lynchings. Lynching returns a supposedly more enlightened post-bellum *socius* to all the abuses of slavery and its inhumane treatment of persons. Its disproportionate, terroristic violence functions within the same structure of fear and revenge that characterized the period of slavery, namely fear of a just vengeance that might now be carried out by blacks against whites, and revenge for any perceived or real violence by blacks against whites. Lynching, like racist practices of capital punishment, aimed to exorcise the fear of black violence by exaggerating it, then preemptively repressing it: "After the Civil War and the end of slavery, the use of capital punishment in the South continued to have strong racial overtones—echoing and being echoed in return by the race-based mob violence of the practice of lynching."[18] Furthermore, the form of black violence that white Southerners feared more (fantasmatically) than anything else was the rape of a white woman by a black man, which was a smokescreen for the very real—and indifferently punished—sexual violence of white men against black women. As a result, though rape was commonly a capital crime until being removed from northern state statutes in the period 1829–60, as of 1954 it remained on the books in sixteen southern states and was used primarily to execute blacks.[19] It was a law decreeing public hanging for rape, as opposed to the electric chair for murder, that brought 20,000 on-lookers, and Rainey Bethea—a black man who had confessed to rape and murder but was charged solely with rape—to the gallows in Owensboro, Kentucky, in 1936.[20] Beyond those judicial examples, the suspicion or charge of black (male) on white (female) rape was a prime mover for lynching: "Never was the (white) crowd's desire to see lethal justice done stronger than in cases involving black rapists."[21] Rape, or even the slightest hint of it, alleged or proven, mobilized lynch mobs like no other crime, as we know from the shocking torture and murder of Emmett Till as late as 1955.

More important, Steiker and Steiker also show the extent to which lynching, and the history of racially motivated capital punishment in the South more generally, infected legislative and jurisprudential debates concerning punishment, particularly capital punishment, for about a century, and all the way to *Gregg* in 1976.[22] They cite the example, in 1906 in Tennessee, of the Supreme Court's decision to review the case of a black man, Ed Johnson, convicted of rape and sentenced to death. He was taken from his cell, hanged from a bridge, and shot more than fifty times, including five times at point-blank range by a deputy sheriff who pinned a message to his chest reading "To Justice Harlan. Come get your nigger now."[23] In the period beginning in the 1890s, when lynching was at its height, until the famous Scottsboro Boys case of 1931, the Court showed itself either unable or unwilling to counter the threat and enactment of mob violence by enforcing due process and other constitutional protections as demanded by cases that came under its review. It would take another three decades, until 1963, for the situation to begin to change significantly, and what occasioned that change would again be a capital case of black on white rape. The Court declined to review the case of Frank Lee Rudolph, from Alabama, but in a highly unusual move—given that the Court was not taking up the case—one of the dissenting justices, Arthur Goldberg, made public his opinion, drafted by his clerk, Alan Dershowitz. Moreover, opening the question well beyond the terms of the litigation, Goldberg invited the Court to "decide whether the Eighth and Fourteenth Amendments to the Constitution permitted the imposition of death for the crime of rape."[24] Although, as we have seen, that particular question would not be resolved until *Coker* in 1977, Goldberg had, in 1963, effectively introduced the terms of debate regarding the constitutionality of the death penalty that would obtain in the Court's capital case deliberations for half a century.

Steiker and Steiker state that "but for the dramatic regional divide [between North and South] on the death penalty, the Supreme Court might never have stepped in at all."[25] Their complex and detailed analysis shows overwhelmingly, as the examples just given reinforce, that the history of capital punishment in the United States since the Civil War is above all a history of convicting and executing black men charged with raping white women. And if the retrograde side of the narrative—lynching, and legislative and judicial impotence or inaction—is racially charged, so is the progressive side, for from the time of Goldberg's memorandum until *Furman* and *Gregg*, it was the Legal Defense Fund of the NAACP that championed the cause of capital punishment unconstitutionality as part of their more general advocacy of civil rights, and their having "developed valuable experience in 'cause' lawyering [i]n the fight against Jim Crow and state-sponsored segregation."[26] Following Goldberg's initiative the LDF acted on what it already knew, "that the death penalty for rape was administered in a racially discriminatory manner."[27]

There is, for that reason, tragic irony in the fact that despite the emphasis placed by the LDF campaign on questions of race in relation to the death penalty, that very issue has remained, as Steiker and Steiker put it, "hiding in plain sight" in the Supreme Court decisions of the past fifty years.[28] One might see it returning, still out of sight, but brought back into the wings, with all the accompanying factors just discussed, by Clarence Thomas in 2015. What greater irony could there be, in this context, than a *black* man, who had accused his opponents of a figurative *lynching* during his Senate hearing, arguing for the reinstatement of the death penalty for *rape?* "The Court has also misinterpreted the Eighth Amendment," he writes in *Glossip*, "to grant relief in egregious cases involving rape" (Thomas concurring, 8) before going on to cite *Coker* (1977) and *Kennedy* (2008). *Coker*, coming hard on the heels of *Gregg*'s 1976 reinstatement of the death penalty, was an attempt by the Court nevertheless to place limits on capital punishment by taking up a case, issuing from a southern state, involving not murder but rape, perpetrated by a white and not a black man. As Steiker and Steiker analyze, the Court's choice of this case for review—two other petitions for rape cases from Georgia, involving black men, were pending—can easily be read as a desire on the part of the Justices to exclude race from the capital punishment equation: "*Coker* represents the height of the Court's avoidance of race, because Georgia's continued authorization of death for rape was simply impossible to explain or understand without examining the racial history surrounding that practice."[29] *Kennedy*, on the other hand, some thirty years later, was the case of a black man sentenced to death for raping his stepdaughter. Though we might seem far from the paradigm inherited from slavery, Thomas cites *Coker* and *Kennedy*, as well as *Roper*'s 2005 decision against capital punishment for a juvenile, as examples of the Court's overreach "in its ceaseless quest to end the death penalty through undemocratic means" (*Glossip*, Thomas concurring, 10). He therefore evokes what he considers to be the *activist* jurisprudence of recent times, but at the same time, no doubt unwittingly, implies and implicates the much longer history that we have just reviewed, with its toxic combination of slavery and racist murder occurring on the edges, or beyond the bounds of constitutionality and judiciality; and similarly implied and implicated in that history is a shamefully *passivist* judiciary that, decade after decade, failed to redress the wrongs of that racist past or stand sufficiently firm on constitutional principle.

A different intersection between slavery and the death penalty occurs in discourses of both abolition and anti-abolition, namely in the concurrence of economic and moral questions that framed the debate concerning slavery, and continue to frame discussion concerning the mechanics of capital punishment. That is to say, slavery was a moral outrage for abolitionists and an economic necessity for nonabolitionists; the death penalty is a moral outrage for abolitionists, and its cost constitutes an important element of debate for both abolitionists (it is far more expensive than incarceration) and retentionists (yes, but that is because of endless appeals). Similarly, fault lines that emerged in American democracy, and its judiciary, during the period of slavery, extend into the practice of the death penalty: opposition between state rights and federalism, or questions of principled leadership on contentious issues versus simple obedience to a perceived or expressed majority opinion. Abraham Lincoln, whatever his hesitations, tergiversations, or convoluted strategizing, made emancipation a matter of principle; similarly, one might say, though with far lesser stakes, Obama led the people toward a more enlightened position on gay and gender rights. But no presidential nominee of either party has expressed opposition to the death penalty since Michael Dukakis in 1988, and no major politician in recent memory has seen fit to make capital punishment a topic for public discussion, let alone make abolition a policy goal. Instead, the country was treated to the "principled" stand of candidate Bill Clinton breaking off his campaign engagements to be personally present in Arkansas for the execution of Ricky Ray Rector in 1992; or to George W. Bush's 152 executions in five years as governor of Texas.

The basic principles of human rights, of life and liberty as enshrined in the Declaration of Independence and developed in the Bill of Rights, principles that served as the basis for the Emancipation Proclamation, have failed over the last century and a half to extend into the question of the death penalty, and, in the period of the abolitions taking place across the globe since World War II, national debate in the United States concerning capital punishment has more or less remained confined to the Supreme Court. That national failure to address the issue produces parallels between how the nineteenth-century slave was freed but denied the rights of that freedom until more than halfway through the twentieth century and the perversions of judicial process that we have seen, such as a convict languishing in prison for decades before finally being executed. Though the parallels by no means run in the same direction or according to the same logic, it is clear in the final analysis, as Derrida summed it up, that "one can understand nothing about the situation of the United States faced with the death penalty without taking into account . . . the history of the federal state, the history of racism, the history of slavery, and the long, interminable struggle for civil rights, the still critical relation of the states to the central government and federal authority" (*DP I*, 74).

The slavery-punishment nexus is further analyzed, in terms that remain coextensive with the death penalty, in the work of Colin Dayan. Her arguments are summarized succinctly in *The Story of Cruel and Unusual* and developed in more detail in *The Law Is a White Dog*.[30] In the first book she reads how, as we have seen, the use of the term "cruel and unusual" in the 1689 English Bill of Rights was taken up and repeated by the 1791 American Bill of Rights, but that, as a result, the latter document failed to prohibit on the grounds of cruelty the principle of excessive punishment as distinct from obviously egregious forms of punishment: "If the methods of punishment used in the United States today—the death penalty, prolonged solitary confinement, extreme force, and psychological torture—seem barbaric by our standards and by those of the rest of the so-called civilized world, this can be traced to the colonial history of the legal stigmatization and deprivation of a group considered less than human."[31]

American law and penal practice all the way to Supermax prisons, solitary confinement, Guantanamo Bay, and black prison sites, Dayan demonstrates, are inextricably linked to the problem of defining the personhood of a slave. Punishment and cruelty became questions precisely in the context of slavery, where it was a matter, in the first instance, of refining harsh treatment of persons deprived of right according to a predominantly economical rationale: A bleeding or injured slave is an unproductive slave. From there the doctrine was imported into the context of incarceration, for, as Dayan emphasizes, the Eighth Amendment prohibition, by specifically speaking of cruel and unusual punishment in the context of bail and fines, "is the only provision of the Bill of Rights that explicitly relates to prisoners."[32] As we saw in Chapter 1, prison and hard labor as excessive punishment are in question in *Weems* in 1910, and Dayan argues that it was the prisoners' rights movements of the 1970s and 1980s that brought about revisions of Eighth Amendment jurisprudence in a way that overlapped with the considerations of such death penalty milestone cases as *Furman*, where, of course, cruel and unusual was also explicitly related to questions of racial inequality.[33] Similarly, practices of detention, as well as treatment of the racial other, are again foregrounded in relation to Guantanamo Bay and the Abu Ghraib scandal, in the context of the post-9/11 constitutional overreach that has also given us assassination by drone.[34]

That history of the personhood of a slave is, as Dayan shows, complex. Its crux is, no doubt, the paradox of treating slaves as chattels or things but rehabilitating their personhood when it came to punishing them: "For this piece of property became a person only in committing a crime. . . . No longer disabled in law, the slave could be recognized as a thinking thing. He was treated as a person, capable of committing acts for which he might be punished as a criminal."[35] Nor is such a paradox without historical precedent; nonhuman animals, for example, were tried, convicted, and punished for crimes in Europe from the Middle Ages to the second half of the seventeenth century. But, as Dayan argues, the status of the slave was defined by reference less to subhuman animals than to the concept, in English law, of the deodand, which extended criminal agency to objects such as a tree or cartwheel.[36] The slave had "liability but no rights," remaining "vulnerable to legal prosecution though deprived of personality," capable of committing "criminal but not civil acts."[37] That novel status of the slave prevented a trader, in *Boyce v. Anderson* (1829), from recovering damages for lost cargo: Slaves were declared in that case not to be simply "a common package," but neither were they recognized as anything more than "mere property."[38] That perverse logic is what prevented slaves from exercising the freedom they were granted by the Emancipation Proclamation, just as it kept open the jurisprudential possibility of forms of dehumanization that are exploited to this day.

Thus, though slavery has disappeared, special categories of (less than complete) personhood persist in the law. Dayan emphasizes in particular two complementary mechanisms, and points to a third, through which certain deprivations of rights have come to be accepted in contemporary American jurisprudence. The first mechanism emerges in a series of cases regarding prisoners' rights that culminated in the 2006 Supreme Court decision in *Beard v. Banks*, which denied prisoners access to certain broadcasts, press, and other documents.[39] Effectively, because the Constitution does not specifically define a prisoner, no more than it defined a slave, jurists were able to reach back to nineteenth-century models of carceral deprivation—even by extrapolation to Benjamin Rush's late eighteenth-century model—in order to determine what passes Eighth Amendment muster when it comes to convicts. Yet one presumes that a Clarence Thomas, whose concurring opinions in some of those cases were striking in their treatment of the prisoner as a special, lesser category of person, would refuse to acknowledge any overlap of doctrine between the definition of the slave and that of a convict.

The second mechanism leads step by step from the latitude accorded prison guards in their treatment of prisoners to the abuses of Abu Ghraib, Guantánamo Bay, and black detention sites. Debate turns not on the acts themselves and their effect on detainees or prisoners, but rather on the intent of the actor. As a result, according to Dayan, "the intangible self—the thinking thing—becomes detached from the prisoner, while his body comes forth as focus."[40] She traces that development from the late nineteenth century, through *Resweber* in 1947—where, as we remember, only "purposeful non-promptness" was judged unconstitutional and no one had intended to inflict unnecessary pain—to the infamous 2002 torture memos issuing from the Departments of Justice and Defense. The latter, Pentagon memo, dwells in particular on the difference between the Eighth Amendment ("cruel and unusual") and the UN Convention Against Torture and Other Cruel, Inhuman, or Degrading Treatment or Punishment, which was ratified by the United States in 1994 with the proviso that the "cruel, inhuman, or degrading treatment or punishment" prohibited by the Convention be interpreted in the light of the Eighth Amendment. In short, for this country, treatment or punishment could be inhuman or degrading as long as it was not cruel or unusual.[41]

If I have dwelled on Dayan's argument here, it is because she essentially maintains that in all the aforementioned cases the slave is presented as a problematic category, existing somewhere between thing and person. Not only did that require, from that point on, that American jurisprudence interpret and reinterpret the rights of a duly constituted person, it also allowed that same jurisprudence to perform step by step contraventions of the very, supposedly inalienable rights upon which the Republic is based: "The mutations generated by law become part of the logic of punishment. It is not indifference to the category of personhood, but rather an obsession with it, that introduced another kind of person, anomalous and somehow extraneous to civil society," producing as a result "connections among the offending animal or inanimate object, the slave, the prisoner, and the newly targeted terrorist or detainee."[42] What I am arguing here is that, coextensive with the same sort of step-by-step abrogation of constitutionality that was enabled by slavery, and coextensive with the practice of the death penalty as intersecting constitutional problem, one finds the practice of targeted killing. The enemy soldier is protected by the Geneva Convention, while the partisan or guerilla who fights in a theater of war without a uniform is not. The enemy combatant, wherever he or she be, may be targeted if he or she poses an "imminent" threat. Conversely, whoever is found in a strike zone will in the majority of cases be posthumously defined as an enemy combatant. Those policies and destitution of rights may be applied to American citizens and noncitizens alike.

The third mechanism that emerges from the nexus between slavery and punishment directly implicates the death penalty. It is the logic whereby incarceration for extended periods of time, or involving solitary or Supermax confinement, is allowed to aggravate to the extent of being considered more cruel than the death penalty. Dayan cites the repeal of the death penalty signed by Governor Bill Richardson of New Mexico in 2009.

Richardson's decision in favor of abolition was partially motivated by a visit to the maximum security unit of the state penitentiary, which gave rise to his assessment that "those cells are something that may be worse than death," which for him made life imprisonment "a just punishment."[43] Without imputing to Richardson any intention to have prisoners suffer a punishment worse than death, the proposed replacement of the death penalty by prison without parole—currently one of the most effective abolitionist arguments in the United States—emerges as a more sinister, slow form of death penalty. It bears little difference from one of the first abolitionist arguments—against capital punishment but for perpetual slavery—famously made in 1764 by Beccaria, and taken up by reformists, and proponents of prison and solitary confinement such as Rush. For Beccaria:

> The death of a criminal is a terrible but momentary spectacle, and therefore a less efficacious method of deterring others, than the continued example of a man deprived of his liberty, condemned as a beast of burden, to repair, by his labour, the injury he has done to society. . . . Perpetual slavery, then, has in it all that is necessary to deter the most hardened and determined, as much as the punishment of death. I say, it has more. There are many who can look upon death with intrepidity and firmness; some through fanaticism, and others through vanity, which attends us even to the grave; others from a desperate resolution, either to get rid of their misery, or cease to live: but fanaticism and vanity forsake the criminal in slavery, in chains and fetters, in an iron cage; and despair seems rather the beginning than the end of their misery.[44]

Death is preferable to being condemned as a beast of burden; perpetual slavery is a more effective deterrent than the death penalty. That is so because slavery is an egregiously intolerable treatment to inflict upon a human person, but also because, in the American context at least, slavery has always shadowed the death penalty, on the imprecise edges of constitutional acceptability, as a slow, lifelong penalty to complement a supposed rapid execution, the white master's dream of a permanent indenture, the capacity to dispose of a human body at will whose cruelty evokes and is evoked by the instant disposal of a life put suddenly to death.[45]

Slavery in America, or more precisely its discriminatory legacy, is represented by Steiker and Steiker as a most significant form of "exceptionalism" contributing to the retention and operation of the death penalty here in contrast to other Western democracies.[46] In summarizing other contributing factors, they point to a high rate of violent crime, particularly in

the South, "unusual embrace of individual gun ownership, and lack of social solidarity, reflected in high levels of income inequality and a relatively
weak welfare state," and cite Frank Zimring's critique of a "distinctive culture of vigilante justice" and "an illuminating connection between a history of lynching early in the twentieth century and the willingness to
conduct executions in the 1980s and 1990s."[47] In the passage quoted earlier where Derrida evokes the inextricable link between the death penalty
and racial inequality, he goes on to mention "the ethics of so-called self-
defense that overarms the population to a degree unknown in any other
country in the world, a feeling of explosive insecurity unknown in Europe,
against the background of social and racial inequality" (*DP I*, 74). Following Dayan's extension of the question into post-9/11 practices, however,
I would argue for a further extrapolation. For not only is America's "excep-
tionalist" death penalty rooted in a violence of so-called self-defense and
constitutional presumptive right that arms the civilian population to a
frightening degree, as well as in a propensity for vigilante justice practiced
in the domestic sphere, armed vigilantism also extends to the national militarism that plays out on the global stage.

We Americans armed ourselves first in order to resist or rise against the
colonial masters who subjugated us; then we armed ourselves against those
who risked rising against us, or so we thought, once our mastery had been
called into question (the KKK was no doubt the first postbellum well-
regulated militia); now we arm ourselves against the possibility that our
government will disarm us; and all too consistently, massively armed as a
country and delightedly arming other countries, we dispense vigilante justice against those we call or make our enemies the world over. Since 2001
the United States has been moving heaven and earth and raising hell in an
attempt to defeat a nebulous coalition of brownish non-Christian malcon-
tents radicalized by our neocolonial connivance in their subjugation, or by
our misguided assaults on their lands. Hand-wringing over domestic gun
violence in general and military assault weapons in particular may or may
not lead to legislation that will better protect American children, but never
has it been allowed, up to the present, to call into question the automatic
reflex of militarist self-defense, the unquestioned presumption of military
might and prerogative as the first and last negotiation on the international
stage. Successive presidents are more than willing to arm the country to
the hilt and attack schools, mosques, and meeting places abroad with premeditated precision, incarnating the extraordinary disconnect between illicit mayhem at home and that we perpetrate abroad, even if their actions
be as judicious as those presidents would have us believe. Similarly, there

is an ocean of difference between genuine presidential and paternal concern shown African American (and just plain American) children, and the reckless disregard, through our militaristic geopolitical strategy, for African and Asian ones, as though the dividing line were as easy to draw in contemporary times as it was for a colonialist sovereign Isabel, George, or Louis.[48]

Slavery and the death penalty also converge in the French Revolution. In May 1791, the Constituent Assembly debated capital punishment prior to legislating it and adopting the guillotine. As we have seen, Robespierre argued strongly against it, as did the Marquis de Sade. But a month later Louis XVI attempted his game-changing escape. The absolute monarchy could thenceforth be definitively overthrown only by being decapitated; only in that way would Article III of the 1789 Declaration of the Rights of Man—"the principle of every sovereignty resides essentially in the Nation"—come to be fully respected; only by that means would sovereignty be transferred from an inviolable monarch to the state itself, and to its people. So, as Derrida reminds us, it was the simple citizen Louis Capet whom the Convention condemned to be guillotined in January 1793:

> By dividing in this way the body of the king in two, the head on one side, the body on the other, this unprecedented event was destined at least to put an end to what Kantorowicz calls the *double body of the king*, the king's two bodies, the empirical and carnal, mortal body, on one side, and the body of the glorious, sovereign, and immortal function, on the other . . . . by dividing in two the body of Louis Capet beneath the blade of the guillotine, the revolutionaries . . . were reducing it to a single body. (*DP I*, 100–1)[49]

Just over a year later, in February 1794, the same Convention abolished slavery, enacting Article I of the Declaration of the Rights of Man: "men are born and remain free and equal in rights." Robespierre was again in the abolitionist vanguard, along with Danton. But by then the revolutionary agenda had been effectively overtaken by the slave revolt—inspired by that same Revolution—that had begun in Haiti in August 1791, two months after Louis XVI was captured in seditious flight. And although Haiti indeed obtained independence in 1804, a few months before Napoleon crowned himself emperor, the same Napoleon Bonaparte, then consul, tried to forestall that ultimate colonial emancipation by reinstituting slavery, in colonies where the abolition of 1794 had not been applied, in 1802.

Thus, the French death penalty, seemingly ready to be abolished in 1791, remained on the books for nearly two centuries, until 1981; and slavery, abolished in 1794, returned in order to restore colonial order in 1802, remaining in force until its abolition by the Second Republic in 1848 (when Victor Hugo and others argued strongly against the death penalty but were not able to have it abolished). Both death penalty and slavery, then, survive the revolution, and, following Napoleon's 1799 coup of the 18 Brumaire, which saw the end of the last revolutionary government (the Directory), the Roman form of absolutism, the *lex curiata* of the Consulate, later to become the Empire, came into force. That gave rise to the modern state of exception or emergency—already promulgated by the Constituent Assembly in 1789—to which, according to thinkers such as Agamben, we all now find ourselves subject.[50]

In other words, through the second great eighteenth-century revolutionary model one can again find intersections between slavery and the death penalty; one finds at the very least the idea being advanced that neither one nor the other is compatible with something called democracy, or the Rights of Man, that what the *Trop* doctrine will call in 1958 "evolving standards of decency" and the "dignity of man" have, since the second half of the eighteenth century, militated in favor of basic respect for both life and liberty. But one also finds that same nexus expanded into an international context: Louis XVI was judged and executed not just for his opposition to the Revolution but also for various acts of sedition. Among the thirty-three charges against him were accusations that he gave tacit support to the August 1791 Declaration of Pillnitz (by Frederick William II of Prussia and Emperor Leopold II, Marie-Antoinette's brother) which allowed for foreign military intervention against France; that he transferred money to, and plotted with émigrés planning to march on Paris; that he conducted secret diplomacy and made alliances with other European powers; and that he delayed by two days military action to counter the August 1792 Prussian invasion of French territory.[51] It was in the light of such assistance provided to sworn enemies for actions against France that Robespierre argued for summary judgment: "he has appealed to . . . the armies of tyrants . . . he is already judged."[52] Repeating his opposition to the death penalty, he nevertheless argues for a capital sentence, using terms that foreshadow his later invocation of terror as a general principle of democracy answering to patriotic demands: "For my part, I abhor the death penalty . . . and have for Louis neither love nor hate: I hate only his crimes. It is with regret that I pronounce this fatal truth . . . Louis must die, because the homeland [*patrie*] must live."[53]

Men are born free and remain free and equal in rights; the principle of every sovereignty resides essentially in the Nation. Alternately: *all men are created equal and endowed with certain unalienable rights; to secure these rights, Governments are instituted, deriving their just powers from the consent of the governed.* There should be no possible place for slavery in such formulations. Indeed, when Thomas Hobbes wrote his seventeenth-century textbook on sovereignty, the slave remained outside the protection of the commonwealth, but by the same token absolved of any responsibility toward those with power over him. In the section of chapter 20 on "Despoticall Dominion" or "dominion acquired by conquest," the slave is mentioned in parentheses following explanation of the covenant between master and servant, by which "is not meant a Captive . . . (for such men, (commonly called Slaves,) have no obligation at all; but may break their bonds, or the prison; and kill, or carry away captive their Master, justly)."[54] Even in 1651 the slave was conceived of, in the light of an emerging modern, Westphalian concept of sovereignty, in the restrictive Greek and Roman terms as one "taken in war."[55] From the Hobbesian point of view, then, the slave "enjoys" the status of an outlaw, mirroring that of the sovereign, who, as Schmitt famously insisted for the twentieth century, "is he who decides on the exception" or suspension of the law.[56]

In his final, 2001–2003 seminar, *The Beast and the Sovereign*, Derrida refers to Hobbes in the context of the sovereign "figured sometimes as what rises, through the law of reason, above the beast, above the natural life of the animal, and sometimes (or simultaneously) as the manifestation of bestiality or human animality."[57] For Derrida, it is in the nature of a sovereign to be both sovereign and beast, one who both personifies the law by virtue of the power to make and suspend it, and is by the same token an outlaw or criminal. Sovereign power is capable of "carrying the human sovereign above the human, toward divine omnipotence (which will moreover most often have grounded the principle of sovereignty in its sacred and theological origin) and, because of this arbitrary suspension or rupture of right, runs the risk of making the sovereign look like the most brutal beast who respects nothing, scorns the law, immediately situates himself above the law."[58] Such a rogue sovereign is described further in *Rogues*, which overlaps with, and grows out of *The Beast and the Sovereign* seminars.[59] Rogue is he who calls others rogues—other states or heads of state—while being himself wholly rogue in the exercise of power: "it is the most powerful sovereign states which, making international right [or law] and bending it to their interest, propose and in fact produce limitations on the sovereignty of the weakest states . . . going so far as to violate or not respect the international right [or law] they have helped institute . . . all the while accusing the weaker states of not respecting international right [or law] and of being rogue states, i.e. outlaw states."[60]

Derrida is here writing in spring 2002, at the beginning of the buildup toward the invasion of Iraq, and he clearly has in mind the excesses of post-9/11 America, as he makes more explicit in *Rogues* and other texts.[61] But one should by no means construe that specific historical context as confining his comments to the actions of the Bush White House. Indeed, as he states, it was the Clinton administration that "invented" and propagated the rhetoric regarding rogue states; and the Clinton administration's bombing of Yugoslavia in 1999 stood out for Derrida as the prime, watershed example, of how the sovereign power of the powerful, bolstered by the discourse of humanitarianism, rides roughshod over the sovereignty of weaker states.[62] So we could well presume that were he to have witnessed the development of drone warfare and its radical intensification under Obama,[63] he would not have neglected its pertinence to any discussion concerning international sovereignty, not to mention the death penalty. As he reminds us at the very beginning of the 2001 seminar, "those of you who followed the last few years' seminars on the death penalty know that the huge and formidable question of sovereignty was central to them."[64]

It would be hard to imagine, especially in the democracies of the twenty-first century, a more Roman, medieval, or at least prerevolutionary, predemocratic practice of the state of exception than the kill list that Obama was said to consult every week or so during his presidency (we have as yet no idea how or whether that practice has continued under Trump). Since 2004, successive consuls-in-chief of the American Sway have declared more than seven hundred such states of exception over the territories of Pakistan, Yemen, and Somalia, outside any declared theater of war, many of them being the handiwork of former constitutional lawyer and Nobel Peace Prize laureate Obama. The drone was his preferred exterminating angel, hovering in the sky with a nonspecific imperial sweep above a population become slaves to airborne terror before unleashing without warning its missiles of vengeance. Divine vengeance, quite clearly, like a flash of lightning out of the heavens. George Bush seeking guidance through prayer before refusing Karla Faye Tucker's request for clemency in Texas in 1998, or on his knees about Afghanistan or Iraq, has nothing to envy Obama, studying writings on war by Augustine and Thomas Aquinas, we are told, to assist in his deliberations over whom next to target on an ever-expanding extrajudicial death-penalty list. Conscious of his responsibility "for the position of the United States in the world," according to his national security adviser,[65] he personally and repeatedly drew the line in the sand to take us back in regress motion across medieval trade routes, back to Yemen and Somalia, to execute its recalcitrants into submission.

My thematic insistence, from the beginning of this chapter, on the trans-African, transatlantic blood meridian is related, finally, less to the historical and geographical nexus among slave trade, death penalty, and targeted executions, than to the particular version of sovereign superterrestriality that is the intercontinental ballistico-technological arc operating, for instance, between Hancock Air Base near Syracuse, New York, or Creech Air Force Base in Nevada, from where the drones are operated, and Waziristan (Pakistan) or Elasha Biyaha (Somalia). It relates to my more general thesis that the drone penalty per se is a function less of conscience, intelligence, or even belligerence than of the technology that seems to come into play only once we get into what is euphemized as the "Naugahyde Barcalounger" or drone pilot's seat at Creech or Hancock.[66] And that relates in turn to my even more general thesis that what appear as technologies that humans have created, at will and of necessity, for our use and convenience, in order to do everything from sharpening flint to waging war or waging executions, are in fact functions of the technics that defines us. Technology is always at work in us, I would argue, from the moment we stood upright, but even before that, from the moment we decided to remember by means of mnemotechnological devices inside or outside our skull; it exists coextensively with the thinking or rhetoric of invention that we presume to be distinct from, while giving rise to, the artifacts that we produce; and it exists coextensively, as I maintain in concluding this chapter, with even the inner recesses of thinking, or praying, that are presumed to inhabit some secret mental space.

The version of technology that emerges as a gravity's rainbow connecting Nevada and Waziristan reposes the question of the expanding spatial parameters of Carl Schmitt's politico-polemical front that I have tried to analyze elsewhere.[67] Schmitt's implied preference, in insisting on the ever-present threat of conflict in order to distinguish friend from enemy and so define the political, is for a form of Spartan or gladiatorial combat, a *mano a mano* struggle along a clearly defined boundary separating political enemies who confront one another with the threat or promise of existential negation. He finds that model of combat problematized once a regular army has to confront a guerilla or "partisan" force: "In partisan warfare, a new, complicated, and structured sphere of action is created, because the partisan does not fight on an open battlefield, and does not fight on the same level of open fronts. He forces his enemy into another space."[68] The other characteristic of the partisan, related to the first, is his mobility, understood as a function of a more generalized technologization of warfare in the two World Wars: "Flexibility, speed, and the ability to switch from attack to retreat, i.e. increased mobility, remains today characteristic of the partisan, and this characteristic is even more intensified through technicization and motorization."[69] Paradoxically, though, the mobility of the partisan would separate him from his most immediate motivation, that is protecting his home territory against an invader or occupier, referred to by Schmitt as the partisan's "telluric character": "Such a motorized partisan loses his telluric character and becomes only the transportable and exchangeable tool of a powerful central agency of world politics, which deploys him in overt or covert war."[70]

While Schmitt seems to have remained blind to the fact that technology, in the form of the prosthetic extension of the body by means of weaponry, was always a factor of combat, he was prescient enough to realize that modern technology signaled the beginning of the end for his classical view of warfare. He viewed the 1949 Geneva Convention as struggling to deal with that transformation; it allowed for new categories of belligerents, such as members of an organized resistance, to be treated as combatants, and it continued to presume that wearing a clearly visible badge of rank still made sense in combat involving long-range weapons.[71] But, true to his first concept of the political—"the specific political distinction to which political actions and motives can be reduced is that between friend and enemy"[72]—he realized that modern warfare's technological problematization of the enemy heralded the more troubling problematization of the political, a "new *nomos* of the earth," as he called it, where war takes place in a "new type of space-appropriation" as combat among "cosmopartisans."[73]

Clearly, then, the twenty-first century has produced that new *nomos*, an exponential increase in telecommunicational expansion appropriating spaces as large as that between Mogadishu and Syracuse, New York, controlled via the ether, and serving as the front in a war among *cosmopartisans*. The intercontinentally removed enemy is little more than a shadowy figure on a screen, hardly a person at all, just the blip of a moving body or vehicle. Once dead, he or she becomes "bugsplat." But that is not a word one hears in the official discourse, sparse though it be, regarding drone strikes. It is not the word Obama would have used in explaining the means by which, Aquinas and Augustine assisting, he would confront the need to defend us, like the gentleman he no doubt is, in a just war. Instead, we are led to believe that little has changed in the classical conception of the enemy, of warfare, or of the political, even when it comes to dispatching an American citizen without more process than a secretive executive discussion, as was the case when Imam Anwar al-Awlaki was killed in Yemen in September 2011, followed by his sixteen-year-old son two weeks later. And we are supposed to produce our own interpretation of how the rules of war are respected in the case of the revenge blitz of a series of strikes unleashed after a suicide bomber killed a whole cadre of CIA operatives in Afghanistan in late December 2009. In general, the target of these killings is presented as far removed from the "towel head" or "dune coon motherfucker" that an everyday grunt screams his hatred at as he wastes him or her on the latter's own sovereign national territory that we happen to have invaded.

The parameters of the transformation of warfare into drone-assisted assassination are numerous. Grégoire Chamayou has attempted to account for them in *A Theory of the Drone*, analyzing in particular the ethical stakes of this new face of warfare, and its transformative effect not just for the combatants involved, but also for the political body that stands behind its soldiers. The spatial reconfiguration of warfare that takes place thanks to the drone does not reduce to the intercontinental expansion that I have just described. In the first place, any theory of the drone is ultimately a theory of a robotization of conflict—well exceeding my particular interest in its use as a form of extrajudicial death penalty—and requiring consideration of technological developments from the "unmanned" soldier to the miniature drone (cf. *Drone*, 56, 207–18). But, as Chamayou makes clear, in virtualizing a theater of operations that reaches from Nevada to Mali, the drone attack is at the same time concentrating its attack, in theory at least, on a single vehicle, a single room, and even a single body: The drone operator is a high-tech sniper. The consequences are twofold. In the first place, "this supposed gain in precision" allows the zone of fire to be extended to the point where it can "take in the whole world" (*Drone*, 56), as we have seen; in the second place, "by redefining the notion of armed conflict as a mobile place attached to the person of the enemy, one ends up, under cover of the laws of armed conflict, claiming the equivalent of a right to extrajudicial execution" (57). As a result, certain foundations of the modern political order are necessarily called into question.

On the level of state sovereignty in the traditional, post-Westphalian sense, drone attacks represent indefensible violations of the airspace and territory of countries such as Yemen, Somalia, and Pakistan. Those violations take place on a regular basis, with constant dispute, and complicated deniabilities on one side or the other, concerning whether permission was requested or granted; by extension, the whole world becomes a potential battlefield. And, as happened from the moment of the first V2 attack in 1944, the triangulation of sovereign space is also transformed, the classical horizontal projection of power being replaced by a new form of spatialization: "in very schematic terms, we have switched from the horizontal to the vertical, from the two-dimensional space of the old maps of army staffs to a geopolitics based on volumes" (*Drone*, 54).

But Chamayou is especially interested in the complicated transformations of political and ethical space that result from drone warfare, its modification of "the State's relation to its own subjects" (177). In the traditional, Schmittian schema, the concept of the political relies on the always potential idea of soldiers exposing themselves to existential risk in fighting an enemy at the front on behalf of a nation; our proverbial "young men and women in uniform putting themselves in harm's way." Chamayou examines the changes that take place along those vectors of exposure and vulnerability once soldiers are no longer in harm's way, at least not in that traditional, existential sense; in particular, what reciprocal effect does that have upon the protection that the state provides its citizens in exchange for their service—particularly military service—to that state. For, he argues, not only is the concept of combat thereby redefined, but so are elements of the contract binding the state to its citizens. One should not of course forget the contrary arguments advanced by proponents of drone warfare: First, it is the moral responsibility of a state and its military planners to do everything in their power to protect and preserve their own soldiers, since that means, by extension, protecting all its citizens; second, the relative precision of drone attacks means far less deleterious effect on a local civilian population, as well as on the armed forces involved, than in a ground war.[74] But those arguments do not effectively alter the analysis and critique advanced by Chamayou.

The form of social contract advanced by a thinker of modern sovereignty such as Hobbes was presumed to put an end to the natural state of war thanks to a monarchical system where the individual's sovereign control over his own life is ceded in exchange for protection from the sovereign (which means in turn that the subject offers his life to protect the sovereign in a time of war). As Chamayou explains, Kant's philosophy of right, a century and a half after Hobbes, introduced a new emphasis on "citizenship" to replace what was effectively a "zoopolitical sovereignty" (182) whose paradigm is slavery.[75] In Kant's republican schema—tending toward what we now call democracy—the sovereign has a more rigorously defined duty toward his subjects; instead of giving obedience in exchange for protection, the citizens of a republic require the sovereign who *exposes* them to obey them (183), especially when they are being asked to risk their lives in a war. That should lead the sovereign to think twice about going to war.

However, once a republican or democratic state is able to wage war without exposing its subjects, its power is no longer bound by the same constraint. In Chamayou's analysis, that overturning of Kant's model began with outsourcing of military operations in the British Empire of the nineteenth century, when troops were commandeered from colonial populations to fight for the English, effectively allowing a Hobbesian monarchic commonwealth to obtain abroad so that the British population could rest easy at home as Kantian citizens. In the age of the drone a similar military outsourcing takes place thanks to the machine: "Once warfare became phantom and remote controlled, citizens, no longer risking their lives, would at the outside no longer even have a say in it" (188).

Such a crisis in, or corruption of the democratic body politic has widespread effects, as we shall shortly see, but it also has the more local effect of a crisis in, or corruption of a military ethos that remains informed by Schmitt's traditional model of the noble Spartan wrestler-warrior, founded on values of courage and sacrifice. The classical warrior must come to terms with a new technical reality (141) that renders him invulnerable: "in the light of traditional values, killing by drones—crushing the enemy without ever risking one's own skin—is still seen as the highest degree of cowardice and dishonor" (98). The idea that war should be waged between roughly symmetrical forces, that it be a type of duel in which combatants on both sides are exposed and at risk, and that the fighting take place on a circumscribable field of combat in some sort of real time, is an ideal that has been challenged and problematized at various historical periods, and between various enemies, notably as a result of technological innovation—bronze, steel, musket, missile, A-bomb, and so on. By the same token, it is a principle that has endured and led to rules of war that essentially forbid the use of "a weapon that by its very nature deprive[s] the enemy of the freedom to defend himself" (159). Prohibitions concerning mustard gas, or other chemical weapons would be a case in point, concerning not just risk to civilians but a type of unacceptable paralysis of warrior virility or physicality. That drone killing is another such case in point is a view shared not only by the victims of such attacks, but by ordinary soldiers in their reactions to the armchair security, and daily return to family, of drone operators who, supposedly, never find themselves in "harm's way": "initially the most virulent criticisms of drones came not from incorrigible pacifists

but from Air Force pilots, in the name of the preservation of their traditional warrior values" (99).[76]

Chamayou does not hesitate to call this transformation of polemologi-
cal standards a "necro-ethics." Once counterinsurgency tactics or strate-
gies are abandoned in favor of antiterrorist tactics, the possibility of a
political treatment of a conflict is excluded (69), with principles of international law being "eviscerated" in favor of "a nationalism of vital self-
preservation" (134). It is no longer a question of changing "hearts and
minds," and indeed the counterproductivity of drone killings, their producing more combatants than they eradicate has been attested to by various official and unofficial bodies, as well as by sources as unsympathetic
as retired General Michael Flynn.[77] Given widespread recognition of such
counterproductivity, one should look for the motivation for pursuing a
drone assassination policy in a type of culling, or grass-mowing, critiqued
by Chamayou in damning terms:

> The strategic plan of air counterinsurgency is now clear: as soon as a
> head grows back, cut if off. And never mind if, in a spiraling develop-
> ment of attacks and reprisals that is hard to control, the perverse effect
> of that prophylactic measure is to attract new volunteers. . . . Never
> mind if the enemy ranks thicken, since it will always be possible to
> neutralize periodically the new recruits, as fast as they emerge. The
> cull [*tonte*] will be repeated periodically, in a pattern of infinite
> eradication [*ce schéma est celui d'un éradicationnisme infini*]. (71)

Yet the most radical, and most fundamentally troubling consequence of
such an antiterrorist policy based on an extreme asymmetricality is to call
into question the traditional respect for a distinction between killing in
war and murder: "The right to kill with impunity in war [seems] based
upon a tacit structural premise: if one has the right to kill without crime,
it is because that right is granted mutually. If I agree to confer upon another the right to kill me or my people with impunity, that is because
I count on . . . the same exemption" (161). Chamayou is adamant that, absent such a reciprocity, "war degenerates into a putting-to-death," to a situation of "execution or [animal] slaughter [*abattage*]" (162); in short, to *a
drone penalty*.

The extrapolemological status of the drone penalty is reinforced in various ways: first, by means of the participation of nonmilitary entities such
as the CIA (who thereby commit war crimes; *Drone*, 170–71), a practice
introduced by Bush, perpetuated and then discontinued by Obama, and
now reintroduced by Trump; second, by the fraught question of how a

targeted combatant is defined (according to Obama's Defense University doctrine, the United States targets only those "who pose a continuing and imminent threat"); third, by the limitless extension of the war zone in both space and time. In the final analysis, the summary drone death penalty kills so-called combatants in a context where there is, in many respects and according to various definitions, no combat.

The strategy of culling has of course many historical precedents, notably in the era of Western colonialism. Scandalized by technological transformations of the battlefield in the late nineteenth and early twentieth centuries, the European powers set in motion discussion that led to such international agreements as the Hague Convention of 1907, laying out principles for naval bombardment, or the Geneva Protocol of 1925, prohibiting chemical and biological weapons. At the same time, they showed much less compunction when employing their technological superiority against military forces and populations in the countries they were colonizing. Chamayou gives the example of Kitchener's slaughter of ten thousand or so opposing soldiers with the newly invented Maxim machine gun in the Sudan in 1898 (93). Also in use for one of the first times in that battle was the expanding "dumdum" bullet. During discussion concerning the legality of such ordnance, which took place during the 1899 Hague Conference, British General Sir John Ardagh intervened with pertinent information relating to colonial situations, a question in which "quite a large number of nations [were] interested." He described colonialism's moral and military quandary in these terms:

> In civilized war a soldier penetrated by a small projectile is wounded, withdraws to the ambulance, and does not advance further. It is very different with a savage. Even though pierced two or three times, he does not cease to march forward, does not call upon the hospital attendants, but continues on, and before anyone has time to explain to him that he is flagrantly violating the decisions of the Hague Conference, he cuts off your head.[78]

The reductive dehumanization of an enemy functions consistently as the justification for extreme military measures, and discourses not so very far in tone and substance from that of General Ardagh are again mobilized in antiterrorist warfare. When sixteen-year-old Abdulrahman al-Awlaki was killed by a drone strike, he was reproached by Obama's press secretary for not having "a more responsible father." After that, the dead father's irresponsibility spread to cause the execution of his eight-year-old daughter also.[79]

Neocolonialist policies worthy of the nineteenth century are strongly on display in the situation that has been fundamental for the development of drone warfare, namely Israeli pacification of the Occupied Territories and of Gaza, following what Eyal Weizman terms "a relatively straightforward process of colonization, dispossession, resistance and suppression."[80] But as he convincingly shows in the final chapter of his comprehensive study, *Hollow Land: Israel's Architecture of Occupation*, following the Israeli withdrawal in 2005, Gaza "has become the world's largest laboratory for airborne assassinations."[81] The evolution of that assassination program from a first Apache helicopter attack in 2000, through the use of drones for reconnaissance, and finally for the assassinations themselves starting in 2004, closely mirrored the development of the American program. The similarities extend into such policies as reliance upon international law governing "armed conflict," and the definition of combatants as "all men of combat age who happened to be in the vicinity of the assassination."[82]

For Chamayou, at the outside limit of the necro-ethics of targeted assassinations there emerges the specter of the "drone state" (31), one that abdicates its responsibilities in several respects: it transforms Kant's citizen-soldiers—fulfilling their duty to the republic—into assassins, thereby betraying its side of the contract that produces the state (271); and, conversely, it removes from that governmental contract the (at least potential) military obligation placed upon its subjects, allowing it to wage war without their consent or even consultation. By introducing a sense of invulnerability, by telling its subjects that they can remain protected through a war, the drone state risks not only reducing the subject's concept of life to "the preservation of physical life at all cost" (181), but, more importantly, introducing a security state that claims to have dispensed with the tension or contradiction between protection and exposure, allowing it to "freely exercise war-waging sovereignty, but within the internal political conditions of sovereign security and protection" (ibid.). The drone state will be a state of compliant subjects, whose contestation of military adventurism is neutralized by an absence of body bags, whose concept of security is wholly determined by the new "democratic militarism" (188) to whose economy they blindly subscribe. And that blind subscription will be a form of subservience, even servility, attached as they are to a state of security whose costs remain invisible to them. They will enjoy that comfort while, a continent away, entire populations remains slaves to fear and violence within the kill zones to which the drone state has transported them.

At the end of a long note in *A Theory of the Drone*, in which Chamayou develops a phenomenology or pragmatics of "copresence," he argues that the teletechnology of the drone radically reconfigures the conditions of intersubjective experience in relation to violence, "introducing a revolution in the modes of co-presence and, at the same time, in the structure of intersubjectivity" (254n).[83] Clearly, the relation between a drone operator who stalks a supposed combatant with a view to killing him from thousands of miles away, and that supposed combatant who can do no more than perhaps hear the humming of the UAV in the sky above him, presents a very different intersubjectivity from the world of everyday relations. That said, from the point of view of a prosthetic teletechnology, which subsumes my whole discussion here, every technology is understood to introduce distance and rupture, which makes every technology a teletechnology, and defines every intersubjective experience, by virtue of distance and rupture, as technologized. The same prosthetic structure links a human body to that of its foe, whether that combat is undertaken on the wrestling mat, in the trenches, or in the "common" space of Washington, Nevada, and Waziristan. The current intercontinental teletechnologization still presumes a face-to-face confrontation with an other whose existential negation I relish, whether that negation ensues from the barrel of a gun I fire or the nose of a missile I activate remotely.

Not only does every intersubjective relation involve such a prostheticity but the very concept of sovereignty whereby a people invents a commonwealth in order to transact its own protection is similarly a fact of artifice, as Hobbes states in his very first paragraph: "For by Art is created that great LEVIATHAN called a COMMON-WEALTH or STATE . . . which is but an Artificiall Man."[84] As Derrida stresses, "this absolute sovereignty is . . . anything but natural; it is the product of a mechanical artificiality, a product of man, an artifact; and this is why its animality is that of a monster as prosthetic and artificial animal."[85] The strings and string pulling of the sovereign prosthesis are explicitly revealed—pointedly laid bare in the discussion Derrida develops around first Valéry and then La Fontaine and later Celan—in the question of the marionette. There he emphasizes in parodic terms the automatic, puppetlike phallic *erectability* of sovereign power: "this is not a figure but an essential feature of sovereign power, an essential attribute of sovereignty, its absolute erection, without weakness or without detumescence, its unique, stiff, rigid, solitary, absolute, singular erection."[86]

There would be nothing particularly reductive about sexualizing the seemingly decisive, muscular potency of the targeted killing program in

similar terms. If Obama was generally careful, during his eight years of
the practice, to refrain from employing that sort of pumped-up rhetoric,
he was nevertheless drawn into the logic of it; the action itself, which each
decision initiates, speaks that very discourse. But the decision to condemn
someone to the drone penalty is of course preceded by a lengthy surveillance that enacts in a different way the erectile verticality of this sovereign performance, operating at "the height from which the state has the
power to see everything . . . having literally, potentially, a right of inspection over everything . . . power to have under surveillance, to observe, take
in, archive from a superterrestrial height, by satellite, the whole globalized
surface of the earth."[87] Not only does the drone enact that sort of surveillance in a "local" manner, in both its lethal and nonlethal modes, but we
have come to understand, thanks to the Snowden revelations, how states,
especially the United States, assert broad global sovereignty by assuming
the prerogative of a universal right of inspection.

The intersubjective copresence of participants acting within drone space
therefore includes, by means of the prosthetic sovereign contraption that
I have just described, not only drone operator and kill-list victim, but also
the sovereign president. Among them there is greater or lesser distance but
never anything other than a degree of closeness. The drone penalty calculates on the technological advantage of mythological distance when a
president presumes that the executive death penalty will obviate having to
put boots on the ground, keeping soldiers and the home front alike out of
harm's way (and keeping the indefinite detention gulag out of the public
consciousness). But that same president is operating within a structural
space that on the one hand keeps him mired in desert sands and on the
other brings his distant war on terror back to being something of a civilian and civil war fought on the same ground as homegrown judicial
executions.

If space both expands and compresses in that strange relation, so of
course does time. The drone penalty, no less than the other forms of technologized or automatized death penalty that we have discussed, produces
a sovereign technicity of the instant. It requires a precision that is as devoid of nuance as any judicial execution, not just in the execution of the
execution itself—location of the target, timing of the attack—but in the
temporal stringency of the whole process of drawing up the kill list, weekly
meetings and decisions concerning victims, and relay along the chain of
command.[88] Not everything happens in an instant, but everything is di-
rected toward what will happen in the critical instant when the missile of
execution strikes. The precision of a White House appointments schedule

is refined to organize the electronic point in time that will cancel inter-continental space: An idealized simultaneity is effected by the decider who decides in Washington, the button that is pushed in Nevada, and the missile that is fired in Yemen.

Any pure instantaneity of the drone penalty is divided and relativized by those serial instances of decision, and such variables as the target's habits and movements, presence of others, and intelligence coming from the ground. The specific temporal force of the drone penalty derives from a different structural effect, namely the veil of state secrecy that extends from "trial" and "verdict" to execution. Under that veil, the time of the sovereign's judgment accelerates to infinite speed, the no-time of a secretive black hole within which, more dramatically than a trapdoor or falling blade, the missile strikes with lightning speed out of the sky, a rainbow meteoric arc of fire sent from executive executioner to those condemned. Indeed, not only does the condemned person remain ignorant of the day or hour of his or her execution, he or she is not even aware of having been identified as a victim. Even more egregiously, in the case of "signature" strikes based on how one behaves and whom and where one frequents, that victim does not even have to have an identity. More egregiously still, supposing that were possible, it can be enough that one comes to the aid of a victim—target or collateral, man or woman or child—to become a victim oneself, since the grim reapers of our high-minded nation of laws are also known to indulge in one of the worst excesses practiced by the terrorists they claim to be fighting, resorting to the practice known as "double-tap," which means sending in a second missile to kill those assisting the victims, or in some cases attending the funeral of the first.[89] In these extraordinary perversions of anything resembling due process, *habeas corpus* is replaced by *habemus cadaver* or rather *habemus cadavera* in the plural, as the single patent fact that reaches the light of day.

The secrecy of the drone penalty thus returns us to the fantasm of the absolute seized only in the instant, the dream of the suicide bomber. The drone penalty verdict is pronounced by a godlike sovereign operating in an instant of which he alone is ultimately master.[90] Justice can be that swift only in such an absolute instant; only in such an instant can it approach, mime or mimic divine justice. And only in the space of secrecy can the instant reach its absolute atemporal ideal, for in absolute secrecy there is neither space nor time for betrayal. The (no-)space and (no-)time of absolute secrecy, of the purest, most ineffable secret, is a divine space, the innermost sanctum where only a god can exist and function, without a name, without even an utterance to in any way identify him as material existence.

A secrecy that figures the absolute seized in the instant, accessible only to a god such as drone executioner or suicide bomber seeks to be, constitutes the space described by Derrida in *The Gift of Death*, some years before drones appeared on the scene. He was referring to the God who sees in secret of Matthew 6:4, one "capable, more than any satellite orbiting in space, of seeing into the most secret of the most interior places."[91] But as he makes clear, that conception of secrecy as a relation of surface to depth appears naïve once it is compared with a secret *outside* of visibility, such as the secret relationship I have with myself, on the basis of which "(there is) what I call God in me."[92] Secrecy produces a chiasmus between an omniscient or *omnipercipient* god from whom no secret can be hidden, and an absolute secret space "within" each of us for which the obvious name is God; my innermost sanctum is also the space only a god can see into but does not really see into, for "in" there vision no longer functions. From that point of view the idealized absolute instant of the drone penalty is not only a technological contrivance of contemporary warfare—a finely tuned combination of intelligence, decision and technical prowess—but also, as currently practiced, a fundamentalist or *integrist* invention of a sovereign godspace.

That has the following implications. First, the national security secret that keeps the assassination program under wraps expands the front or border of the secret every time it carries out an execution. It presumes that the essential kernel of its secret can be protected throughout its operation—and the recourse by government agencies to selective leaking is no doubt a function of that presumption—but the murderous flash of light that confirms each time the success of the secret also functions as a revelation. The temporalizing and spatializing relays of the secret, culminating in its manifestation as explosion within a kill box, also render it visible. Now, while that gives no assurance that we will some day know the whole truth about these sovereign states of exception, it does mean something: not only that each time a missile explodes elements of the secret are disclosed—for example the lie concerning precision—but also that the secret remains susceptible to discovery whenever what Glenn Greenwald has so aptly called "an impotent Congress, a supine media, and a subservient federal judiciary" see fit to perform the duties entrusted to them.[93]

Second, in contrast to the secret godhead of supervisory and supervisual surveillance represented by high technology in the service of intelligence agencies, the interiorized crypt of secrecy known only to a god who sees otherwise than by vision, who by seeing in me comes to produce or inhabit a space in me that is accessible to him alone, raises the question of, say, an Obama's relation to the secret sacrosanct space within him where his kill-list decisions are made. We might imagine that space to overlap with the secrecy, the little godspace that we all possess and call soul or conscience; we might say that he delves deep into his innermost conscience or soul in order to justify giving permission to pull the trigger. However, we would have also to concede that space being shared with or by the so-called terrorist operative in Africa who hatches his own secret plan, or quietly detonates a bomb. It must be presumed that he too possesses that very same ownmost god within him; not some *version* of that god, which we could dismiss as a *perversion* of it, but the *very same god or secret conscience of an Obama*. For we are talking not about different gods or religions or even about anything religious at all, rather about the capacity, on the part of each player, for his own secret recess.

Third, in light of that, and in consonance with the logic I have outlined, the intercontinental ballistico-technological arc again comes into play to connect intimately the president executioner with whomever he condemns in secret, to connect the secret space of one to the secret space of the other, as if the two of them were exchanging a silent but deadly handshake across the oceanic expanse, an American president giving the order to kill while the other activates his bomb, both thanks to the secret inaccessibility that is called god within them. And, in the case of the Obama who spent all eight years of his mandate exploiting what he took to be the advantages of the drone penalty, such a connecting arc projects him like some automatically piloted historical missive back to the Africa he would have wanted both to own and disown—passing back, therefore, to the continent where the madcap "birther" movement (epitomized of course by his successor Trump) always wanted to relegate him. That would find the American president—whether Bush, Obama or Trump—tethered there to a repetition of the geopolitical history from which we are all supposed to have been emancipated, back floundering somewhere in the sinking Sahara sands of a blind and failing militarism that is no respecter of persons, parties or successive administrations, bound to the mission creep of a violent *raison d'état* functioning as the only possible final recourse, bequeathing to the world the failure of an Afghanistan ripe with opium and still threatened by the Taliban, the failure of an Iraq, and a Syria, where flesh explodes every other day, the failure to defeat a terrorism that obeys a no-brain-science logical reaction to the brutalization practiced by America and its allies in country after country, seemingly without end.[94]

One cannot easily imagine an end to the death penalties of geopolitical sovereignty; one cannot presume to change the fabled sovereign logic, or "reason of the strongest" that La Fontaine's *Wolf and the Lamb* so simply yet so devastatingly represents.[95] But the tautological certainty of the idea that might makes right, the structural "requirement" that sovereign power "pervert" itself, does not render any less culpable a given historical "perverting" instance such as extrajudicial assassination by drone. How, then, is one to respond to the brute violence of an overreaching sovereignty taken to its illicit murderous extreme? The question arches back from Yemen's bewildered orphan faces and resolute militant rage alike, and includes all of us living supposedly safe and sound—as a consequence—on this side of the drone trade meridian, and elsewhere within the current first world protectorate.[96] Where might there be a resistance or defiance that also resisted the logic of a violent or militarized response? Some combination of national or international public outcry, and more specific political or judicial activism, may bring about changes in the current practice of the drone penalty, but the change of heart, or abolition of reflex militarism that one really wishes for, can by no means be presumed as a result of those arguments and actions.

The secret space of a god in us, if that is what we want to call it, is the source of every intersubjective relation. From within it—though necessarily disturbing any absolute purity we assumed that it had—comes an impulse, need, or desire to reach (out to) another. That inevitably means that any solicitation of another, however welcome it be, will somehow "disturb" the other, encroach however minimally upon her space, and more specifically, her time. The resulting interaction can amount to total abandonment to, and relish of such a disturbance, ecstatically allowing oneself to get lost in the other as though outside of time; or it can amount to an unwanted form of surveillance or intrusion, the tyranny of sovereign power and violence. In that absolute extreme case the other is destroyed, annihilated, allowed no more time, erased from time; that is the violence of the death penalty.

One can understand the original impulse to reach out, the need or desire for another, as a type of "innocence"; a first such solicitation would be something like a prayer. That is the sense of the word: In praying, one approaches, asks, begs, or implores, but it begins in the form of a simple "excuse me." Every such relation begins more or less with that type of prayer, in the form of an "I pray you" or "I beg your pardon." As Derrida analyzes it: "Can one address oneself to someone or indeed to any living being at all—or even something not living—without some implicit prayer coming to bend, to inflect the discourse, or even the simple silent look which, addressing itself to the other, cannot fail to ask of him or her 'listen to me, please [*je t'en prie*], listen, I pray you, look at me looking at you, please, turn toward me, turn your attention toward what I'm saying or doing to you, be present to what is coming from me.'"[97]

What one is inevitably begging or praying for in such an interruption is forgiveness for encroaching upon the other's time, or time-space. That "innocent" interruption of another's time and attention operates within the same structure as the institutional or political power to *detain*—definitely or indefinitely, unexceptionally or exceptionally—using up a subject's time of life by means of incarceration, or cutting it short by means of execution. For as Derrida notes, "the torturer also prays his victim to receive and to be present, to be aware [*sensible*] of the blows he is giving him."[98] The drone penalty mocks that temporal relation, the retention or detention of one by another, by means of an absolute reduction, where the first approach to the other, the first hailing or greeting, is an instantaneous death sentence.

One might not expect to find an affirmative politics of the time of the other, and by extension a politics of resistance to sovereignty run amok, in a discourse on poetry. But in an important passage in his "Speech on the Occasion of Receiving the Georg-Büchner-Prize" in 1960, known as *The Meridian*, Paul Celan refers to how the poem makes its address by letting "the most essential aspect of the other speak: its time."[99] As Derrida explains:

> It is not even, here, a poetics, still less a politics of dialogue, a dialogue during which, with help from experts and communications counselors, one would laboriously learn to let the other speak. It is not a matter of a democratic debate, during which one leaves the other his speaking time. . . . It is not a matter of speaking time but of letting the other, and thus of *giving* the other, without there being any act of generosity, effacing oneself absolutely, of giving the other its time. . . . *It is time that one must let speak, the time of the other.*[100]

One might therefore imagine a dialogue with a drone-wielding president where one patiently explained how to give the other its time in contrast to perpetrating a rogue sovereignty, where one attempted to explain—perhaps with the aid of Augustine and Aquinas—how absolute effacement is not the same as impotence or defeat. One might manage to retain or detain him for a little or a long time, with little or no hope or chance of dissuasion or persuasion, but, whatever the result, such an intervention would not for all that itself be a discourse of pure impotence.

Or one might try a more direct approach. Given the framework within which Celan makes his case for poetry, poetry's seeming effacement in favor of the time of the other should also be read as an expression of defiance. That is because the mouthpiece for the poetry he advocates is a figure from that paroxysm of political violence with which we are now familiar, the Terror. Lucile Desmoulins is the twenty-four-year-old wife of Camille Desmoulins, whom she has married in 1790, with Robespierre as one of the witnesses. In late 1793 her husband founds a newspaper, *Le Vieux Cordelier*, and in January 1794 Desmoulins writes an article that strongly condemns Robespierre for the increasingly tyrannical activities of the Committee for Public Safety. He is arrested, along with Danton, at the climax of the Terror on March 30, 1794. There follows a travesty of a trial by the Convention, at which those accused are prevented even from appearing, thanks to a new decree proposed by Saint-Just "that anyone accused of conspiracy who resists or insults national justice will be immediately expelled from the debate."[101] On April 5, Robespierre declares that the enemies of freedom will not be defeated by half measures, but "by going right up to them, attacking head on, relentlessly; it is by plunging into their heart the dagger of justice that we will be able to deliver freedom from all the villains who seek to destroy it."[102] Desmoulins and Danton are guillotined that same day.

Georg Büchner ends his 1835 play *Danton's Death* by having Lucile Desmoulins linger near the guillotine following her husband's execution before provoking her own arrest by crying out, "Long live the king!"[103] She will subsequently be executed on April 13. Celan calls her cry a "counterword [*Gegenwort*] . . . the word that no longer bows down. . . . It is an act of freedom." However, it is to be understood not as "a declaration of loyalty to the ancien régime" but as poetry: "This . . . has no fixed name once and for all, but I believe that this is . . . poetry."[104] Logically speaking, the poetry that no longer bows down is also the poetry that lets the time of the other speak. It is both decision, a punctual even perfunctory declaration, and deliberation, a slow, even passive allowance for the other. It is also, I would argue, justice, not the national dagger seized in the instant by a Robespierre already drenched in blood, but a judgment that comes at the end of a process, following due process in due time.

CHAPTER 6

Lam Time

According to the logic of Eighth Amendment interpretations made by Clarence Thomas, the egregious violence or cruelty of the crimes of the worst of the worst is contrasted with the next-to-no-pain instant of execution by lethal injection. In the Western, post-Enlightenment era of capital punishment, of course, there is no converse or corollary to that, no prolonged torturous punishment to match an exalted crime of *lèse-majesté* such as was meted out to Robert-François Damiens in 1757. When it comes to the death penalty, there is no corollary for the shorter or longer prison terms that match other crimes. Instead, time obeys its own peculiar logic, or series of logics, all of which turn around the instant: It can be divided and its duration called into question; it is as much a machine that gives life its rhythm as it is a moment that the machinery of death attempts to capture; it disappears as readily into the ether of its absolutization as into the atemporality of secrecy.

In this final chapter, I will attempt to put the problematic instant of the moment of execution, and the various attempts to appropriate that instant that we have seen, into relation with the time of the act or crime that gives rise to it. That will be to pose—counter to Thomas's matching of punishment to crime—the question of a type of reverse chronology, or *chrono-alogicality* whereby the effect (death penalty) reaches back to problematize the cause (crime). An understanding of what that might mean will involve, in the first place, examining the time of an act, especially as it comes to be complicated, if not by a psychoanalytic unconscious, then by the effect of irrationality upon criminal responsibility;[1] and in the second place, accounting for the ways in which the judicial process of deliberation and decision comes to be complicated by what I will call narrative time. My privileged example for this analysis will be the strange case of a multiple homicide that occurred at a key moment in the history of the death penalty in France, an archive that was unearthed by a team of researchers led by Michel Foucault and first published in 1973.[2] That story of Pierre Rivière is an exceptional one (but isn't every crime?), and it brings into extraordinary focus the questions I wish to raise. It does so, especially, by means of Rivière's memoir, which was conceived before but written following his commission of the crime. That narrative account is drawn into the means by which Rivière himself, and also the prosecution and defense, attempt to explain his motive. But in a more troubling sense, it opens up the temporal space between conception and act in a way that problematizes the very time of the criminal act: first, with respect to the juridical sense of intent or premeditation; second, by inserting within that space the narrative time of fiction in general, linking the killing time of a murderous act to certain functions of the literary machine.

In Chapter 2 the horrific accounts of crimes, exploited by Justices Scalia and Thomas in rebutting the compunctions of their colleagues concerning the potential pain of certain executions, were interpreted as obeying a type of photographic logic of truth: Look at this and see it for the horror that it is, and see that it merits the ultimate penalty. But as I noted then, the plain-as-day evidence that Thomas offers is verbal, and it is verbal discourse that dominates judicial proceedings in general. By way of comparison, I offered the example of the hanging sermon, where the event of the execution itself receives an extensive discursive and illustrative overlay; and, at the other end of the historical scale, the mediatic manipulations of gruesome executions performed by the Islamic State. The case of Pierre Rivière provides another peculiar discourse in the form of the criminal's memoir. Yet, unusual as it is, even unique, Rivière's narrative has as its general institutional structure the confession, which, in a strangely analogous way to how the suicide bomber's autoexecution preempts the judicial process, functions in a relation of tension with the requirement of evidence and proof. Trial by ordeal, in medieval times, sought to extract the very confession that substituted for the trial, and confession remains the goal of every prosecutorial venture (to the extent of permitting all the abuses one can imagine).[3] That is because it offers the most self-evident proof.

At 1:00 P.M. on June 3, 1835, authorities were called to a rural village house in Normandy following reports of a grisly murder. There they found three corpses: a woman of about forty years killed while preparing the family gruel, her neck and the back of her skull slashed; a seven- or eight-year-old boy with his head split open in the back; and an adolescent girl lying on her back with her feet out the door, her lacework on her chest, a large clump of hair clenched in her fist, the right side of her face and her neck "cutlassed to a very great depth" (*PR*, 4). Seventy-four-year-old Marie Rivière, the children's grandmother, testified to having attempted to prevent the murder of her granddaughter, and to being the first to find the other bodies. Two other witnesses allegedly encountered twenty-year-old Pierre Rivière leaving the scene with a bloody pruning bill (7–8). According to one of them the murderer said that he had just delivered his father from all his woes: "I know that they will put me to death, but no matter" (8). It was almost a month later, on July 2, 1835, that Pierre Rivière was arrested, having wandered on foot throughout the region in the interval, remaining more or less, but not entirely out of sight. Four different trajectories each lasting about a week had taken him as far as the Channel coast, and amounted to a total distance covered of about 310 miles.[4] Rivière's trial took place in the middle of November 1835, and he was found guilty and condemned to death. His appeal was heard and rejected in January 1836, but on February 10 King Louis-Philippe commuted his sentence to life imprisonment. Rivière hanged himself in his cell on October 20, 1840.

That linear chronology of Rivière's crime and punishment, his life and death, could be further filled in by facts concerning his preparations for, and premeditations concerning the crime, mostly by his own account: he has his pruning bill sharpened on May 24; dresses in his Sunday best on Saturday, May 30; plans, then defers the act twice on May 31; then again while plowing on June 2; and finally commits the murders at about noon on June 3. And, perhaps, more significantly, his crime is inscribed within the longer time frame of ten years of humiliations and financial hardships that he believes his mother inflicted on his father, and which constitute the motive for the murders. He kills his mother because she is the direct cause of his father's misfortunes, and his sister because she is in league with her mother. When it came to the young brother, things were more complicated: of course, the little boy loved his mother and sister (24), which was perhaps cause enough, but, given the fact that both Pierre and his father also loved the boy dearly, the murderer reasoned that he could secure his father's happiness only by making himself utterly abject in his father's eyes. If he were to kill the innocent boy, "my father w[ould] conceive such an abhorrence of it that he will no longer regret me and will even wish for my death" (130).

As I mentioned earlier, however, two other factors disturb that chronology. The first appears with hindsight to be a purely juridical issue, but whose status was much less clear in the first half of the nineteenth century, namely the introduction of medical testimony inflected by the emerging psychological sciences of human behavior.[5] If I say the issue appears now to be a juridical one it is because such testimonies were in turn a function of the application of extenuating circumstances, which, in spite of strong opposition, became an accepted element of French law beginning in 1811. Its applicability was extended to cover all crimes only three years before the Pierre Rivière case. As Patricia Moulin clarifies in one of the commentaries (which their authors call "Notes") accompanying the archival dossier in the volume *I, Pierre Rivière*, two possibilities existed by 1835 for reducing penalties: an appeal to the King, or a plea of extenuating circumstances that limited culpability and allowed a lesser punishment (*PR*, 212). As we have learned, the French penal code was overhauled in 1791, following the Revolution; a further reform in 1811 instituted minimum and maximum punishments and introduced the term *circonstances atténuantes*, limiting that plea to certain crimes. The number of relevant crimes increased in 1824, but as of 1832 the doctrine of extenuating circumstances was applied generally, and it was left to the discretion of the jury whether to accept or reject such a plea (213).

The period of Rivière's crime is also important in the more general history of the post-Enlightenment death penalty in France, and beyond. Most proximately, less than two months after his crime an infamous attempt was made on the life of King Louis-Philippe, an attempt that no doubt revived memories of the crimes and punishments of Damiens in 1757 and Ravaillac in 1610. But the assassination attempt is also notable for ushering in new, automatized, and remote-controlled forms of assassination, and it is pointedly contemporaneous with the development of photography. The 1835 plot—one of a series of attempts against Louis-Philippe, whose constitutional monarchy was a considerable improvement over the previous regime of Charles X, but who never enjoyed widespread popularity—put serious pressure on penal reform, and led to severe restrictions on the freedom of the press as part of a progressive clampdown against the opposition that would ultimately lead to the uprisings of 1848.[6]

Giuseppe Marco Fieschi, of Corsican origin, developed his assassination plan with a fellow conspirator and the assistance of a section of the Society for the Rights of Man, a widespread grouping of Jacobin-style republicans that developed out of the 1830 July Revolution. Fieschi's plan involved an "infernal machine," a primitive volley gun whose twenty-five barrels, each containing bullets as well as buckshot, were to be fired simultaneously from an apartment window overlooking the king's parade route for the commemoration of the Revolution. Four of the barrels failed to fire, and another four exploded, seriously wounding Fieschi, but eighteen military personnel and others were killed, and many more were injured by the approximately four hundred projectiles. The king received a graze to the forehead but barely flinched, seeing the ceremony to its conclusion.

Between the murders committed by Rivière and Fieschi there is a world of difference: a provincial family feud culminating in a bloody artisanal slaughter by pruning bill, and a highly technologized and high-stakes political massacre. Those differences are also temporal, differences in the time or temporality of the crime. In the first case, Rivière chooses his moment as a function of the rhythms of rural life and labor; in the second case, Fieschi requires the precision of the moment when the king is within range, and develops a technology of momentous overkill, either to insure the success of his regicide, or to produce mass casualties. For those times of crime also correlate with different mediatic temporalities, hence my reprise of the role of photography: Rivière's memoir will show him to have a somewhat megalomaniacal relation to his historical position that remains essentially mythological, drawing on Napoleon as well as figures from Roman and Maccabean history and the Vendée counterrevolution; Fieschi, on the other hand, produces an event in and of the present, a sudden flash of glory and gore—an absolutization, if not of the instant, then of the mediatic moment—inaugurating what would eventually become a format that has lasted all the way to Stephen Paddock's October 2017 Las Vegas massacre.

In spite of those contrasts, one can point to significant resonances between the cases of Rivière and Fieschi, especially once they come to trial. The Court of Cassation rejected Rivière's appeal "at the very moment when the complicated examination was being conducted at the Fieschi trial" (*PR*, 220), and the commutation of Rivière's sentence by the king took place one day after Fieschi's conviction and one day before the latter's execution. But where the crimes of Rivière and Fieschi have their most significant convergence is in the age-old juridical analogy between patricide (here, matricide) and regicide. We remember from Chapter 2 that it was a simple citizen, not a king—referred to familiarly by Robespierre as "Louis"—who was guillotined in 1793. Indeed, the crime of regicide had disappeared from the penal code by then, associated as it was with the torturous excesses of the old regime. As Barret-Kriegel points out, regicide was still absent in name in 1832, and subsumed instead under the term "parricide": "The penalty for a criminal attempt against the life or person of the sovereign is the punishment for parricide" (cf. 220). Resistance against allowing extenuating circumstances to be considered in cases of parricide remained strident throughout the 1830s (223–24). In addition, it was only three years prior to Rivière's crime, in 1832, that the requirement that a parricide be mutilated before being executed—"the sheriff reads the writ of sentence aloud to the people. He [the parricide] shall then have his hand struck off and shall immediately be executed"—was abolished (cf. 221).[7] One can therefore see how the wheels of jurisprudence had come full circle, from the Revolution's first rejection of mutilation in relation to capital punishment to this second rejection forty years later.

Another wheel was turning during the same period. In 1829 an anonymous author published a novel entitled *The Last Day of a Condemned Man*. It was republished in 1832, signed by Victor Hugo, and accompanied by a long preface in which Hugo made an impassioned plea for the abolition of the death penalty, a cause that the thirty-year-old had already been supporting for nearly ten years. Indeed, from the time that an abolitionist bill was rejected in the wake of the July Revolution (1830), until, as a representative of the Constituent Assembly, Hugo himself militated forcefully but unsuccessfully to have capital punishment abolished by the Constitution of the Second Republic (1848), and essentially for the rest of his days, he was a tireless advocate for abolition. In that, he was part of a European, and also North American abolitionist trend that saw Michigan lead the way in 1846, followed by Rhode Island in 1852 (later reinstated, but no executions took place after 1845), Wisconsin in 1853, and Maine in 1887.[8]

As Hugo states, his novel was "nothing more than a plea, direct or indirect . . . for the abolishment of capital punishment," a cause that represents the "great right of humanity urged and pleaded by every voice before mankind, which is the highest court of appeals; it was the ultimate principle [*cette suprême fin de non-recevoir*], *abhorrescere a sanguine*, established before the existence of the criminal courts themselves."[9] In his eyes, and as the conceit of his novel demonstrates, the supposed rejection, by the revolutionary penal code, of a torture that *endures* in favor of an instantaneous decapitation, is belied by the "torture" represented in the ritual of anticipation of, and preparation for each execution. Particularly disappointed by the French failure to abolish the death penalty after 1789, a disappointment that Hugo felt even more keenly when the winds of liberty seemed again to blow with the July Revolution of 1830—not to mention what he would have to relive in much more personal terms in 1848—he concludes that "the scaffold is the only thing which Revolutionaries do not demolish. It is seldom indeed that a revolution spares human life; and coming, as it does, to prune, cut, hack, and behead society, capital punishment is one of the instruments [*une des serpes*] which it is most loath to give up."[10]

Hugo's novel represents an abolitionist literature whose argument, however laudable, remains parallel to the illustrative intentions of the execution sermon or the photographic shock tactics of Thomas and Scalia. It falls clearly within the tradition of realism, in all its forms, that dominated the literature of the nineteenth century. Nevertheless, reaction to it, both positive and negative, indicates the extent to which France in the first half of the nineteenth century continued to struggle with the legacy of the monarchy—restored, of course, for much of that half-century—and the association of the monarchy with punitive excess.

Echoes of the abolitionist sentiment incarnated by Hugo, and continuing debate over extenuating circumstances, can be heard among reactions to the condemnation of Pierre Rivière published in press accounts of the time.[11] On one side, newspapers such as the *Journal de Rouen et du Département de la Seine-Inférieure* editorialized that Rivière was a paradigm of corruption whose naïve judges indulged his crooked ways like a doctor who troubles himself with "eradicating the corns from the foot of a gangrenous leg already ripe for amputation" (*PR*, 148). That metaphor of disease is extended to cover the moral condition of "a society given over to every sort of unbridled material appetite" (150). On the other side, the *Gazette des Tribunaux* gives voice to an anonymous subscriber of "personal standing" (157) who believes Rivière should have benefitted from extenuating circumstances or be accorded royal clemency so that "corrected by good education [he may] some day repay the preservation of his life by some great service to mankind" (159). More pertinently, the *Pilote du Calvados* sees fit, in spite of its editors' personal opinions on the topic, to publish a letter entitled "Yet another capital sentence," lending "the hospitality of our columns to these remarks as at least one of the elements in the solution to a problem which has for some time been exercising the most distinguished moral philosophers of our age" (151). The author of the letter, who takes Rivière to be "a wretched, a diseased, an unfinished being" (152), considers that because the young man's judges could not classify his

form of insanity they sought to cut "through the tangle of such questions
[by] . . . cutting off a man's head" (153). Though not willing to go as far as
the defense counsel, and call the death penalty judicial murder, the writer
deplores "from the depths of our heart the fact that once again we have
had to resort to the executioner to cure the maladies . . . of persons and
societies" (154). And in terms that approach Hugo's descriptions of the
bloody guillotine, the letter concludes:

> Blood should answer for blood, it is said. . . . Well, the fatal sentence
> has been delivered; the blood will flow if it is not arrested in time. . . .
> But may we be permitted to lodge our own appeal . . . and to cry to the
> judges before whom Rivière will have again to appear or to the
> Sovereign who may be called upon to exercise his prerogative of
> mercy: pity for him, pity, but not infamy; and, above all, not the
> scaffold! (153–54)

Pierre Rivière's extenuating circumstance is his state of mind. At the outset, in plain contrast with appearances of insanity, that mind is found to
be a prodigious one. In referring the case for prosecution, the Pretrial
Court (*Chambre d'Accusation*) has difficulty reconciling Rivière's acts with
"the gifts so liberally imparted to him by nature without any assistance
whatever from education: a remarkable memory, a great aptitude for the
sciences, a lively and strong imagination coupled with an eagerness for in-
struction and the achievement of glory" (45). That perplexity is produced
especially by Rivière's having completely changed his story between the
first interrogation, when he claimed to have been acting under God's
commands, and the second, nine days later, based on the memoir he had
written in the interval, which justified the crime on the basis of his parents' marital and financial distress, more precisely the torment to which,
he believed, his mother had subjected his father. A similar perplexity is
emphasized in the prosecutor's indictment. Rivière's "unconcern [*insou-
ciance*]" (*PR*, 48; *Moi*, 67) for his crime, and an appearance of "mental derangement" (ibid.) in his explanations raised the question of a faked
insanity, but his keen intelligence supported instead the idea of crimes that
were "meditated, calculated, and prepared" (ibid.). He was therefore considered to have "full and entire knowledge [*la conscience la plus complète*]"
(49; *Moi*, 67) of his actions.

A small arsenal of medical opinions was mobilized to decide on the
soundness of Rivière's mind. Before the trial, two opinions were sought.
Dr. Bouchard found him in good health, if "of a bilious-melancholic
temperament" (122), but showing no sign of "any derangement of the

mental faculties" (123). The doctor professed a lack of qualifications when it came to making a phrenological assessment and so attributed the crime to "a state of momentary over-excitement [*exaltation*] brought on by his father's tribulations" (124; *Moi*, 152). Dr. Vastel, who claimed to be "more fitted than anyone else" (125) to give an opinion, wrote a much longer report that developed precisely a theory of hereditary "mental alienation" that was alleged to have produced a "originally defective organization of Rivière's brain" (127). "Truly, I have never seen a more manifest case of insanity among the hundreds of monomaniacs I have treated," he declared (131), concluding therefore that Rivière should be found not guilty of the crime.

At the trial itself, depending on which archival report is consulted, two, three, or four more doctors were called to testify; some supported Dr. Bouchard's judgment, while others supported Dr. Vastel's. Once the guilty verdict was returned, and the appeal rejected, final recourse was had to King Louis-Philippe. On that occasion, according to *Le Pilote du Calvados*, "a considerable number of leading Paris medical experts [*sommités médicales de Paris*]" (163; *Moi*, 205) were asked to give an opinion. Indeed, a statement was signed by seven such august persons as the chief medical officer of the asylum of Charenton, the dean of the Paris Faculty of Medicine, the king's court physician, and the permanent secretary to the Royal Academy of Medicine. In it, the experts roundly rejected the reasoning of Dr. Bouchard, whom they reproached for declaring Rivière sane solely because he did not fit any of the categories of insanity that were familiar to him, and agreed instead with Dr. Vastel that the convict had shown signs of madness since he was four years old and that his crimes were "due solely and exclusively to delirium" (165).

Though in 1835 we are some sixty years before Freud's discovery of the unconscious, the nascent science of psychiatry is developing in significant ways. We noted in Chapter 2 how Philippe Pinel had gone from witnessing the first test of the guillotine at La Bicêtre Hospital in 1792 to freeing deranged patients from their chains at La Salpêtrière asylum in 1795, setting up another uncanny parallel between post-Enlightenment inroads, successful or unsuccessful, into treatments of criminality and insanity. By the middle of the century, the parallel is reinforced by the coincidence of the Second Republic Constituent Assembly's attempts to abolish the death penalty, and further reforms represented by the English Lunacy Act of 1845 and the work of Bénédict Morel in France.[12] At the time of Rivière's crime, his disease could be diagnosed as monomania but, as we saw, phrenology competed with other scientific research in prescribing treatment or in inflecting conceptions of criminality. On one side, then, there existed an idea of delirium that was increasingly related to heredity; on the other, a presumed physiological defect susceptible to phrenological diagnosis. It could be said, though, that whereas criminological medicine had not yet been called upon to deal with the radical temporal disjunction that is the unconscious, it was beginning to understand a crime within a causal context whose time far exceeded that of the act itself; a time that reaches back into previous generations, or back to the formation of an individual's skull. In the case of Rivière, what will indisputably emerge is the idea that such a time of the criminal act must be extended on either side of the fateful noontime moments of June 3, 1835, thanks to his memoir. Thus, if the *time* of the mind has not yet been complicated by theories of traumatic memory or the operations of the unconscious, Rivière's memoir will nevertheless provide a sufficient reservoir of accumulated symptoms and motivations to seriously complicate or *extenuate* the cause and effect logic of the crimes he has committed, and, as we shall see, to expand discussion beyond the bounds of the purely jurisprudential.

The memoir is therefore the second factor disturbing the chronology of Pierre Rivière's crime. It is a fifty-page manuscript—composed in an imperfect written French that the editors of *I, Pierre Rivière* leave as is, except for adding capital letters and some punctuation—written between July 10 and 21, 1835. In making his report to the director of criminal affairs following the conviction, the presiding judge notes that the memoir shows both "great intelligence and the greatest possible aberration of judgment," adding that "though Rivière received only a village education, the style is tolerably correct, and it contains passages of remarkable eloquence" (145). The sage Paris doctors find in it further signs of Rivière's delusion, inasmuch as it "demonstrates a profound and consistent aberration of his intellectual faculties and moral feelings," in spite of "the soundness of memory and the sequence in the ideas" that the narration displays (164).

Much could be said about the memoir on its own terms, and indeed the members of the research group that published *I, Pierre Rivière* were very frank in admitting that what led them to spend more than a year on the project "was simply the beauty of Rivière's memoir. The utter astonishment [*stupéfaction*] it produced in us was the starting point" (*PR*, x; *Moi*, 11). But of particular interest to me is a certain mechanics of interference in what we might call the *chronologicality* of the Rivière case, the memoir's disruption of the time machine of this death penalty.

Rivière announces his memoir at the end of his first questioning session on July 9, 1835. He had maintained throughout that interrogation that he performed the murders on God's orders, the same God who, as he read in Deuteronomy, ordered Moses to slay the adorers of the golden calf, "sparing neither friends nor father nor son" (cf. *PR*, 20). But when asked again to "tell us frankly today, what cause could have led you to murder your mother, your sister, and your brother," he replied that he no longer wished "to maintain the system of defense and the part which I have been acting. I shall tell the truth" (23). According to the examining judge, there then followed Rivière's detailed account, lasting more than two hours and narrating the "innumerable afflictions which . . . his father suffered from his wife. Rivière promises to communicate to us in writing what he has stated to us by word of mouth" (24). In that sense, the memoir represents the confession that the examining judge had asked for earlier in the interrogation: "You claim to excuse your crimes by saying, which is absurd and impious, that they were ordered by God; confess rather that, being unluckily born with a ferocious character, you wished to steep yourself in the blood of your mother whom you had long abominated" (21). It represents that confession, and, within the logic of a confession, it functions as a form of exculpation that might eventually constitute an extenuating circumstance. But, according to a somewhat predictable prosecutorial trap, the facts recounted in the memoir came, in the second interrogation, on July 18, to provide evidence of a sound criminal motive and so reinforced the charge of premeditated murder. Questioning, based both on the memoir and on witnesses' accounts, concentrated on behavioral anomalies, most of which allegedly pointed to Rivière's penchant for cruelty: holding his brother's legs to the fire, frightening children, crucifying frogs and birds, carrying nails or brads in his pockets, threatening his brother, maltreating horses, conducting a mock funeral for a jay, taking his clothes off in the stable, and—*pièce à conviction*, to which I will return—inventing and naming an instrument for killing birds (34–38).

The memoir begins thus: "I, Pierre Rivière, having slaughtered my mother, my sister, and my brother, and wishing to make known the motives which led me to this deed, have written down the whole of the life which my father and my mother led together since their marriage. . . . I shall then tell how I resolved to commit this crime" (54–55). He recounts much further along that that resolution was fixed after meditating on it for about a month (105). His original plan was to write the memoir before committing the crime, "to put an announcement of the deed at the beginning and my reasons for committing it at the end . . . then to commit my deed, to take my letter to the post, and then to take a gun I would hide beforehand and kill myself" (107). He stayed up several nights writing "the announcement of the beginning," but his sister discovered his nocturnal activity and asked to see the document, which caused him to hide it and later burn it. He then reasoned it would be better to keep the announcement of the deed until the end, and so began over a sequence of nights to write the story of his parents' marriage, but invariably fell asleep. That led him to yet "another decision, [and] I gave up writing." Instead of writing the memoir before the murders he would go to the police immediately afterward and "make my declarations" (ibid.), but that would require his dressing in his Sunday clothes in order to show appropriate respect to his judges. A series of dress rehearsals and false starts ensued before he resolved that he could explain himself "quite as well without wearing good clothes" (111), and eventually the fateful Wednesday arrived.

Conceived in order to assist in or even bring about the crime, the memoir was treated from the moment of its appearance as though it formed part of that crime. In his commentary on the archive, entitled "Tales of Murder" (*Les meurtres qu'on raconte*), Foucault takes that interpretation further:

> The fact of killing and the fact of writing, the deeds done and the things narrated, intersected as elements of a like nature. . . . The murder and the narrative of the murder were consubstantial. . . . For in Rivière's behavior memoir and murder were not ranged simply in chronological sequence—crime and then narrative . . . a whole web of relations is woven between the one and the other; they support one another and carry one another in ever-changing relations. (200–1)

Before returning to that analysis of the relations between word and deed we should note Foucault's other emphasis, in his commentary, on the extended sociological context within which Rivière's memoir appears. That context is one of a general narrative discursivity that was regularly committed to writing, constituting "a kind of popular memory of crimes" (*PR*, 203–4) that is reminiscent of the proliferation of textual records that, as we saw in Chapter 2, existed in America from the time of the execution sermon and into the nineteenth century. Foucault understands the purpose of such broadsheets, at least in France, to be to enlarge the compass of the human interest story to the point where "the village or the streets, of their own accord and with no outside intervention, came to produce history" (205). So it was that a flysheet eventually appeared under the title "Judgment of the Caen Assize Court," recounting the story of Pierre Rivière, but with significant inaccuracies: the case was dated 1836; Rivière was said to have been executed in February 1837; and he supposedly killed two brothers for a total of four murders. As was often the case, the account of the crime was followed by a "Sorrowful Lamentation" in four verses to be sung to the tune of "Un chien fidèle."[13]

In other words, one way to treat Rivière's memoir would be as part of the more or less fictionalized accounts of such events that would come eventually to constitute folklore, notwithstanding the ability of those accounts to perform an important role on the fringes of the judicial, and notwithstanding the exemplary features of this particular text. But Foucault's thesis is a much stronger one, according to his theory of discursivity made explicit at the time, namely that "Rivière . . . accomplished his crime at the level of a certain discursive practice and of the knowledge bound up with it" (*PR*, 209).[14] With or without the memoir, Rivière as fact of history (the crime) could not but constitute a discursive practice relating to knowledge as a function of power. At a certain level, this lowly peasant living in a village outside the recognized institutional forms of knowledge and power came nevertheless by his act and his words to participate in that nexus in a significant way, even if it ultimately meant activating a type of powerlessness. But once there was his memoir, the configuration of that nexus came to be altered much more significantly: the fact of history became inextricably tied to his peculiar narrative of it.

Foucault summarizes that complicated mechanism in this passage, which I quote at length:

> In all these transformations [Rivière's changing plans regarding the crime and the memoir] the text and the murder kept changing places, or, to put it more precisely, moved one another around. The narrative of the murder, originally intended to come at the beginning of the memoir, fuses with it and becomes diffused in it; it is concealed by the text, which would not now narrate a premeditated murder, but would be a secret codicil to it; and in the end, the proclamation of the murder is placed not only at the end of the memoir but after the murder itself. The murder, too, has been reversed and has gradually become disengaged from the memoir; from the original intention that it should happen after the memoir was written and simply for the purpose of triggering its dispatch it has broken free and has at length arisen to stand alone and to happen first, propelled by a decision which had determined the narrating of it, word for word, but without being written down. (202)

It is clear, on Rivière's admission, that his crime required the writing of his memoir, that his action required an elaborate discursive apparatus that, however much it have the appearance of a simple, if detailed exculpation—my father's treatment at the hands of my mother necessitates the just resolution that I alone can provide—quickly began to interfere differently with the commission of the act: I cannot commit the murders until I have written the memoir, and now that my sister knows I am writing, I have to destroy what I have said, reorganize the order of events in my writing, and do so in greater secret; but the crime will have to wait as a result. Or: Having abandoned the memoir because it is proving too difficult to write, I will now have to commit the murders in my Sunday clothes in order to be able to go straightaway to the authorities to tell them what I had wanted to write in the memoir; but dressing in my Sunday clothes on a day other than Sunday draws attention to myself and delays the crime again, differently. Similarly, once he has been arrested: I won't tell you why I did it except to say that God commanded me, even though I have a whole rational explanation in my head; on second thought, I *will* tell you, and indeed I will write it all down.

Only once he has written the memoir will he feel that his complicated task has really been accomplished. At that point the memoir takes on another, juridical life that is of course no less intricately woven into the crime; it is taken to be confirmation either of Rivière's monstrously calculating mind or of his absence of reason. But for Rivière himself there was no question of seeking exculpation or of providing extenuating circumstances. As he concludes, logically and teleologically rounding out what he had begun:

> They told me to put all these things down in writing, I have written them down; now that I have made known all my monstrosity, and that all the explanations of my crime are done, I await the fate which is destined for me, I know the article of the penal code concerning parricide, I accept it in expiation of my faults . . . so I therefore await the penalty I deserve, and the day which shall put an end to all my resentments. (121)

No doubt, then, that Pierre Rivière slaughtered his mother, brother, and sister, fled and wandered, was arrested, wrote his memoir, and was tried and convicted, all in that order. That is the chronological, narrative order of the crime. But Rivière's own narrative, in the form of his memoir, orders things differently. That is so in the first place because its account is entirely retrospective, which means that it conjures up the whole, mysterious temporal order of memory; and memory, however meticulous, produces its own compressions and accelerations, its priorities and peripheralities. In the second place, his narrative reveals an intricate, and confused ordering of telling, imagining, motivating and acting. As a result, the memoir attaches to the crime a *narrative time* that opens the space of fiction, a space that is subject to a complicated play of analeptic, suspensive, and proleptic structures.[15]

Crime necessarily begins as a fiction, fantasy, or imagining, one that can be short or long. That is what we think of, and what the law requires, as some form of premeditation. If a crime such as murder is not to be considered as a pure reflex action—as, say, automatic self-defense—then it will require some nonreal imagining of the act. In Western jurisprudence, criminal intent or premeditation, what is called *mens rea*, is required as the basis for the criminal liability of an *actus reus*. From that perspective, the deliberate account and explanation produced before commission of the act, which Rivière set in motion by undertaking to write his first, later destroyed, version of his memoir, would be but an exceptionally elaborate narrative form of the intent that is understood to be formed in the mind prior to every criminal undertaking. Like any crime, Rivière's begins as a type of narrative fantasy or fiction that only rarely is put down on paper.[16] One could say the same of any act, but the obvious difference is that criminal law incorporates this necessity as a formal structure that—and this is what counts for me—*has its own time*. If fictive intention were to coincide with the act such that one could not be distinguished from the other, then *there would be no crime in the first degree*. Premeditation, or malice aforethought, is understood to have its own chronological status distinct from the act that it motivates and directs: An "I want to kill you" that also means "I imagine myself killing you" functions as a fictionalized enactment of the event before the event; and it is, furthermore, recognized or even required by the law. It is as if, once the event of a crime takes place, then judicial process will be required to go back over that preexisting space of fiction and reconstitute it as truth, precisely by proving its attachment to the criminal fact that it will have produced. What was aforethought without commission, pure imagining, will come instead to be understood as a seamless relation of intent and event.[17] But the law will continue to require both a recognizably temporal and conceptual separation of intent from act, and a melding of that same intent—become motive—to that same act.

The first two-thirds of Rivière's memoir, as initially envisaged, operate within the ficto-discursive time that I have just described. His "Summary of the tribulations and afflictions which my father suffered at the hands of my mother from 1813 to 1835" is as meticulously biographical, hence factual, as he can make it, but it is entirely constructed as a proleptic announcement of "this fearful resolution, I determined to kill all three of them" (106). If things had gone as he originally planned, the document would have existed in its own discursive time, expanding to allow whatever detail he chose to include, potentially ad infinitum; and it would have been interrupted or concluded only by the murders themselves. At that point, it would have become both confession and suicide note, the only relevant element, apart from official statements, of any judicial process. Conversely, should the crime not have been committed, Rivière's narrative would have remained a type of hallucinatory fiction, suspended in its own time, failing to produce any criminal act.

The subsequent and actual, retroactive form of the memoir causes it to function differently, as a form of confession as already mentioned. But that analeptic structure retains within it the prolepsis that originally constituted the text, giving to the memoir a time of its own prior to the event of the murders. The "Particulars and explanation of the occurrence on June 3 in Aunay at the village of La Faucterie written by the author of this deed" (54), which are in fact recounted only some fifty pages into the text (in the English edition)—and which are followed by another ten pages describing Rivière's wanderings during the month preceding his arrest—thus have as countercurrent the intervening forty-five-page "Summary of the tribulations and afflictions which my father suffered" (55). That summary constitutes the malice aforethought of the fearful resolution Rivière will then announce as its consequence.[18] Yet, prior to the act described by the text's first words there was an intention that gave rise to an aborted version that nevertheless now resides within the final version.

On the other side of the act, there exists a whole other digressive possibility, or narrative divagation, in Rivière's account of his month-long wanderings. Following the murders he is less a man on the run—or if he is that, it is only half-heartedly so—than someone developing the story of a new, solitary, and self-sustaining existence. If is as if, in deciding not to turn himself in to the authorities but instead to begin a month-long meander, he were opening a new narrative chapter that would surprise and alter the memoir's ending just as his sister's intrusion had surprised and altered its beginning, surprising and altering also the chronology of the murderous acts themselves.

As I understand it, the opening of the ficto-discursive time of intent represents the first in a series of what I have already referred to in passing as *deliberative* times of the judicial process, which exist in tension with its *decisive* moments. The conceit of my whole discussion is to cite the instant of the death penalty as the decisive moment par excellence, appropriated for its absolute finality. But the processual rhythm—deliberation, then crime; investigation, then indictment; trial, then verdict; hearing, then sentencing—works according to an alternation between deliberation and decision, where the suspensive time of deliberation cedes to the sudden time of decision. Each of those moments of decision is also an instantanization; in French it is called an *arrêt*, an arresting or stopping of time, as in the term *arrêt de mort* for "death sentence." At the end of each phase of the proceedings there occurs that type of arrest of time by the instantanization of the decision. Although legal proceedings involve a particular formalization of such a logic, it operates throughout our understanding of action in general.

The rhythm of deliberation and decision might also be understood to continue once a convicted criminal is required to serve a sentence, for example a prison sentence: It has a duration and an endpoint (even if, in cases of life in prison without parole, that endpoint is death), and in many cases it offers the possibility of being interrupted, for example by a positive decision at a parole hearing, and in more general terms by the presumption of rehabilitation and the paying of the criminal's debt to society. But of course the opposite is true in the case of a death sentence. The death sentence not only interrupts deliberative time with an absolute decision, but it also brings to a halt any possible future decision. For, as Derrida explains in the pages where he outlines the principle of mortal time that underwrites my whole project here, what permits the future for a mortal being is precisely the undecidability of that being's future. Not knowing when one will die allows one to envisage—without knowing—that future: "It belongs to life not necessarily to be immortal but to have . . . some life before it. . . . Where the anticipation of my death becomes the anticipation of a calculable instant, there is no longer any future" (*DP I*, 256). Once that principle of indetermination—the suspension of death, the arresting or reprieve of the ordinary mortal's death sentence—is replaced by the determination, imposition, and calculation of a time of death, then mortality is not reaffirmed but instead foreclosed:

> What we rebel against when we rebel against the death penalty is not death, or even the fact of killing, the fact of taking a life . . . [but the fact of being told] you will die on such and such a day, at such and such an hour, in that calculable place, and from blows delivered by several machines, the worst of which is perhaps neither the syringe nor the guillotine, but the clock and the anonymity of clockwork. The insult, the injury, the fundamental injustice done to the life in me, to the principle of life in me, is not death itself . . . it is rather the interrup-

tion of the principle of indetermination, the ending imposed on the opening of the incalculable chance whereby the living being has a relation to what comes. (ibid.)

Although life and fate, being itself, will have decided, from the moment we are born, that we are to die, we will nevertheless live in the suspension of that sentence. But paradoxically, we can enjoy that suspension of our death sentence only because we know we are going to die. If we were born immortal we would not have that possibility, we would not have available to us the opening onto a future that comes from knowing our future is not open-ended. Similarly, and similarly paradoxically, "what is ended by the possibility of the death penalty is not the infinity of life or immortality, but on the contrary, the finitude of 'my life.' It is because my life is finite, 'ended' in a certain sense, that I keep this relation to incalculability and undecidability as to the instant of my death" (*DP I*, 256).

That is the logic according to which the death penalty disjoins mortal time, a disjoining that this book has examined from various angles. Although Rivière will have his death sentence commuted, definitively suspended, his memoir will have opened the strange temporality of such a sentence, and, as it were, will have produced the disarray of times that we have just analyzed. Granted, he began by envisaging nothing less than a self-imposed death sentence, a decision to commit suicide which he ultimately carried out, but that decision is countermanded and complicated by the decision to write an explanation that immediately begins to function as an attempt to forestall the fate he had in store for himself; as long as he was explaining why he had to commit the murders, those acts remain suspended in narrative time. Hence, on the one hand, one could simply say that he needed to talk (or write) himself into (or perhaps out of) the actual commission of the awful act, an idea that is reinforced by his false starts once his "fatal resolution" was made; and, by his own admission as the time approaches, that "I am no coward yet I will never be able to do anything. . . . I was held back by what I then called my cowardice" (109). On the other hand, whether one subscribes to an idea of writing as therapeutic or simply distinguishes among different ways of occupying oneself, one understands the act of writing about, supposing, or imagining murder to function in a different space from the act of murder itself, as we have seen; and specifically, from my point of view, one understands it to function in a different, suspensive time.

We encountered a form of that suspensive time in chapter four: first as an intolerable moment that the suicide assassin Ch'en had to break through;

then, very differently, as the strange atemporality of the "unexperienced experience" of death that Blanchot writes about in *The Writing of the Disaster*, and that his narrator stages in *The Instant of My Death*.[19] In his commentary on the latter text Derrida orients his analysis through what he terms the "disturbing complicity between fiction and testimony" (*Demeure*, 43) deriving from the dual status of a testimony: it must be a unique account by a singular witness who, in a sense, "alone" saw or heard what he or she recounts; but it must also recount what anyone else in the same place at the same time would have seen or heard, and it must be able to be recounted in contexts that are radically separated from the original event that gave rise to it, which ruptures its very uniqueness and opens testimony to the structure of fiction (40–42). Rivière's memoir instantiates precisely that unstable status of testimony, but not just because, as confession made by the murderer himself, it is less deserving of our trust and will necessarily be received as an attempt at exculpation. More precisely, the memoir comes across as unmoored in time in the way that Foucault describes, but which Derrida ascribes to any testimony to the extent that it shares the space of fiction: the fact of its breaking with "a certain commonsense ordering of time" (*Demeure*, 49). From its opening moment, when the memoir states what should be its singular truth—I, Pierre Rivière, have slaughtered my mother, my sister, and my brother—its reconstruction of that singular moment stretches and warps it: back into the part-private, part-public, part-familial, part-socioeconomic time of Pierre's father's tribulations; sideways into the fantasmatic time of his childhood antics and libidinal disarray; forward into the meandering time he spent *on the lam*; and upward into the feigned time of his initial God-told-me-to-do-it defense. Each of those temporal warps constructs and recounts a different crime: a humanitarian retribution, the act of a sociopath, a function of amnesia, a crusade; and each operates as a fictional narrative in its own right, suspended in its own time.

Once narrative or suspensive time—that of Rivière's memoir, that of literary fiction in general—comes into play, something else opens up: the extreme abyssal structure of words themselves. The free flow of the memoir, like the seemingly limitless quality of the literary, comes not only from the capacity of narrative to spin out its yarn endlessly or repeatedly—the Scheherazade mechanism—but also from the way in which this or that word opens up its own suspensive depth of nuance, evocation, cross-reference, and so on. For that reason Foucault argues not only that "the text and the murder kept changing places" (*PR*, 202), but also that Rivière's imaginings gave rise to "verboballistic inventions" (203) such that the murder appears a little like "a projectile concealed at first in the engine of a discourse which recoils and becomes unnecessary in the propulsion discharging it" (202). That is to say: Whereas, according to Rivière's original plan, the murder would be first verbal or discursive before bursting forth as act to replace that discourse, the young man's investment in verbal discourse as displayed in the memoir also reveals itself as an investment in the idiosyncratic force of words in their own right, as "acts," one might say, their being a type of imaginary weaponry. As we learn from the memoir itself, his words were indeed being used to aggress or ward off attack, and his most inventive language was reserved for apotropaic purposes. Some forty-five pages into his memoir, after completing his review of his father's tribulations, and now promising "to explain my character and the thoughts I had before and after this deed" (100), Rivière tells us that he "displayed singularities" (101) that attracted the mockery of schoolmates. That peculiar behavior included: cutting heads off cabbages as though they were troops arrayed for battle (ibid.); avoiding getting close to female members of the family because of his troubling "carnal passion" and "horror of incest" (102); being "preoccupied with my excellence" (ibid.); imagining he could take his revenge on those who mocked him (or the girls who, knowing his neurosis, ran after him to kiss him) by "making writings about all of them . . . put them to scorn and have them driven out of the district" (103); and crucifying frogs and birds or attaching them "to a tree with three sharp nails through the belly. I called that enceepherating [*enceepharer*] them" (104).

More interesting, though, are the machines he imagined he would invent—a self-propelled butter churner, a carriage driven by springs, "which I wanted to produce only in my imagination" (ibid.)—including, in particular, "a tool to kills birds such as had never before been seen" to which he gave the name *calibene* (ibid.). In a way that is strikingly similar to his approach to the memoir itself, he worked on the machine "for a long time on Sundays and in the evening, and finding that it did not succeed as I had expected, I went and buried it in a meadow and later I dug it up again and it is still on the floor in one of the houses" (ibid.). Along with the calibene there were "bows which I called albalesters [*albalêtres*], and I busied myself in trying to get one to go off" (104). The albalester—first a word, then a functional object—opens up a whole new proleptic time and space within the memoir and within Rivière's acts and lives, for "I was arrested with one and though I said I had made it in order to pass for mad, yet it was not exactly that" (ibid.). That is, even though the plan to announce the murders in writing before committing them failed, the albalester begins as an invention of both word and thing that fails, but keeps itself afloat as a possibility until he is living his new life on the lam, at which point he fabricates such a bow, so successfully that he is able to use it both to hunt birds and to get himself apprehended. For, even though it doesn't catch him a bird, it does allow him to be noticed in town as "a fellow carrying a bow" (120), and eventually to be captured. Where the memoir failed to denounce his intentions as planned, the albalester succeeded, identifying him as a stranger in town, as the strange madman he wanted to be taken for, and ultimately as the hunted criminal murderer of his family members.

Rivière is asked about the bow during his first questioning, and about the *calibene* during his second interrogation. In the first case the examining judge suggests that the weapon was an offensive one, whereas Rivière asserts it was for killing birds. In the second case the judge names the word Calibene, and it is indeed not clear from the memoir whether it is intended as a common noun or proper name when Rivière writes that he "named it 'calibene'" (103), a doubt that persists in the course of the questioning. When asked about the meaning of the word Rivière emphasizes the fact of invention, the invention of the word perhaps even more than the invention of the thing: "I imagined that word; I tried hard to find a name that could not mean any other instrument" (37).

Rivière's memoir therefore sets in motion a suspensive time machine that will regulate his relation to his crime, and at the same time puts into operation the hauntingly resonant time of the word, of the word as machine. The word will always be the motor of the deliberative process of justice, the narrative and rhetorical instrument of court proceedings, even though it function with the prospect of bringing an end to deliberation by means of verdict, sentence, or committal. It will be enacted right up to and including the sentence of death and execution, each of those events requiring the formulaic performance of a decree, all the way to the medical and administrative pronouncement of death itself having occurred at such and such a time. But throughout that process and those procedures, the word will haunt decision as its deliberative other, as if threatening to suspend the decision indefinitely, holding up the judicial act as long as rhetorical ploy or pleading—or the presiding judge—allows. Pierre Rivière's memoir focuses on the fact and acts of verbal discourse functioning in their own time, overlapping with the murder itself and uncannily disturbing the time of both crime and punishment.

The word-machine would be the opposite of the trap door image. In opening suspensive time "beyond" the sentence it will allow for a literature that can potentially digress ad infinitum: words on automatic pilot that produce their own perpetual motion. None of that flow of words will ever prevent, in the sense of substituting for, a real execution, even though, like literature of any persuasive or militant nature, an abolitionist literature such as that of Victor Hugo remains capable of inflecting attitudes toward the death penalty; and literature *of* the death penalty, some examples of which have been mentioned in earlier discussions, constitutes a relatively abundant genre.[20]

Among writers of the Western tradition who have made penalty, penality, and death their subjects, one stands out clearly, having lent his name for a word that describes par excellence the machine of a suspensive time that, unfortunately, has nothing redemptive about it. It is thanks to the name and fictions of Franz Kafka that we have a word for the labyrinthine operations of a justice that is more mad than blind, operations that we call "Kafkaesque." We could use that word to describe the cruel and absurd injustice of a death penalty as experienced so far by Richard Glossip in Oklahoma. I say "experienced so far" because he has continued to *experience* or live through that death penalty after eating his last meal three times, awaiting the next time he will be led, following his nearly two-score-year limbo on death row, to be strapped again to a gurney. During the years that have elapsed since I began to write the Introduction to this book in 2014, he has continued to inhabit that Kafkaesque space and time.[21] We could also use the word "Kafkaesque" to refer to a secret process that targets for instant killing an unidentified person spotted behaving aberrantly by a drone operator some nine thousand miles, two continents, and an ocean away. Or, consonant with my emphasis throughout this book, we could call Kafkaesque the decision to impose categorically on a given fellow human a time that is foreign to human time, a time whose opening to the future is defined instead as the progressive closing of the doors of possibility and potentiality.

When it comes to the death penalty in Kafka the text of reference would of course be "In the Penal Colony." There, Justice Blackmun's machinery of death finds its literal application in the inscription of the law in real time upon the body of the condemned. As the officer explains to the explorer, "Our sentence does not sound severe. Whatever commandment the prisoner has disobeyed is written upon his body by the Harrow."[22] That grotesque procedure reminds us again, as if we needed to be reminded at this late stage, that punishment as a concept is inseparable from duration, that in many respects the pain that punishment inflicts is the very time of its infliction, *the duration during which it must be endured.* For the execution machine of "The Penal Colony" is designed to puncture the body, writing the law at an increasing depth, and with increasing pain, for a period of twelve hours: "So it keeps on writing deeper and deeper for the whole twelve hours. The first six hours the condemned man stays alive almost as before, he suffers only pain."[23] But the second half of the punishment brings about a consciousness beyond pain, something approaching Hegel's absolute knowledge, inculcating in the condemned person the very spirit of punishment and of the sentence:

> But how quiet he grows at just about the sixth hour! Enlightenment comes to the most dull witted. It begins around the eyes. From there it radiates. A moment that might tempt one to get under the Harrow oneself. Nothing more happens than that the man begins to understand the inscription, he purses his mouth as if he were listening. You have seen how difficult it is to decipher the script with one's eyes; but our man deciphers it with his wounds. To be sure, that is a hard task; he needs six hours to accomplish it. By that time the Harrow has pierced him quite through . . . [24]

"In the Penal Colony" illustrates, however figuratively, that no technology can be attached to the human body without being accompanied by time, without that technology being inscribed as a form of time. As I have argued previously, technology is most obviously about saving time for the human; a machine that works gives the time it saves back to the human. But it is also because technology functions in time: time itself is its medium and substance. Technology begins as soon as the human, supposedly secure in its self-enclosed existence, reaches outside itself to encounter the time of the inanimate: Objects that predate it, have their own history, are capable of outliving it, can still be functioning once a given human has ceased to function. So it might be said that before there is any encounter with the inanimate object itself, there will have already been an encounter with its time, with time as the artificial construct that is required if the human is to know that object, for the human to articulate and negotiate with it as technological object, as a result of which she can use it to save time. It is in that sense that time might be called the first technology, what comes into play immediately as another pulse, rhythm, or speed the moment that the human reaches outside itself.

Yet, of course, what has just been described as "beginning" once the human reaches outside itself also reaches back to disturb the supposed watertight distinction between what is inside and what is outside the human, the extent to which technology is limited to inanimate objects constructed by the human outside itself. We saw how that problematic functioned in the case of the blood, as Hegel understood it, in Chapter 3. In Hegel's terms the internal pulse of the human finds its way to the surface on the way to reacting with the inanimate outside that it hopes to subdue: that encounter is effected, and the victory of the human affirmed, as blood overcomes and assimilates air, taking it back in and putting it into circulation as its own matter to assure its sustenance. But that blood cannot in fact reach out to sublate the "purely negative immaterial life" of air without somehow recognizing an interruption in, and problematization of its idealized circulation. Either the blood that flows internally to preserve the intact sustenance of the human is imagined to "step outside" itself, or we realize that it was never in fact flowing without interruption, being subject rather to the rhythm of the mammalian body's own internal machine called the heart.

Kafka's penal colony execution machine, his time-inflicting punishment machine, or punishment-inflicting time machine of death, is a perverse staging of time being used not to open the mortal future but to foreclose it. When the human encounters, discovers, or invents time as an external apparatus to measure her days, she gives it an autonomy that is precisely an automatism, allowing it, as I have just described, to function indefinitely into the future. The penal colony time machine is instead an apparatus for interrupting that mortal time. For the period of its functioning it grotesquely mocks the mortal invention of time by superseding it, inflicting a defined and limited time, six hours of pain and six hours of enlightenment. Time as mortal law, the law of finitude, is mechanized and perverted into an apparatus that will sew itself back into the human as finitude. The Harrow *punctuates* such a time, indeed *punctures* the body with its force and truth; it gives back the time it has saved for the human with a vengeance, brutally marking out points of time on the exposed spaces of the victim's body, and eventually subjugating and destroying that body by piercing the seat of its consciousness.

Granted, in Kafka's narrative the time-inflicting execution machine breaks down. It coughs and splutters, requiring the endless tinkering that the officer describes, as a result of worn cogwheels, unavailability of spare parts, broken wrist strap, filthy felt, insufficient funding. But it breaks down far more fundamentally once the explorer refuses to represent to the new Commandant the officer's plea for a return to a smooth-functioning death-dealing machine. In the face of that refusal, the officer declares that "'the time has come [*dann ist es also Zeit*].' 'The time for what?' [*Wozu ist es Zeit?*] asked the explorer uneasily, but got no answer."[25] The reader soon finds out that what it is now time for is for the officer to subject himself to the machine, to execute himself with the maxim "be just," to show how staggeringly well "he managed it and how it obeyed him," such that he does not even have to activate the lever to set the Harrow to work. It obeys him and begins to function without "even the slightest hum."[26] It seems then as if the punishment machine were about to inscribe not the law but rather the loftier ideal of justice. Justice, however, is precisely what cannot be designed; it cannot be written, it does not have sufficient intricacy for translation and transmission from Designer to Harrow. Thus the cogwheels of the Designer fly off one by one until "the Harrow was not writing, it was only jabbing." As a result, what is supposed to take twelve hours of exquisite torture is reduced to "plain murder [*unmittelbarer Mord*],"[27] and the Harrow grinds to a halt holding the corpse with its spikes, like a guillotine blade to which the head remains attached. The officer dies "with the same expression as in life," deprived of "the promised redemption; what the others had found in the machine the officer had not found."[28] So it is that through all these different killing times—those of the previous victims for whom the machine functioned as planned, that of the current condemned man who is given a last-minute reprieve, and that of the officer, subject to a machine run amok, who is denied the insight of *incisively* learning to be just—the tethering of a human to a machine means not just the execution of that human, but also the replacement of its time by a mechanized and punctual law.

It is clear that Kafka's "In the Penal Colony" can be read as a parable for much more than what I call "killing times." It is a fully fledged literalization of Blackmun's machinery of death, of all its labyrinthine and cruel ironies, as well as its notorious botchings. Whatever precise textual flourishes of the commandment that the prisoner has disobeyed are to be written into his body, once the lid of the Designer is shut, and the cogwheels set in motion; then the instruments of death set about their business of foreclosing mortal time in favor of seconds that precede extinction. But if "The Penal Colony" is Kafka's most obvious text regarding the application of the death penalty, it is in another famous story, "The Metamorphosis," that time as interruption becomes the very mechanism of the death penalty itself.

Gregor Samsa, transformed into a gigantic insect, is not subject to a formal sentence, but when he awakes "one morning from uneasy dreams," his time begins to be interrupted and reduced by the closing of doors; from that moment on his confinement becomes the progressive imposition of a death penalty.[29] At 7:10 that morning, the chief clerk knocks at the front door. Gregor opens it to expose his strange state and appearance to the world. At that moment, and immediately following that moment, when Gregor props himself in strengthening light, against one half of the double door leading from his room to the living room, when he looks from there and sees clear out the open door leading to the hall, to the front door beyond that, to the landing and stairs, seeing in that way the whole layout of his possible escape, at that moment the doors begin, inexorably, to be slammed shut. His incarceration and execution begin. After being driven back into the room by his father, his fate is irrevocably sealed. The different doors leading to his room—just how many there are remains a question—are fully functional at the beginning of the story, but decrease in operationality from the beginning of the second chapter. His room becomes a cell, and the door to the hallway is increasingly the single point of entry or exit, used regularly only by his sister to bring in food, and by her or the charwoman to keep things clean. The word "captivity" or "imprisonment" (*Gefangenschaft*) is used once, and before his father attacks him with apples his sister announces that he has "broken loose [*ausgebrochen*]."[30] But while it is easy to recognize his incarceration as a form of quarantine, as the family's rejection of Gregor's ontological and species difference ("human beings can't live with such a creature [*Tier*]"),[31] I interpret the doors as less performing a simple spatial confinement than articulating the instant of sentence itself. Each door closed is another end to the future, a closing of future possibility, a further restriction of mortal time. Hence, at the end, with the door to his room "hastily pushed shut, bolted, and locked," his sister crying "at last [*endlich*]," and Gregor saying to himself "what now [*und jetzt*]?" Samsa's time has been decided and its countdown has begun.[32]

Everywhere in Kafka's writing, the time of the law—its process as much as its sentence—operates by means of the door. His haunting performance of legal limbo, "Before the Law," is, from the outset, all doors and gates: "Before the law stands a doorkeeper."[33] If a doorkeeper stands before the law, then it follows that the law *is* the door. And of course the short fragment that bears that title will come to be placed *en abyme*, as if behind a series of doors, in *The Trial*, recessed or secreted inside the ninth chapter of that novel within a complex layering of allegory and commentary. It inhabits the semidarkness of K's encounter with the priest, deep within the protagonist's endless labyrinth of incomprehension and self-deception. In *The Trial* itself, the moment or episode of before the law comes just when K. has all but escaped from the cathedral ("at the moment he was still free; he could walk on and leave through one of the three small dark wooden doors not far from him"), and he knows that "if he turned around he was caught [*festgehalten*]."[34] But he doesn't carry on walking, doesn't exit through the door; instead he stays and is trapped into hearing the priest recount the trap of the law as experienced by the man from the country:

> "Don't deceive yourself," said the priest. . . . "In the introductory texts to the Law it says of this deception: Before the Law stand a door-keeper. A man from the country comes to this doorkeeper and requests admittance to the Law. But the doorkeeper says that he can't grant him admittance now. The man thinks it over and then asks if he'll be allowed to enter later. 'It's possible,' says the doorkeeper, 'but not now.' Since the gate to the Law stands open as always, and the doorkeeper steps aside, the man bends down to look through the gate into the interior. When the doorkeeper sees this he laughs and says: 'If you're so drawn to it, go ahead and try to enter, even though I've forbidden it. But bear this in mind: I'm powerful. And I'm only the lowest doorkeeper. From hall to hall, however, stand doorkeepers each more powerful than the one before.'"[35]

And so it goes, ending the only way it possibly could, with the man from the country wasting his entire life in waiting, and finally dying before the law. The paragraphs that introduce the law, supposedly opening it, as the priest explains, exist only to describe a law that is closed, progressively and successively, to anyone naïve enough to address it.

The trap of the law into which the man from the country falls, the same trap within which K. finds himself ensnared, the supreme weapon wielded by the law, is time. The door to the law is a door into a suspension of time; it emblematizes the whole Kafkaesque nightmare of *The Trial* ("the pro-ceedings gradually merge into the judgment," the priest tells K.).[36] The naivety of the man from the country who finds himself before the door of the law consists in presuming he can sit it out, even if it takes "days and years."[37] But however immobilized before the law he be, however insatia-ble his patience, for all his misfortune and wasted time, he remains in mor-tal time, from manhood to old age and death. Conversely, Joseph K's life inside the law gives the appearance of being all active resistance, but be-ginning with his incomprehensible arrest in the novel's first sentence, it comes to be revealed as an abyss of missed appointments, delays, and de-ferments, continuing until, at the extreme, K. dies within sight of one last open window whose invitation to a mortal future remains beyond his reach. He is executed, by his own admission, "like a dog."[38]

With Kafka's fictions we therefore return to the trap doors of Chap-ter 2, to various allegorizations of a death penalty that means shutting the door on the future of a mortal. A death sentence brings about the ensuing time warp of what is at the same time a limitation (your life will be over at such and such a time on such and such a date) and a delimitation (you are no longer mortal in the normal sense; you are robbed of your finitude, suspended in a type of deferred *un*-mortality). As we saw in our earlier discussion, the image of one deserving such a condemnation is drawn so as to evoke a repulsion like that enacted by Gregor Samsa's family in "The Metamorphosis." The creature that Samsa becomes—and it is as if his crime is precisely the fact of metamorphosing into such a creature under the cover of uneasy dreams—remains specifically unidentified. In German it is *Ungeziefer*, which the standard English translation makes an insect. It could also be bug or vermin, but the etymological derivation refers to what is unworthy of sacrifice, a type of pariah animal, something like the worst of the worst of creatures.[39] But not only does the reader of "The Metamorphosis" remain in the dark concerning the specific creature that Samsa has become; we are also deprived of a clear image of it. We understand well enough that Gregor is all legs, that he is sticky and has feelers, but at no point do we really see what the chief clerk, the family, the maids, or the lodgers see. We see the horror those spectators experience without really seeing Gregor. For all the visual starkness or graphic visuality of the story, it remains remarkably devoid of a satisfactory version of what in cinema is called the reverse shot; the other characters are as if photographed from Gregor's point of view without our having access to their own point of view shots.

Kafka's "Metamorphosis" thus gives us the other side of the *instamatic* reality of the death penalty—an egregious crime, an irredeemable criminal, a humane execution—that its proponents would have us see. The story has us understand how that image is developed in a dark room such as that to which Gregor is consigned and confined. The darkness of Gregor's room covers the awful truth that the family doesn't want to have to face, but it also creates the *camera obscura* by means of which we are able to see the metamorphosis for what it is. On the one hand, that means seeing the Gregor that the world hides from sight, being privy to the place where he is able to be other—insect, bug, creature, becoming animal—*as such*. It means seeing the real Gregor in a way that we can understand neither from the word used to describe him, nor from his family's reactions; it means seeing the real Gregor as he now is. On the other hand, considered from the photographic perspective of the shutter (and the trap door), metamorphosis is understood as the transformation of an instant, of *the* instant. Gregor's change takes place in the darkness of his sleep, in a moment when all that can be perceived is a difference between dark and light, but in the moment of development or revelation that is his awakening it comes to light as his metamorphosis. When he awakes and finds himself transformed in his bed, he finds—in one and the same moment—himself, transformation, and the new ontological status produced by that transformation. And each time his attempts to reassimilate are rebuffed and the door to his room is shut, he finds himself again, as if suddenly transformed again, returned to nothing but the company of his transformed self.

Kafka gives us, via Gregor Samsa, the experience of being condemned to an inassimilable otherness, allowing us to share its dark place of ostracism and ultimate death. Gregor's metamorphosis is an interspecies transformation, but in the dark room of instamatic change there also occurs what I would call an *inanimation*, whereby the human reveals its intimate relation with inorganic or technological otherness. For the fate of our mortality in general, and the most natural experience in the world, is for a mortal animate being, from the moment its life begins, to have to negotiate with the inanimate, and finally to become inanimate. In that way every mortal human immediately starts metamorphosing into part-thingness; indeed, we must do so if we are to function among the things of the world and integrate them as necessary into our daily dealings and into our bodies. But it is one thing to understand that such a prosthesis of human and technology is coextensive with being human in general; it is quite another matter to be attached, by decree, to a clockwork inanimating machine called the death penalty; a machine that will close the door on your future, and condemn you, by the fiat of a sentence, to the status of the worst of the unworthy-to-be-sacrificed worst on the way to disposable thingness. That is what happens to Gregor Samsa: his metamorphosis is first a reduction to an unnamable liminal creature unworthy even of sacrifice, and ultimately, as the charwoman makes clear, he is merely a "thing" that she is proud to have disposed of.

As this book has demonstrated, death penalty advocates advance their own version of the metamorphosis of human into thingness by relying on an all but instantaneous speed of technology and machine, one capable of transforming the instant of death into the supposed humanitarian advances of the guillotine or lethal injection. Capital punishment, in their view, can be rationalized as performing an almost blissful prosthetic union of human and technology that allows the law to be imposed with humanitarian efficacy. The technological speed of contemporary executions, in the United States, presumes to transform the human into inanimate thing without any loss of humanity; it presumes to effect a metamorphosis that does not produce anything like the unacceptable creature that is Gregor Samsa.

   As I have also consistently argued, the recourse to an increasingly refined technology of the death penalty, in its post-Enlightenment Western
moment, is used by proponents of a modern or contemporary capital
punishment to give us a supposedly convincing *image* of its justness. And
that, in turn, relies on a different appropriation and idealization of the
instant. In the same, quasi-imperceptible instant, it is presumed, the machinery of death operates painlessly to fit, as if picture perfect, punishment to crime for only the worst of the worst. The operation is repeated
again and again, mechanically reproducing itself with the same confidence.
That is what allows it to go on. As if Kafka's story were being recounted
by Justice Blackmun, *within days, or perhaps hours, the memory of* Gregor
Samsa *will begin to fade*, Grete will spring to her feet and stretch her young
body, and *the wheels of justice will churn again*; another such judicial metamorphosis of the human will take place.

So it is that in the years since 1994, when Blackmun made his vow never
more to tinker, and since his death in 1999, the wheels have churned, the
tinkering has continued: America's exceptional death penalty experiment
has persisted; its time has not yet run out. The wheels of that machine
continue to turn through time, but, as I have attempted to show throughout this discussion, they also turn *in time*, turning time into something
else. The death penalty machine turns the time of ordinary mortals into a
time outside mortal time, a time programmed to end. The way that that
operates for the person *condemned to death* is incommensurable with how
it operates for the rest of us simply *condemned to die*. Those subject to a
death sentence have their future taken from them and must suffer that
dislocated time as duration or endurance of suffering or pain itself. Their
prosthetic condition involves first that disjunctive temporality, and second, a forcible technological attachment that ends their life. But, as this
book has argued, those whom the death penalty does not condemn are
required to deal otherwise with that conversion, or perversion of what we
presume to be ordinary mortal time.
   What the death penalty requires all of us to face is the *prostheticity* of
our prosthetic relation to time. Whether we knew it or not, from the moment we understood ourselves to be mortal, we became subject to a type
of countdown that functioned as a putatively external system of control
over our lives; we adopted and adapted to time as that prosthesis, even if
we claimed or pretended to be able to avoid or outwit it. Once there is the
death penalty, however, and because there is the death penalty, human or
mortal time can no longer conceal its technicity. We can no more pretend

to experience a prosthetic time as though it were natural. That is not to say that mortal time becomes technological only once there is the death penalty; time, as I have just said, will have always been a prosthesis for all of us. Nor is it even to say that the death penalty reveals the relation that prosthetic technology has both to time and to death; every prosthesis has a different time and life from the human it is attached to, and whom it will likely survive; every prosthesis has the status of an artifact. It is rather that, once the moment of death is situated at a specific point along the time of life—and once prostheses are mobilized to bring about that death—then time reveals its specific artificiality. Time becomes something that is no longer one's own, and it does so in a very different, particularly contrived way.

Or, to put it differently, we have always been involved in prosthetic relations that extend beyond what we conceive of as "us proper." That prosthetization is also a temporalization: first, because what we call time is one of its most obvious forms; second, because the prostheses that we attach ourselves to—from simple tools to elaborate memory machines or life support systems—operate in a different temporal mode, and are presumed to survive us, which is how they also relate us to our death. A machine that is set up in order *to put someone to death* is but an extreme, and noxious, example of that.

In arguing the prosthetic technicity of mortal temporality, as revealed by the death penalty, this analysis advocates more than passively adopting the vague or impersonal idea that as long as capital punishment exists, being so condemned remains possible for everyone. Far from being an obstacle to thinking the ethico-political consequences of the death penalty, an approach to the question that examines temporal technicity has led here to conclusions that are activist or abolitionist, even militantly so. Based on analysis of the instant, the preceding chapters have drawn conclusions as diverse as the contention that because executions take time, the death penalty will always be more or less painful; that the presence or absence of blood is not a measure of the cruelty of the death penalty; that the death penalty is intimately linked with forms of terrorism. In this final chapter we have seen the death penalty time-altering machine operating at the opposite end from the appropriation of the instant consistently highlighted in previous discussions. For all that it requires that pure decisiveness of the instant, the death penalty time-altering machine conversely activates very different extensions of time: the suspended time of death row that we have noted from the beginning; and here, vagaries of process that include, at the outside, stretchings such as those of literary fiction. By concentrating on that outside in this chapter, I seek neither to redeem the death-dealing machine's appropriative gestures nor to indulge some fantasy of the indefinite suspension of its mechanism, no more than have I, here or earlier, floated the fantasy of our sharing the experience of someone on death row. For the death penalty is still claiming victims in the country that perceives itself as the most evolved of all democracies, and still choosing those victims, for the most part, among the most economically and sociologically vulnerable of its citizens.

The death penalty is still with us. I hope to have shown to what extent it is *in us*, how intimately it is *ours*, even in a sense being *in our blood*. Inasmuch as time makes us, or at least, in my argument, makes us technological, death penalty time remakes us down to the core. The end of the death penalty will not restore to us natural time, for time never was natural. Abolishing capital punishment will not detechnologize time. But it will disconnect us from the mechanics of the special technologizing of time that reduces to pure program. It will unhinge that trap door, blunt that blade, and detoxify that cocktail. The instant will no longer be prescribed or circumscribed in the same way but instead allow access to another, in a time of the future. We will have, in some respect, reconfigured our time being mortal.

The time will now be—open.

Atkins v. Virginia, 536 U.S. 304 (2002). 6–3 majority rules that execution of intellectually disabled violates the Eighth Amendment.

Baze v. Rees, 553 U.S. 35 (2008). Kentucky's lethal injection combination upheld by 7–2 majority. Ginsburg joined by Souter dissented; separate concurring opinions by Stevens, and Scalia and Thomas, debate broader constitutional concerns.

Beard v. Banks, 548 U.S. 521 (2006). 6–2 decision denying Pennsylvania prisoner's access to reading and media materials.

Boyce v. Anderson, 27 U.S. 150 (1829). Slaves being transported by ship found not to constitute cargo but rather intelligent beings.

Callins v. Collins, 510 U.S. 1141 (1994). Denial of petition by death row inmate provides context for Blackmun's famous rejection of death penalty.

Coker v. Georgia, 433 U.S. 584 (1977). 7–2 majority rules death penalty a "grossly disproportionate" punishment for the crime of rape.

Enmund v. Florida, 458 U.S. 782 (1982). Death penalty held to be unconstitutional for someone who aids and abets a murder but neither kills nor intends to kill.

Furman v. Georgia, 408 U.S. 238 (1972). Landmark 5–4 decision striking down all capital convictions until states were able to remedy arbitrary and discriminatory application of death penalty.

Glossip v. Gross, 576 U.S. (2015). Oklahoma's use of midazolam as initial drug in protocol upheld by 5–4 majority. Notable dissents by Breyer joined by Ginsburg, and Sotomayor joined by Breyer, Ginsburg, and Kagan.

Gregg v. Georgia, 428 U.S. 153 (1976). 7–2 majority reinstates death penalty following adjustment of procedures to satisfy objections raised in *Furman*.

In re Kemmler, 136 U.S. 436 (1890). New York State electric chair found to satisfy Eighth Amendment.

Kennedy v. Louisiana, 554 U.S. 407 (2008). 5–4 majority extends *Coker* ruling, prohibiting death penalty for rape of a child.

Lockett v. Ohio, 438 U.S. 586 (1978). Ruling that mitigating circumstances may not be excluded from consideration in capital cases.

Louisiana ex rel. Francis v. Resweber, 329 U.S. 459 (1947). Second attempt at electrocution after failure of first found not to contravene Eighth Amendment. Four justices join in notable dissent.

McCollum v. North Carolina, 512 U.S. 1252 (1994). Denial of petition by intellectually disabled man whose crime provides textbook justification of death penalty for Thomas and Scalia. DNA evidence later proves his innocence.

McGautha v. California, 402 U.S. 183 (1971). Bellwether pre-*Furman* case raising doubts concerning unequal application of death penalty.

Stanford v. Kentucky, 492 U.S. 361 (1989). 5–4 decision upholding capital sentence for crime committed by sixteen-year-old (decided one year after *Thompson*).

Roper v. Simmons, 543 U.S. 551 (2005). 5–4 decision overturning *Stanford* and prohibiting death penalty for juveniles under eighteen.

Thompson v. Oklahoma, 487 U.S. 815 (1988). Execution of a juvenile under the age of sixteen ruled unconstitutional.

Trop v. Dulles, 356 U.S. 86 (1958). Stripping soldier of citizenship for desertion considered cruel and unusual punishment.

Weems v. United States, 217 U.S. 349 (1910). Punishment imposed for defrauding the government found to be cruel and unusual.

Wilkerson v. Utah, 99 U.S. 130 (1879). Utah's firing squad law deemed constitutional.

Woodson v. North Carolina, 428 U.S. 280 (1976). North Carolina's mandatory death penalty law deemed unconstitutional (in contrast to decision in *Gregg*).

ACKNOWLEDGMENTS

In the late 1980s or early 1990s I was casting around in search of someone foolhardy enough to publish the strangely heterogeneous book that I was then working on. I do not remember how it came about, but I was introduced to Helen Tartar, who convinced me to throw in my lot with the somewhat fledgling series that Werner Hamacher and David E. Wellbery had launched with her at Stanford University Press. So it was that my title (*Prosthesis*), the artefact of an Antipodean interloper, came to be happily sandwiched in the Meridian Series between Maurice Blanchot, *The Work of Fire* (copiously cited in Chapter 4 of this book), and Jacques Derrida, *On the Name* (an author, if not a book, whose inspiration accounts for much of what I have written here). Ten years later I would be fortunate enough to publish a second title that Helen accepted for the same series, but by then she had moved on to her position at Fordham. Out of fidelity to her confidence in my work, I always wanted to submit a manuscript to Fordham, but although my name appeared on the cover of more than one translated work, I was not able to offer her a volume before her untimely death. This book represents, therefore, a meager attempt to repay the immense debt that I owe to Helen Tartar, and to her memory.

Helen Tartar's legacy at Fordham has been ably continued by Tom Lay. My book owes much to his unshakable support, as well as the assistance of his editorial team, including especially my copyeditor, Gregory McNamee; and to the strong endorsements given by two external reviewers. For all that support I am very grateful.

The work that has culminated in this book began in the context of the Derrida Seminars Translation Project summer workshops over a four-year period from 2010 to 2013. I remain most grateful to my fellow team members—Geoffrey Bennington, Pascale-Anne Brault, Peggy Kamuf, Michael Naas, and Elizabeth Rottenberg; as well Ellen Burt, Katie Chenoweth, and Kir Kuiken; and the students who participated during those years—for their attentive and provocative comments in response to presentations I gave during those workshops.

Subsequently, *Killing Times* took shape via a series of invited lectures, keynote addresses and conference papers, and the feedback to which those papers gave rise, in a variety of venues. That included lectures at the following institutions: Brown University, University of Sussex, Texas A&M University, University of Auckland, and Rice University; and conferences at De Paul University, the University of California, Irvine, Brown University, the University at Albany-SUNY, the University of California, Santa Barbara, Harvard University, Indiana University, and the University of California, Riverside. For all of those invitations I sincerely thank, beside those already mentioned, Nicole Anderson, Kevin McLaughlin, Nicholas Royle, Adam Rosenthal, Laurence Simmons, Cary Wolfe, Amanda Anderson, Elisabeth Weber, Hall Bjørnstad, Sherryl Vint, and Peter Boxall. Other conference papers were delivered at Derrida Today, Fordham University, at the Society for Science, Literature and the Arts, Houston, and at the 20th/21st Century French and Francophone Studies Conference, Bloomington.

I have profited greatly from discussions formal and informal among a circle of friends and a valued intellectual community that includes Sharon Cameron, Ross Posnock, Timothy Bewes, Obrad Savić, Elissa Marder and Vesna Kuiken, and particularly my dear friend and Brown colleague Thangam Ravindranathan.

Mrdjan Bajić's rich visual imagination and acute political and historical intelligence has made him one of the most important artists currently working in the countries of the former Yugoslavia. His generous offer of a piece of his work to grace the cover of *Killing Times* is a gesture that I will never forget. I record here my heartfelt thanks.

Earlier versions of certain chapters in this book were published as follows: "Machinery of Death or Machinic Life," *Derrida Today* 7, no. 1 (2014); "Drone Penalty," Copyright © Board of Regents, University of Wisconsin System, first published in *SubStance* 43, no. 2 (2014): 174–92. Reprinted with permission by Johns Hopkins University Press; and "The Time of the (Trap) Door," *Belgrade Journal of Media and Communications* 4, no. 8 (2015). I am grateful to those journals for permission to reuse that material here.

As always, during the preparation of this volume and beyond, the time of my mortal life will have been immeasurably enhanced by the unfailing presence, love, and support of Branka and Emma.

INTRODUCTION

1. Indeed, as discussed in chapter 1, on June 29, 2015, the Supreme Court decision in *Glossip* gave rise to important new positions taken by different justices with respect to the constitutionality of the death penalty.

2. UN resolution 69/186, cosponsored by ninety-five countries, was adopted on December 18, 2014. The following countries voted against the resolution: Afghanistan, Antigua and Barbuda, Bahamas, Bangladesh, Barbados, Belize, Botswana, Brunei Darussalam, China, Dominica, Egypt, Ethiopia, Grenada, Guyana, India, Iran, Iraq, Jamaica, Japan, Kuwait, Libya, Malaysia, North Korea, Oman, Pakistan, Papua New Guinea, Qatar, Saint Kitts and Nevis, Saint Lucia, Saint Vincent and Grenadines, Saudi Arabia, Singapore, Sudan, Syria, Trinidad and Tobago, the United States of America, Yemen, and Zimbabwe. See Amnesty International, "Death Sentences and Executions in 2014" (https://www.amnesty.org/en/documents /act50/0001/2015/en/), Annex IV.

3. See https: //www.amnesty.org/en/what-we-do/death-penalty; and https://deathpenaltyinfo.org/states-and-without-death-penalty.

4. See Roland Barthes, *Criticism and Truth*, trans. Katrine Pilcher Keuneman (London: Continuum, 2007 [*Critique et vérité*. Paris: Minuit, 1966]); *On Racine*, trans. Richard Howard (Berkeley: University of California Press, 1992); *Mythologies*, trans. Annette Lavers (London: Macmillan, 1972). See also Raymond Picard, *Nouvelle critique ou nouvelle imposture* (Paris: Pauvert, 1965).

5. See attempts to explain the outlier status of the United States in relation to the death penalty in Franklin E. Zimring, *The Contradictions of American Capital Punishment* (New York: Oxford University Press, 2003), esp. 42–66; and David Garland, *Peculiar Institution: America's Death Penalty in an Age of Abolition* (Cambridge, MA: Harvard University Press, 2010), 20–24.

6. *Furman v. Georgia* 408 U.S. 238 (1972), 406. Further references in text.

7. Most recently, on March 14, 2018, Oklahoma announced that it would henceforth perform executions using nitrogen gas, although a protocol for such usage has yet to be developed.

8. See my *Prosthesis* (Stanford: Stanford University Press, 1995), *Dorsality* (Minneapolis: University of Minnesota Press, 2008), and *Inanimation* (Minneapolis: University of Minnesota Press, 2016).

9. Michel Foucault, ed., *I, Pierre Rivière, having slaughtered my mother, my sister, and my brother*, trans. Frank Jellinek (Lincoln: University of Nebraska Press, 1982).

10. Jacques Derrida, *The Death Penalty*, Vol. I, trans. Peggy Kamuf (Chicago: University of Chicago Press, 2014), 219. See also *The Death Penalty*, Vol. II, trans. Elizabeth Rottenberg (Chicago: University of Chicago Press, 2017). Further references to these two volumes will appear in text, preceded by the mentions *DP I* and *DP II*.

1. MACHINERY OF DEATH OR MACHINIC LIFE

1. *Callins v. Collins*, 510 U.S. 1141, 1143–45 (1994). Following initial citation, references to this and all subsequent Supreme Court decisions appear in text and are identified by petitioner's name (e.g., *Callins*) followed by page number.

2. See *Furman v. Georgia*, 408 U.S. 238 (1972); *Gregg v. Georgia*, 428 U.S. 153 (1976).

3. See *Baze v. Rees*, 553 U.S. 35 (2008).

4. See *Glossip v. Gross*, 576 U.S. (2015).

5. See, for example, Derrida's extension of the machinery of death to "so many techno-scientifico-capitalist mechanisms for distributing, in a terribly unequal way, the right to life, to longevity, and which therefore not only condemn to death a calculable number of individuals but also condemn to die prematurely an incalculable number of living beings, human and nonhuman." Jacques Derrida, *The Death Penalty*, Vol. II (hereafter *DP II*), trans. Elizabeth Rottenberg (Chicago: University of Chicago Press, 2017), 199–200.

6. See *Weems v. United States*, 217 U.S. 349 (1910); *Louisiana ex rel. Francis v. Resweber*, 329 U.S. 459 (1947); *In re Kemmler*, 136 U.S. 436 (1890); *Wilkerson v. Utah*, 99 U.S. 130 (1879).

7. Immanuel Kant, *Critique of Pure Reason*, trans. and ed. Paul Guyer (Cambridge: Cambridge University Press, 1998), 179, 181, 182–83. See also Kant, *Critique*, Transcendental Aesthetic, sect II, esp. "Elucidation"; and Jacques Derrida, *The Death Penalty*, Vol. I (hereafter *DP I*), trans. Peggy Kamuf (Chicago: University of Chicago Press, 2014), 225–26: "Time is sensibility or receptivity, affection (a major vein of philosophy from Kant to Heidegger . . .); time is suffering; the time of execution is endurance, passion, the pathetic, pathological *paskhein*—which sometimes means not only 'to undergo' but 'to undergo a punishment,' and the fact of passively undergoing can already be interpreted as the suffering of a punishment:

sensibility is in itself a punishment." As Derrida also suggests, a converse reasoning emerges to challenge any trend toward an ever more instantaneous death penalty. For if suffering is a function of duration, any reduction in the time of the punishment tends to eliminate punishment itself: "One might often be tempted to say: . . . No one suffers the death penalty. The condemned one, once executed, disappears before even being able to pay any penalty whatsoever." Derrida, *DP II*, 50.

8. The 1888 State Commission complied the following list of possible modes of execution: auto-da-fè, beating with clubs, beheading/decapitation, blowing from cannon, boiling, breaking on the wheel, burning, burying alive, crucifixion, decimation, dichotomy, dismemberment, drowning, exposure to wild beasts, flaying alive, flogging/knout, garrote, guillotine, hanging, hara-kiri, impalement, Iron Maiden, *peine forte et dure*, poisoning, pounding in mortar, precipitation, pressing to death, rack, running the gauntlet, shooting, stabbing, stoning, strangling, suffocation. Cited in David Garland, *Peculiar Institution: America's Death Penalty in an Age of Abolition* (Cambridge, MA: Harvard University Press, 2010), 70.

9. Such an assessment is reinforced by Justice Alito in the 2014 Missouri case of Russell Bucklew, who had his execution temporarily stayed on the basis of a claim that, because of the disease from which he suffered, administering pentobarbital would produce excruciating pain. See *Bucklew v. Lombardi*, Missouri, No. 14–2163 (8th Circ. 2015), and *Bucklew v. Lombardi*, 134 S. Ct. 2832 (2014).

10. *Trop v. Dulles*, 356 U.S. 86, 101 (1958).

11. *McGautha v. California*, 402 U.S. 183, 241 (1971); *Kennedy v. Louisiana*, 554 U.S. 407, 420 (2008); *Baze*, 80.

12. *Thompson v. Oklahoma*, 487 U.S. 815 (1988); *Stanford v. Kentucky*, 492 U.S. 361 (1989); (1989), *Atkins v. Virginia*, 536 U.S. 304 (2002); *Roper v. Simmons*, 543 U.S. 551 (2005); *Kennedy*, 407.

13. *Coker v. Georgia*, 433 U.S. 584 (1977).

14. See Derrida's complicating the question of age as a singular concept in relation to the execution of juveniles: "Suppose that I kill: at what age will I have killed, or will I have been killed? . . . There is in us simultaneously . . . something of the old man and of the child but also of the man of the twenty-first century, of the fifth century BCE, of Cro-Magnon man of the Neanderthal." *DP II*, 12–13.

15. Order, Rehearing denied No. 07–343, Statement of Justice Scalia, 554 U.S. (2008), 948–49.

16. Carol S. Steiker and Jordan M. Steiker discuss obstacles to progress in Eighth Amendment jurisprudence because of the understanding, prior to 1962, that it applied only to federal law. See their *Courting Death: The Supreme Court and Capital Punishment* (Cambridge, MA: Belknap Press of

Harvard University Press, 2016), 29–32, 52–53; and Franklin E. Zimring, *The Contradictions of American Capital Punishment* (New York: Oxford University Press, 2003), 68–70.

17. See *Enmund v. Florida*, 458 U.S. 782 (1982).

18. *Lockett v. Ohio*, 438 U.S. 586 (1978).

19. *Woodson v. North Carolina*, 428 U.S. 280, 304 (1976). Cf. *Callins*, 1149.

2. THE TIME OF THE TRAP DOOR

1. See https: //www.theguardian.com/world/2015/jun/04/north -carolina-pardons-brothers-pardoned-1983-rape-murder-of-girl. McCollum was North Carolina's longest serving death-row inmate. He petitioned the Supreme Court in 1994 but his Writ of Certiorari was denied (*McCollum v. North Carolina*, 512 U.S. 1254 (1994). Blackmun was the sole dissenting judge, acting on his vow made in *Callins* earlier that year, but also on the question of mental retardation, which, as we saw in the previous chapter, was resolved in *Atkins* in 2002.

2. Henry McCollum's innocence was a factor in Breyer's *Glossip* dissent (*Glossip*, Justice Breyer dissenting, 5, 30), discussed later. Despite the fact that Breyer drew attention to McCollum's being innocent of the rape and murder for which he was convicted—Scalia's example in rebutting Blackmun in *Callins*—neither Scalia nor Thomas mentions that injustice in *Glossip*, preferring to draw on, and draw, the graphic cases I mention here.

3. Jeffrey Toobin, "Clarence Thomas's Disgraceful Silence," *The New Yorker*, February 21, 2014.

4. See Thomas's statement at http://www.americanrhetoric.com /speeches/clarencethomashightechlynching.htm. For the Beitler photo-graph, see https: //iconicphotos.org/tag/lawrence-beitler.

5. See, for example Austin Sarat, *When the State Kills* (Princeton: Princeton University Press, 2001), which devotes a whole chapter to "Narra-tive Strategy and Death Penalty Advocacy." Sarat acknowledges that "all lawyers traffic in narrative," but emphasizes its "particularly important role in the work of lawyers trying to end state killing" (181). My intention here is not to discount the importance of narrative itself, but to point to the specific rhetoric of what I will call "photo-graphic visuality" within certain narra-tives. I return to the question of narrative in Chapter 6.

6. Stuart Banner, *The Death Penalty: An American History* (Cambridge, MA: Harvard University Press, 2002), 45–46. Michel Foucault records the first usage of trap door gallows in England in 1760; *Discipline and Punish: The Birth of the Prison*, trans. Alan Sheridan (Harmondsworth: Penguin Books, 1979), 18; see also Austin Sarat et al., *Gruesome Spectacles: Botched Executions and America's Death Penalty* (Stanford: Stanford University Press,

2014): "In 1759, Tyburn's infamous 'Triple Tree' was torn down and replaced by a portable gallows outfitted with a trapdoor" (34).

7. Banner, *Death Penalty*, 45. See also Sarat et al., *Gruesome Spectacles*, 32.

8. Cotton Mather, *Pillars of Salt* (Boston: Samuel Phillips, 1699), 62, cited in Banner, *Death Penalty*, 45.

9. See Banner, *Death Penalty*, 46.

10. Casanova, *The Memoirs of Jacques Casanova de Seingalt*, trans. Arthur Machen (New York: Putnam's, 1959), 3:21, 26–28; cf. Casanova, *Storia della mia vita*, ed. Piero Chiara and Federico Roncoroni (Milan: Mondadori, 1984), 2:182, 186–88.

11. Cited by Foucault, *Discipline and Punish*, 3.

12. Ibid., 3–6.

13. A detailed account of the execution of Louis XVI is given by Daniel Arasse, *The Guillotine and the Terror*, trans. Christopher Miller (London: Penguin Books, 1991), 48–72.

14. Banner, *Death Penalty*, 25.

15. Hugo Adam Bedau, ed., *The Death Penalty in America*, 3rd ed. (New York: Oxford University Press, 1982), 13.

16. Ibid., 146. Louis P. Masur links the move to private executions to urbanization and the development of middle-class values regarding privacy: "The concern with public assemblies and public space accelerated the shift to a faith in privacy and the creation of an urban environment characterized by class segmentation and social exclusion. . . . At the same time that classes cut themselves off from one another, middle-class families turned inward to the private realm of the sanctified home." *Rites of Execution: Capital Punishment and the Transformation of American Culture, 1776–1865* (New York: Oxford University Press, 1989), 102–3.

17. The specter of the death penalty as public spectacle returns in debate surrounding photographs taken by the Florida Department of Corrections following the execution of Allen Lee Davis. Those photos were appended to Justice Shaw's dissent in *Provenzano v. Moore*, demonstrating again how graphic visuality is not limited to those, like Scalia and Thomas, who are arguing that the death penalty spares criminals the pain that they caused their victims. See https://partners.nytimes.com/library/tech/99/10/cyber/cyberlaw/291aw.html.

18. Walter Benjamin, "The Work of Art in the Age of Technological Reproducibility," *Selected Writings. Vol 3, 1935–1938*, ed. Howard Eiland and Michael W. Jennings (Cambridge, MA: Harvard University Press, 2002), 102.

19. Masur, *Rites of Execution*, 26.

20. Ronald A. Bosco, "Lectures at the Pillory: The Early American Execution Sermon," *American Quarterly* 30 (1978): 163.

21. Banner, *Death Penalty*, 7.

22. Samuel Danforth, *The Cry of Sodom Enquired into* (Cambridge: Johnson, 1674), cited in Bosco, "Lectures at the Pillory," 157.

23. *Diary of Cotton Mather*, cited in Banner, *Death Penalty*, 33.

24. Cited in Bosco, "Lectures at the Pillory," 171–72. See also Banner's accounts of other execution documents (*Death Penalty*, 48–51).

25. Foucault, *Discipline and Punish*, 8.

26. Ibid., 9, translation modified. In *The Death Penalty*, Vol. I (hereafter *DP I*), trans. Peggy Kamuf (Chicago: University of Chicago Press, 2014), Jacques Derrida questions Foucault's idea of a disappearance of the spectacle of punishment with the birth of the prison, arguing instead that it be understood as a shift in regimes of a visibility that always remains operative in the death penalty (*DP I*, 43); see also Jacques Derrida, *The Death Penalty*, Vol. II (hereafter *DP II*), trans. Elizabeth Rottenberg (Chicago: University of Chicago Press, 2017), 220.

27. Foucault, *Discipline and Punish*, 49.

28. Ibid., 257, translation modified: The Alan Sheridan translation includes a number of inaccuracies. Notably, "public execution" is here used for *supplices* where Foucault is clearly referring to putting to death by torture, even if *supplice* is elsewhere a synonym for execution. Cf. *Surveiller et punir* (Paris: Gallimard, 1975), 261.

29. Ibid., 60.

30. Ibid., 61.

31. Ibid., 63, translation modified. For Derrida on autoimmunity, see Giovanna Borradori, *Philosophy in a Time of Terror: Dialogues with Jürgen Habermas and Jacques Derrida* (Chicago: University of Chicago Press, 2003), 94–102; Jacques Derrida, *The Beast and the Sovereign*, trans. Geoffrey Bennington (Chicago: University of Chicago Press, 2011), 2:83–85; and my discussion in *Inanimation* (Minneapolis: University of Minnesota Press, 2016), 103–5.

32. Ibid., 92.

33. For a full account of the theatrical spectacle of the guillotine in the revolutionary period see Arasse, *Guillotine and Terror*, 88–132. It was not until 1832 that there began "the slow process by which the guillotine was finally withdrawn from the public eye" (ibid.,109), displaced first to a public square closer to the prison, and in 1852 to the prison gates. In 1872 the guillotine was removed from its scaffold and placed on the ground; the last public guillotining, that of Eugen Weidmann, took place in 1939. See my discussion in Chapter 4.

34. Foucault, *Discipline and Punish*, 33.

35. J. Madival and E. Laurent, E. Clavel, eds., *Archives parlementaires de 1787 à 1860: Recueil complet des débats législatifs & politiques des Chambres*

françaises (Paris: Librairie Administrative de P. Dupont, 1877), 9:393, all translations mine.

36. Ibid., 11:279, my emphasis.

37. Ibid., 31:326.

38. *Le Moniteur,* December 18, 1789, cited in Arasse, *Guillotine and Terror,* 17.

39. Cited in Arasse, *Guillotine and Terror,* 17.

40. Jacques Delarue, *Le métier de bourreau* (Paris: Fayard, 1979), 149, all translations mine. See also Arasse, *Guillotine and Terror,* 22.

41. Quoted in Delarue, *Métier,* 127.

42. Pierre-Jean-Georges Cabanis, "Note sur le supplice de la guillotine," *Oeuvres completes de Cabanis. Tome II* (Paris: Bossange Frères, 1823), 171, all translations mine. See also Delarue, *Métier,* 128–29.

43. Foucault, *Discipline and Punish,* 13.

44. Madival and E. Laurent, et al., eds., *Archives parlementaires* (22 February–14 March 1792), 39:686, my translation, my emphasis.

45. Grégoire Chamayou, "La querelle des têtes tranchées: Les médecins, la guillotine et l'anatomie de la conscience au lendemain de la Terreur," *Revue d'histoire des sciences* 61, no. 2 (2008): 333–65. English translation ("The Debate over Severed Heads: Doctors, the Guillotine and the Anatomy of Consciousness in the Wake of the Terror") at http: //www.cairn-int.info /article-E_RHS_612_0333—the-debate-over-severed-heads.htm.

46. Chamayou, "Debate," §57.

47. Chamayou has the latter position represented by the Edinburgh vitalist Robert Whytt (1714–1766); cf. "Debate," §62–69.

48. Ibid. , §84.

49. Ibid. , §103.

50. Cf. Arasse, *Guillotine and Terror,* 37.

51. Chamayou, "Debate," §85.

52. Ibid., §94.

53. Ibid., §108–9.

54. Cabanis, "Note sur le supplice de la guillotine," 171.

55. Ibid., 170, 176.

56. Ibid., 173. It is important to note that in no way did Cabanis's faith in the machine prevent him from arguing for the abolition of the guillotine. See ibid., 180.

57. Ibid., 180.

58. Ibid., 172.

59. Arasse, *Guillotine and Terror,* 35.

60. *Journal des états généraux,* quoted in Arasse, *Guillotine and Terror,* 17.

61. Arasse, *Guillotine and Terror,* 13.

62. Ibid., 35.

63. Ibid., 36.

64. Fernand Meyssonnier, *Paroles de bourreau*, ed. Jean-Michel Bessette (Paris: Éditions Imago, 2002), 14, all translations mine. See also the novel by Mano Gentil, *Le photographe* (Paris: Éditions Syros, 2009), narrated by the "photographer" responsible, according to narrative clues, for the last execution in France, that of Hamida Djandoubi in 1977.

65. Patrick Wald Lasowski, "La guillotine dans le texte," *MLN* 103, no. 4 (1988): 840, all translations mine. Lasowski's essay was pointed out to me by Elissa Marder, in her excellent commentary "The Elephant and the Scaffold: Response to Kelly Oliver," *Southern Journal of Philosophy* 50 (2012): 95–106. See also Kelly Oliver, "See Topsy 'Ride the Lightning': The Scopic Machinery of Death," in ibid., 74–94. Arasse also analyzes, first, the relation between the guillotine and portraiture, and second, the coincidence of guillotine and photography, but that analysis takes him in a direction that is different from mine here (cf. *Guillotine and Terror*, 139–40).

66. Ibid., 840, 845–46.

67. Arasse, *Guillotine and Terror*, 27.

68. Ibid., 17.

69. Ibid., 10.

70. Meyssonnier, *Paroles de bourreau*, 114–17. Having watched photographs of the execution of Weidmann in 1939, Meyssonnier accuses that "photographer" of not doing his job, for he seems to have stepped away from the guillotine before the blade falls. He also describes the additional time pressures brought to bear—especially on the photographer who had to dispose of one head, then raise the blade in preparation for the next victim— in the case of multiple executions such as occurred during the Algerian War; and accuses "photographers" of low professional standards in other cases (ibid., 118–23, 127–28).

71. Cf. Sarat et al., *Gruesome Spectacles*. See also Victor Hugo's 1832 Preface to *The Last Day of a Condemned Man* regarding botched executions of the period, the most infamous imputed to an executioner's valet's interference with the workings of the guillotine as revenge for losing his job. Hugo, *The Last Day of a Condemned Man*, trans. Arabella Ward (Mineola, NY: Dover Publications, 2009), xxiv.

72. Bazin, "The Ontology of the Photographic Image," in *What Is Cinema?* trans. Hugh Gray (Berkeley, Los Angeles, and London: University of California Press, 1967), 1:13

73. Ibid., 15.

74. Ibid.

75. Banner, *Death Penalty*, 53–70.

76. See Arasse regarding the "representative quality" of the guillotine in terms of both physical laws and the rationality that subtends them: "the very

shape of the guillotine gave substance to the principle of justice it represented—a justice humane enough, no doubt, but as inexorable as a universal axiom. . . . The guillotine had something of the simplicity and austerity of a diagram: its abstract shape was a declaration of the universal validity of the laws of geometry and gravity. The decapitating machine made public execution a celebration of the mechanical and geometrical, and so ensured the spectacular triumph of these forms of 'just' and 'reasonable' thought" (*Guillotine and Terror*, 55).

77. Ibid., 36, translation modified. I return to this passage in Chapter 3.

78. Bazin, "Ontology," 13.

79. http: //www.amnestyusa.org/research/reports/death-sentences-and -executions-2015

80. Unverified or unverifiable press reports have also included the following among recent methods of execution practiced by Islamic State groups: nitric acid bath, crushing of head with a boulder, explosion, crucifixion, stabbing.

3. THE FUTURE ANTERIOR OF BLOOD

1. Jacques Delarue, *Le métier de bourreau* (Paris: Fayard, 1979), 384. Charles-Henri Sanson was appointed Royal Executioner in 1778 and continued as High Executioner until 1795, counting among his three-thousand-odd "patients" Louis XVI himself. Sanson was the fourth in a dynasty of six generations of *bourreaux* that lasted from 1684 to 1847.

2. http://www.deathpenaltyinfo.org/some-examples-post-furman -botched-executions.

3. Immanuel Kant, *The Metaphysics of Morals* in *Practical Philosophy*, trans. and ed. Mary J. Gregor (Cambridge: Cambridge University Press, 1996), 498.

4. Justice Shaw dissenting in *Provenzano v. Moore*, 744 So.2d 413 (1999), 428–29. The full context of his barbaric spectacle remark is this: "The color photos of Davis depict a man who—for all appearances—was brutally tortured to death by the citizens of Florida. Violence begets violence, and each of these deaths [Davis, Jesse Tafero, Pedro Medina] was a barbaric spectacle played by the State of Florida on the world stage. Each botched execution cast the entire criminal justice system of this state—including the courts—in ignominy" (490). See also the potential return of blood in response to the lethal injection crisis in the United States, in recent proposals by lawmakers in Wyoming, Missouri and Utah to return to the firing squad—permissible in Utah and last used in 2010—as the most humane method of execution.

5. http://www.perseus.tufts.edu/hopper/text? doc=Perseus% 3Atext% 3A1999.04.0059%3Aentry%3Dcruor.

6. See also Jacques Derrida, *The Death Penalty*, Vol. II (hereafter *DP II*), trans. Elizabeth Rottenberg (Chicago: University of Chicago Press, 2017),

220: "From the beginning of this seminar last year we became aware of a certain necessity . . . of seeking, if not finding, some correlation, a law of kinship . . . between the history of the death penalty and the history of blood."

7. Beyond the history of Western art, see the mythology that developed concerning Louis XVI's blood at the time of his guillotining. Daniel Arasse, *The Guillotine and the Terror*, trans. Christopher Miller (London: Penguin Books, 1991), 61–65.

8. The other botched Florida executions to which Shaw refers—Tafero and Medina—were marked by fire, which evokes a different historical form of capital punishment, namely the stake that returns in *Resweber* and in Sotomayor's *Glossip* dissent.

9. See André Leroi-Gourhan on the heart (along with stars, seasons, days, walking) as one of the "few regular rhythms that the natural world offers." *Gesture and Speech*, trans. Anna Bostock Berger (Cambridge, MA: MIT Press, 1993), 316. I thank Francesco Vitale for drawing this reference to my attention.

10. *Phaedo*, 58b. Plato, *The Collected Dialogues of Plato*, ed. Edith Hamilton and Huntington Cairns (Princeton: Princeton University Press, 1980), 41.

11. *Crito*, 43d. Ibid., 28.

12. *Crito*, 44a. Ibid., 28–29.

13. *Phaedo*, 54 and 678e. Ibid., 46 and 50.

14. *Apology*, 29a. Ibid., 15.

15. *Apology*, 38c. Ibid., 23.

16. *Phaedo*, 116e–117a. Ibid., 96–97.

17. Albert Camus, "Reflections on the Guillotine," trans. Justin O'Brien, in *Resistance, Rebellion and Death: Essays* (New York: Vintage International, 1995), 202.

18. Ibid., 233. A somewhat similar sentiment can be found in the thinking behind Nevada's introduction of the gas chamber in 1921, where some advocated that the execution should take place while the condemned person was asleep. See Sarat, *Gruesome Spectacles*, 91.

19. Ibid.

20. Martin Heidegger, *Being and Time*, trans. Joan Stambaugh (Albany: State University of New York Press, 2010), 7. Further references to this edition will be included in text, preceded by the mention *BT*.

21. "To have to do with something, to produce, order and take care of something, to use something, to give something up and let it get lost, to undertake, to accomplish, to find out, to ask about, to observe, to speak about, to determine. . . . These ways of being-in have the kind of being of *taking care of [Besorgen]*" (*BT*, 57).

22. The German words are *Entschlossenheit* (resoluteness) and *Vorlaufen* (anticipation). The first expresses both determination and the idea of being unlocked; the second conveys the sense of running forward, or toward, which is obviously very different from avoiding death, or even sitting back and waiting for it.

23. Section 74 of *Being and Time*, in which the term *Schicksal* occurs frequently, is also where Heidegger refers to the destiny (*Geschick*) of a people (*Volk*) (*BT*, 366). In the light of Heidegger's subsequent association with National Socialism, the use of the two terms and their context remain highly controversial.

24. Arasse, *Guillotine and Terror*, 36.

25. Ibid. See again Derrida on Guillotin's "four-stroke verbal machine" as "coming from on high . . . falling, striking down . . . from the transcendence of the Most High." Jacques Derrida, *The Death Penalty*, Vol. I (hereafter *DP I*), trans. Peggy Kamuf (Chicago: University of Chicago Press, 2014), 222.

26. Arasse, *Guillotine and Terror*, 36. See also Derrida, for whom a gesture such as Heidegger's deconstruction of the now nevertheless relies on commonsense knowledge, "judged to be indubitable, of what separates a state of death from a state of life . . . that is, of the supposed existence of an objectifiable instant that separates the living from the dying, be it of an ungraspable instant that is reduced to the blade of a knife or to the *stigmē* of a point. Without the supposed or supposedly possible knowledge of this clear-cut, sharp limit, there would be no philosophy or thinking of death." *DP I*, 238.

27. Dasein's everyday instants, its state of "entangled being-together-with," which Heidegger also refers to as "falling prey to [the] things at hand and objectively present that we take care of" (*BT*, 313), amounts to yet another way in which it gets—as it were ecstatically—taken out of any possible authentic relation to the present. That sense of being too preoccupied with the mundane to enjoy the moment is easily understood. If Dasein does manage to come back to itself it is precisely by being shaken out of its distractedness, being reminded in the blink of an eye or "Moment" (*Augenblick*) what it is effectively missing. Heidegger's word for that moment of instantaneous authenticity has a strong mystical sense of ecstasy, being carried away or carried off, enrapt or in *rapture (Entrückung)*.

28. See Aristotle, *Physica*, in *The Basic Works of Aristotle*, ed. Richard McKeon (New York: Random House, 1941), 292–99.

29. See Derrida, *DP II*, 148: "we have been and might still be surprised (once again drawing significant consequences from this symptom, as is the case with every philosopher), surprised, therefore, to discover . . . that this

great thinker of being-toward-death never shows any interest in the death penalty."

30. So little does Heidegger feel compelled, in concluding his volume, to engage in any complicated analysis, that he consigns substantial elements of his critique of Hegel to a long footnote in which he similarly rejects Bergson's idea of duration, again insisting that "this is not the place for a critical discussion of Bergson's concept of time and other present-day interpretations" (*BT*, 410n). Heidegger's critique of the Aristotelian-Hegelian(-Bergsonian) axis of temporality forms something of a matching bookend to the pages he dedicates to Descartes and Kant, in chapter 2 of the introduction to *Being and Time*. There it is stated that "despite all his essential advances, Kant dogmatically adopted Descartes' position" (23); and later, that "Kant's fundamental ontological orientation—despite all the differences implicit in a new inquiry—remains Greek" (25), which again means Aristotelian.

31. Jacques Derrida, "*Ousia* and *Grammē*: Note on a Note from *Being and Time*," in *Margins of Philosophy*, trans. Alan Bass (Chicago: University of Chicago Press, 1982), 34.

32. Ibid., 38. For Derrida, Hegel repeats Aristotle on two counts: his disappearing of time in the pure Notion of absolute knowledge, discussed below, reverts to an understanding of time as a distraction or degeneration of presence, a contingent means by which presence gets extended toward or into absence; and his subject of self-consciousness, "thinking itself, and assembling itself near itself in knowledge" (ibid., 59), amounts to a transformation of Aristotle's prime mover conceived of as pure presence.

33. Derrida also critiques Heidegger's recourse to the primordial and authentic as versions of a "proper" that risks anchoring Heideggerian ontology within the very metaphysics of presence that it seeks to deconstruct: "The primordial, the authentic are determined as the *proper (eigentlich)*, that is, as the *near* (proper, *proprius*), the present in the proximity of self-presence. One could show how this value of proximity and of self-presence intervenes, at the beginning of *Sein und Zeit* and elsewhere, in the decision to ask the question of the meaning of Being on the basis of an existential analytic of *Dasein*. And one could show the metaphysical weight of such a decision . . ." (ibid., 64n).

34. G. W. F. Hegel, *Hegel's Philosophy of Nature*, trans. A. V. Miller (Oxford: Oxford University Press, 2007), 29. Further references appear in text preceded where necessary by the mention *Nature*. In quotations from Hegel I have consistently substituted "concept" for "notion" in the Miller translations.

35. G. W. F. Hegel, *Hegel's Phenomenology of Spirit*, trans. A. V. Miller (Oxford: Oxford University Press, 1977), 487. Further references appear in text, preceded where necessary by the mention *Phenomenology*.

36. *"Plasticity* . . . will be presented as the 'unforeseen' of Hegelian philosophy. . . . The process of plasticity is dialectical." Catherine Malabou, *The Future of Hegel: Plasticity, Temporality, Dialectic*, trans. Lisabeth During (London: Routledge, 2005), 7, 12. The translation is sometimes slightly modified.

37. Ibid., 53.

38. Quoted in ibid., 54.

39. Ibid., 55.

40. Ibid., 128.

41. Jacques Derrida, "A Time for Farewells: Heidegger (Read by) Hegel (Read by) Malabou," in Malabou, *Future of Hegel*, xvi. Derrida's essay appears as a Preface to the English translation of Malabou's book. It was originally published in *Revue Philosophique de la France et de l'Étranger* 188, no. 1 (1998).

42. Ibid., 58, 59.

43. Ibid., 59. Malabou discusses in more detail the relation between contraction and habit in "Who's Afraid of Hegelian Wolves," trans. David Wills, in *Deleuze: A Critical Reader*, ed. Paul Patton (Oxford: Blackwell, 1996, 114–38).

44. Ibid., xxvii. As Malabou also wants to have understood, plasticity is, especially in Hegel, something other than elasticity, malleability or adaptability; it includes the radical transformability or becoming that she will ultimately call "metamorphosis" (*Future of Hegel*, 134), and renders problematic distinctions between inorganic and organic, artificial and natural.

45. Derrida, "A Time for Farewells," xiii.

46. See my discussion, in relation both to Jacob's *Logic of Life*, and Freud's death drive, in *Inanimation* (Minneapolis: University of Minnesota Press, 2016), 13–16, 70–77.

47. Malabou, *Future of Hegel*, 55.

48. In *Zusatz* comments in the *Philosophy of Nature* relating to the practical side of involvements with the outer world, Hegel phrases the organism's relation to externality or exteriority in particularly stark— psychological if not psychoanalytic—terms, as though the organism were functioning not just according to physiology but as a consciousness. The blood's struggle with air is repeated by ingestion in general, and by "the whole process of digestion" whereby the organism "angrily oppos[es] itself to the outer world" (402). If the organism is to find a way beyond that anger, it will be in terms that return us again to the logic of the *Phenomenology*, such that the animal—beginning, presumably, with some lowly organism— advances way past its digestive disorders to achieve a type of self-consciousness:

The animal . . . is angry with itself for getting involved with external powers and it now turns against itself and its false opinion; but in so doing it
throws off its outward-turned activity and returns into itself. The triumph
over the non-organic "potency" is not a triumph over it *qua* non-organic
"potency," but a triumph over animal nature itself. The true externality of
animal nature is not the external thing, but the fact that the animal itself
turns in anger against what is external. The subject [the animal has now become a consciousness] must rid itself of this lack of self-confidence which
makes the struggle with the object appear as the subject's own action, and
must repudiate this false attitude. Through its struggle with the outer thing,
the organism . . . compromises its dignity in face of this non-organic being.
What the organism has to conquer, is, therefore, this its own process, this
entanglement with the outer thing. (403–4)

49. In French, *étancher* means "to staunch" (hence *étanche*, "watertight"),
whereas *épancher* is "to shed (blood), pour out." In discussing blood here,
Derrida plays between those two verbs.

50. In returning to the question in the final session Derrida will concede
that the link he establishes "doesn't mean that I understand what sacrifice
is," but that nevertheless "we must think what 'sacrifice' means, if we are to
approach the question of the animal, as well as the question of the death
penalty, from both sides" (*DP II*, 245). His subsequent, and last seminar
cycle will be on the animal. Cf. Jacques Derrida, *The Beast and the Sovereign*,
Vol. I, trans. Geoffrey Bennington (Chicago: University of Chicago Press,
2009); Vol. II, trans. Geoffrey Bennington (Chicago: University of Chicago
Press, 2011).

51. Gil Anidjar, *Blood: A Critique of Christianity* (New York: Columbia
University Press, 2014), xii. Anidjar does not reference Derrida's death
penalty seminars, the first volume of which no doubt appeared after he had
completed his study.

52. Ibid., 22, 84.

53. Ibid., 92.

54. Ibid., 156. For Anidjar, even if blood represents a universal cultural
"concern," "the difference—and the distinct range—of this concern clearly
leaves Christianity in a class of its own" (ibid.). That will lead him, in a way
that my discussion to follow finds highly instructive, to transition in his final
chapter from a *hemato-political* axis produced by the seventeenth-century
contemporaries and friends William Harvey and Thomas Hobbes, an axis
that links the circulation of blood and of money within the commonwealth
called Leviathan, to the nineteenth century of *Moby-Dick*, where "Melville
lays out the history of Christianity as the history of blood" (206) and

produces an unmistakable conjunction between consumerism and bloodletting, the original form of "blood for oil" (207).

55. See Rainer Brömer, "The Nature of the Soul and the Passage of Blood through the Lungs: Galen, Ibn Al-Nafis, Servetus, Itaki, Attar," in *Blood, Sweat and Tears: The Changing Concepts of Physiology from Antiquity to Early Modern Europe*, ed. Manfred Horstmanshoff, Helen King, and Claus Zittel (Leiden: Brill, 2012), 339–62.

56. Ambroise Paré (1510?–90) became the surgeon of Henri II of France during the period when there was an exponential increase in battle wounds caused by handheld artillery and mobile cannon. See my discussion in *Prosthesis* (Stanford: Stanford University Press, 1995), 215–19, where I argue that ligature of the arteries not only revolutionized surgery but also inaugurated the modern possibility of a prosthetic member.

57. Cf. Malabou, referring to the collapse of time in absolute knowledge: "The dialectical sublation of a specific temporal form, as presented in the chapter on Absolute Knowledge, would not be possible . . . if teleological time—the circular unrolling of *dynamis* and *energeia*—did not lie behind it." *Future of Hegel*, 130.

58. See Derrida's comments on the vulgar or "current" concept of time critiqued by Heidegger but "dominated by the schema of the flux." "A Time for Farewells," xxviii.

59. Malabou, *Future of Hegel*, 76.

4. SPIRIT WIND

1. Jacques Derrida, *The Death Penalty*, Vol. I (hereafter *DP I*), trans. Peggy Kamuf (Chicago: University of Chicago Press, 2014), 278.

2. Michel de Montaigne, "A Custom of the Isle of Cea," *Essays*, book 2, chap. 3, trans. Donald Frame (New York: Knopf, 2003), 306, translation slightly modified. Cf. Michel de Montaigne, *Les essais* (Paris: Gallimard, 2007), 369.

3. Montaigne, "Custom," 306.

4. Ibid., 311, 316; quotation at 313; for the woman of Cea, see 317–18.

5. Robert A. Pape, *Dying to Win: The Strategic Logic of Suicide Terrorism* (New York: Random House, 2006), 35; and Christoph Reuter, *My Life Is a Weapon: A Modern History of Suicide Bombing*, trans. Helena Ragg-Kirby (Princeton: Princeton University Press, 2004), 133.

6. For the history of suicide bombing, see Pape, *Dying to Win*, 11–15. Pape identifies the first female suicide bomber of the contemporary era as sixteen-year-old Sana Youssel Mhaydali (138; see also 205–10, 226–30). See also Reuter, *My Life Is a Weapon*.

7. In his thoroughly reasoned and reasonable analysis of suicide bombing, Talal Asad states that, despite the etymological relation between "martyr" and *shahīd*, "the Qur'an, incidentally—and perhaps significantly—doesn't make explicit use of the word *shahīd* to signify someone who dies in God's cause. . . . The concept of *istishhād* as a technique of jihad in which the combatant (*mujāhid*) annihilates himself is an entirely modern idea." Talal Asad, *On Suicide Bombing* (New York: Columbia University Press, 2007), 51–52. Asad convincingly argues that the Western assessment of—especially—the Muslim terrorist as cruel, barbaric, or suicidally fanatical is warped by the role of (holy) sacrifice in the Judeo-Christian tradition (43), and by the paradigm case of the crucifixion: "In short, in Christian civilization, the gift of life for humanity is possible only through a suicidal death; redemption is dependent on cruelty or at least on the sin of disregarding human life" (86).

8. André Malraux, *Man's Fate*, trans. Haakon M. Chevalier (New York: Vintage Books, 1990), 243. Further references to this edition included in text. Here and elsewhere the translation is slightly modified. Where necessary, page references are added in brackets from Malraux, *La condition humaine*, in *Oeuvres complètes*, Vol. 1 (Paris: Gallimard, 1989).

9. Marc Redfield introduces two separate but important ideas for consideration in the context of the "rhetoric" of terror that are apposite to its representation as a form of ecstasy in Malraux. The first is a complex relation to the sublime; the second is his astute acknowledgment of Heidegger's disturbing use of the word *Schrecken* to emphasize what Dasein requires as an antidote to everyday emptiness in *The Fundamental Concepts of Metaphysics*. Marc Redfield, *The Rhetoric of Terror: Reflections on 9/11 and the War on Terror* (New York: Fordham University Press, 2009), 32–35, 125–26.

10. On this point see Asad, *On Suicide Bombing*, 89–90.

11. Albert Camus, "Reflections on the Guillotine," trans. Justin O'Brien, in *Resistance, Rebellion and Death: Essays* (New York: Vintage International, 1995), 191, 192. See Derrida's discussion of this passage by Camus (*DP I*, 247–49). Earlier (51–52), Derrida comments on the death wish of the infamous Claude Buffet, whose 1972 case is recounted by his accomplice's lawyer, Robert Badinter, in *L'exécution* (Paris: Grasset, 1973). Badinter, a militant abolitionist, would go on to oversee the abolition of the death penalty in France in 1981.

12. Jean Genet, *Our Lady of the Flowers*, trans. Bernard Frechtman (New York: Grove Press, 1991), 120–21.

13. Ibid. Cf. Jean Genet, *Notre-Dame-des-Fleurs*, in *Oeuvres complètes* (Paris: Gallimard, 1951), 54.

14. Genet, *Our Lady*, 51.

15. The dedication to Pilorge reads, "Were it not for Maurice Pilorge, whose death never stops poisoning my life, I would never have written this book. I dedicate it to his memory." Pilorge, who was executed in February 1939 for slashing the throat of his (presumed) male lover, is celebrated in Genet's poem "Le condamné à mort" (*Oeuvres complètes*, 177–86). According to Genet's biographer, Edmund White, the writer falsely claimed to have known Pilorge. Edmund White, *Genet: A Biography* (New York: Knopf, 1993), 180. Derrida calls Genet's poem "a kind of chant of mourning and resurrection that describes but also poetically provokes, produces, performs, and glorifies the *elevation*, the *ascension* of the victims of the scaffold" (*DP I*, 33). Derrida mistakes the date of Pilorge's execution.

For the execution of Weidmann, see https://www.youtube.com/watch?v=VJdhePPvxjY and https://www.youtube.com/watch?v=Ybp-EZe7PoQ.

16. Franz Kafka, *The Trial*, trans. Breon Mitchell (New York: Schocken Books, 1999), 230–31. I return to this text in Chapter 6.

17. In the Kantian context, Derrida's deconstruction weighs, more precisely, on the former's distinction, developed in his *Metaphysics of Morals*, between a self-inflicted (moral) punishment (*poena naturalis*) and one imposed by a legal authority (*poena forensis*). See *The Death Penalty*, Vol. II (hereafter *DP II*), trans. Elizabeth Rottenberg (Chicago: University of Chicago Press, 2017), 68–69, 84–86.

18. See Lisa Stampnitzky, *Disciplining Terror: How Experts Invented "Terrorism"* (Cambridge: Cambridge University Press, 2013) for the contemporary transition from policy and academic discussion of "insurgency" to "terrorism," a shift that she dates to the 1972 Munich Olympics hostage-taking by Black September (21–23). On suicide bombing, see 144–45. See also Derrida's discussion in Giovanna Borradori, *Philosophy in a Time of Terror: Dialogues with Jürgen Habermas and Jacques Derrida* (Chicago: University of Chicago Press, 2003), 101–9.

Regarding violence against property, the Animal Enterprise Terrorism Act of 2006 provides the "Department of Justice the necessary authority to apprehend, prosecute, and convict individuals committing animal enterprise terror" involving damage to or loss of "any real or personal property (including animals or records) used by an animal enterprise." See https://www.gpo.gov/fdsys/pkg/PLAW-109publ374/html/PLAW-109publ374.htm.

19. "Discours de Robespierre sur les principes de morale politique qui doivent guider la Convention dans l'administration intérieure de la république," *Réimpression de l'ancien Moniteur*, Convention Nationale (Paris: Henri Plon, 1863), 19:404, my translation. Cf. Marcel Reinhard, Georges Lefebvre, and Marc Bouloiseau, eds., *Archives parlementaires de 1787–1860* (Paris: CNRS, 1962), 84:333.

20. http://www.larousse.fr/encyclopedie/divers/la_Terreur/146370. On the Revolution's progressive imposition of the state of siege, see Giorgio Agamben, *State of Exception*, trans. Kevin Attell (Chicago: University of Chicago Press, 2005), 4–5, 11–12.

21. I discuss the role of the pamphlet at length in my *Dorsality* (Minneapolis: University of Minnesota Press, 2008), 183–91. Cf. Marquis de Sade, *Justine, Philosophy in the Bedroom, and Other Writings* (New York: Grove Press, 1990), 296–339.

22. Maurice Blanchot, "Literature and the Right to Death," in *The Work of Fire*, trans. Lydia Davis (Stanford: Stanford University Press, 1995), 320. Further reference in text following the abbreviation "Right to Death," translation sometimes slightly modified; cf. "La littérature et le droit à la mort," *La part du feu* (Paris: Gallimard, 1949), 310 (earlier version in *Critique* 4, 20 [1948]: 30–47). Pages numbers from *La part du feu* are added in brackets where necessary.

23. Maurice Blanchot, *The Infinite Conversation*, trans. Susan Hanson (Minneapolis: University of Minnesota Press, 1993), xii.

24. Ibid.

25. Space does not permit me to discuss here how the second half of "Literature and the Right to Death" provides what is in many ways a reasoned theoretical explanation for the more programmatic logic of its first half. See, in that regard, *DP I*, 112ff. One should also note that when Blanchot includes his article in *La part du feu* the whole essay is printed in italic script, as though it were a particular hypothetical form, a separate opuscule within, or special postface to that volume; or as though it were written in a different mood, quoted, or translated from another language. That special status is not reproduced in the English translation.

Blanchot's essay is clearly in conversation with Hegel's chapter on "Absolute Freedom and Terror" in G. W. F. Hegel, *Hegel's Phenomenology of Spirit*, trans. A. V. Miller (Oxford: Oxford University Press, 1977), 355–63. One should also note its other, very different background source: Jean Paulhan, *The Flowers of Tarbes or, Terror in Literature*, trans. Michael Syrotinski (Urbana: University of Illinois Press, 2006), published in 1941. Paulhan defines terror as "those moments in the history of nations . . . when it suddenly seems that the State requires not ingeniousness and systematic methods . . . but rather an extreme purity of the soul, and the freshness of a communal innocence" (24). Blanchot discusses Paulhan's book in 1943, in "How Is Literature Possible?" without for all that extending the discussion in the directions taken in "Literature and the Right to Death." In a sense, that makes the latter essay another, very different take on how literature is possible. See Maurice Blanchot, "How Is Literature Possible?" in *Faux pas*, trans. Charlotte Mandel (Stanford: Stanford University Press, 2002), 76–84. For a fine reading of these questions, and analysis of Blanchot that overlaps with my own, see Redfield, *The Rhetoric of Terror*, 81–84.

26. Blanchot, *Infinite Conversation*, xii.

27. Sade was imprisoned in the Bastille starting in February 1784. It was there that he wrote a number of his works, most notably the unfinished manuscript of *120 Days of Sodom*. On July 2, 1789, during his permitted walk along the towers of the prison he created a disturbance by shouting, supposedly with the aid of an improvised loudspeaker, that the jailers were cutting prisoners' throats, inviting the crowd to come and liberate him. He was transferred to the Charenton asylum two days later and, of course, ten days after that, the Bastille was stormed, launching the Revolution. See Gilbert Lély, *Vie du Marquis de Sade*, in Lély, ed., *Oeuvres complètes du Marquis de Sade* (Paris: Cercle du livre précieux, 1962), 2:190–92.

28. See again Dolmancé's pamphlet in *Philosophy in the Bedroom*, 318–19, 337.

29. See *DP I*, 97–122. Derrida's fourth session of the first year of his seminar, within which the discussion of Blanchot's "Literature and the Right to Death" is found, begins and ends with Hugo's appeal to the Constituent Assembly for what would become the Second Republic in 1848: "I vote for the pure, simple, and definitive abolition of the death penalty." See also my discussion in Chapter 6.

30. In subsequent pages of Derrida's analysis of Blanchot's article, he tempers "the properly terrifying and sinister resonances and connotations of this terrorist, terrorizing thinking of literature, of this literature as Terror" (*DP I*, 117) by discussing literature's contradictory language, the relation of death to resurrection, and death as the impossibility of dying (117–20). See the following discussion.

31. The Universal Declaration of 1948 will add more explicitly as Article 3: "Everyone has the right to life, liberty and security of person."

32. Montaigne, *Essays*, 305.

33. According to François Billacois, though the duel remained the principal form of trial by ordeal in the sixteenth century, the continued use of trial by water for sorcery led the Paris Parliament to forbid it as late as 1601. *The Duel: Its Rise and Fall in Early Modern France*, ed. and trans. Trista Selous (New Haven: Yale University Press, 1990), 15.

34. Maurice Blanchot, *The Instant of My Death* and Jacques Derrida, *Demeure: Fiction and Testimony*, trans. Elizabeth Rottenberg (Stanford: Stanford University Press, 2000), 3. Although Blanchot's and Derrida's texts appear in the same volume in English, further references appearing in text will be distinguished as *Instant* and *Demeure*. In one or two instances the translation is slightly modified.

35. For the biographical and historical record see Christophe Bident, *Maurice Blanchot: Partenaire invisible* (Paris: Champ Vallon, 1998), 228–31. Cf. also Blanchot, *The Madness of the Day*, trans. Lydia Davis (Barrytown, NY: Station Hill Press, 1981): "I was made to stand against the wall like many others. Why? For no reason. The guns did not go off" (6).

36. Maurice Blanchot, *The Writing of the Disaster*, trans. Ann Smock (Stanford: Stanford University Press, 67.

37. Ibid., translation modified; cf. Maurice Blanchot, *L'écriture du désastre* (Paris: Gallimard, 1980), 110.

38. See Sharon Cameron's excellent analysis of this episode from Dostoyevsky in *The Bond of the Furthest Apart* (Chicago: University of Chicago Press, 2017), 44–50.

39. Philippe Lacoue-Labarthe points to the noteworthy echoes between Blanchot's reflection here and Bataille's "Hegel, Death, and Sacrifice." Lacoue-Labarthe, *Ending and Unending Agony*, trans. Hannes Opelz (New York: Fordham University Press, 2015), 32–33.

40. See, for example, Blanchot, *Writing of the Disaster*, 117. Derrida does not make any connection to Heidegger in *Demeure*.

41. Since 1326, according to the Centre National de Ressources Textuelles et Lexicales. See http://www.cnrtl.fr/etymologie/attentat.

5. DRONE PENALTY

1. More than any other chapter in this book, this one remains hostage to current events and to the speed of academic publishing, as discussed in the Introduction. I have attempted to account for new facts based on statistical and other information that was revised for the last time on September 30, 2018.

2. Grégoire Chamayou, *A Theory of the Drone*, trans. Janet Lloyd (New York: New Press, 2015), 84. Further references will be included in text, preceded where necessary by the mention *Drone*. The translation is sometimes slightly modified.

3. See https://www.thebureauinvestigates.com/projects/drone-war; http://www.reprieve.org.uk/investigations/drones; https://www.facebook.com/DronesWatch; http://www.thebureauinvestigates.com; http://www.longwarjournal.org. The figures cited are those provided by www.thebureauinvestigates.com, restricted to actions in Pakistan, Somalia, and Yemen, accessed September 30, 2018. They do not take into account deaths from drone strikes in Afghanistan from January 2015 to the present (3,918–5,256), or actions in the recently opened or reopened theatres of Syria and Iraq (see https://airwars.org).

4. http://www.deathpenaltyinfo.org/executions-year. Accessed September 30, 2018.

5. Édouard Glissant, *Poetics of Relation*, trans. Betsy Wing (Ann Arbor: University of Michigan Press, 1997), 5.

6. https://theintercept.com/2016/02/25/us-extends-drone-war-deeper-into-africa-with-secretive-base.

7. http://www.huffingtonpost.com/2013/06/27/obama-goree-island_n_3511414.html.

8. On March 6, 2013, Paul filibustered for almost thirteen hours to prevent a vote on the confirmation of John Brennan, Obama's choice to lead the CIA, drawing attention to the potential for a drone strike against an American citizen on American soil. See https://www.theguardian.com/world/2013/mar/07/rand-paul-drones-policy-filibuster.

9. "That the President is authorized to use all necessary and appropriate force against those nations, organizations, or persons he determines planned, authorized, committed, or aided the terrorist attacks that occurred on September 11, 2001, or harbored such organizations or persons, in order to prevent any future acts of international terrorism against the United States by such nations, organizations or persons." (https://www.congress.gov/107/plaws/publ40/PLAW-107publ40.pdf).

10. http://www.nytimes.com/2013/05/24/us/politics/transcript-of-obamas-speech-on-drone-policy.html. Since that speech, a leaked Pentagon document has become available (https://theintercept.com/document/2015/10/14/small-footprint-operations-5-13/); and The Intercept has published its "Drone Papers" with further documentation and extensive commentary (https://theintercept.com/drone-papers).

11. For the current state of play, see Matthew C. Weed, "A New Authorization for Use of Military Force against the Islamic State: Issues and Current Proposals," https://fas.org/sgp/crs/natsec/R43760.pdf.

12. See https://obamawhitehouse.archives.gov/the-press-office/2016/07/01/executive-order-united-states-policy-pre-and-post-strike-measures; and https://www.justice.gov/oip/foia-library/procedures_for_approving_direct_action_against_terrorist_targets/download.

13. "Report of the Special Rapporteur on Extrajudicial, Summary or Arbitrary Executions, Philip Alston," A/HRC/14/24/Add.6, §87. https://documents-dds-ny.un.org/doc/UNDOC/GEN/G10/137/53/PDF/G1013753.pdf. The report refers to practices by Israel, the United States, and Russia.

14. Ibid., §4.

15. See Peshawar High Court Writ Petition No. 1551-P/2012. If the Peshawar decision cannot have immediate consequences for U.S. policy and actions, unless Pakistan were to develop some vigorous follow-up; and if the United States remains mostly immune to international action by virtue of its not being a signatory to the World Court, that is not the case for allies who are complicit in carrying out the drone program, such as Australia, as has

recently been pointed out (http://www.theguardian.com/commentisfree
/2013/jul/29/australia-drones-pine-gap).

16. Elements of what follows were outlined in my *Matchbook* (Stanford:
Stanford University Press, 2005), 16–18.

17. Carol S. Steiker and Jordan M. Steiker, *Courting Death: The Supreme
Court and Capital Punishment* (Cambridge, MA: Belknap Press of Harvard
University Press, 2016), 7.

18. Ibid., 20.

19. See Stuart Banner, *The Death Penalty: An American History* (Cambridge, MA: Harvard University Press, 2002), 131, 222, 228, 230.

20. Steiker and Steiker, *Courting Death*, 25.

21. Ibid., 24.

22. Cf. ibid., 67. See also David Garland, *Peculiar Institution: America's
Death Penalty in an Age of Abolition* (Cambridge, MA: Harvard University
Press, 2010), which uses an "archetypal Southern lynching scene . . . to
orient [its] study of American capital punishment and its peculiar character-
istics" (36); and Franklin E. Zimring, *The Contradictions of American Capital
Punishment* (New York: Oxford University Press, 2003), 88–99.

23. Steiker and Steiker, *Courting Death*, 34.

24. Ibid., 40.

25. Ibid., 26.

26. Ibid., 54.

27. Ibid., 55.

28. See *Courting Death*, 78–115. "Hiding in plain sight" is a section
heading at 79. The authors discuss in detail the relative absence of race from
the *Furman*, *Gregg*, and *Coker* opinions.

29. Ibid., 97. See also Sheri Lynn Johnson, "*Coker v. Georgia*: Of Rape,
Race, and Burying the Past," in *Death Penalty Stories*, ed. John H. Blume and
Jordan M. Steiker (New York: Thomson Reuters/Foundation Press, 2009),
171, 190–95.

30. Colin Dayan, *The Story of Cruel and Unusual* (Cambridge MA: MIT
Press, 2007), and *The Law Is a White Dog* (Princeton: Princeton University
Press, 2011).

31. Dayan, *Cruel and Unusual*, 7–8.

32. Ibid., 17.

33. Ibid., 17–21.

34. For a recent, profound analysis of links between drone warfare,
torture and illegal detention see Elisabeth Weber, *Kill Boxes: Facing the
Legacy of US-Sponsored Torture, Indefinite Detention, and Drone Warfare* (New
York: Punctum Books, 2017).

35. Dayan, *White Dog*, 89.

36. On animal prosecutions see E. P. Evans, *The Criminal Prosecution and Capital Punishment of Animals* (London: William Heinemann, 1906); and, for a more recent assessment, Anila Srivastava, "'Mean, dangerous, and uncontrollable beasts': Mediaeval Animal Trials," *Mosaic* 40, 1 (2007): 127–43. According to Evans, "as late as 1864 at Pleternica in Slavonia, a pig was tried and executed for having maliciously bitten off the ears of a female infant aged one year" (137). Evans also discusses the jurisprudence of the deodand (186–92). Conversely, in the final chapter of *White Dog*, Dayan takes up the question of contemporary treatments of "wayward" species of dogs.

37. Dayan, *White Dog*, 147, 148.

38. Cf. ibid., 152–53.

39. Cf. ibid., 96–112. See *Boyce v. Anderson*, 27 U.S. 150 (1829)

40. Ibid., 195.

41. Cf. ibid., 200–1.

42. Ibid., 181.

43. Cited in Dayan, *White Dog*, 86. Steiker and Steiker point to the converse characterization of how death row currently functions in California, made by federal judge Cormac J. Carney in 2014, as "life in prison with the remote possibility of death" (*Courting Death*, 1).

44. Cesare Beccaria, *An Essay on Crimes and Punishments* (Albany: W. C. Little & Co., 1872), 99–100, 101.

45. Except for passing reference toward the end of Chapter 1 this study has, for fear of being derailed, refrained from addressing the dubious constitutional justification for the death penalty found in the Fifth Amendment: "No person shall be held to answer for a capital, or otherwise infamous crime . . . nor be deprived of life, liberty, or property, without due process of law." However, that dubiousness comes into particular focus in this context. It seems quite clear that the clause that contemplates capital punishment also contemplates slavery, to the extent that a slave is not there presumed to be a person with access to redress for being deprived of liberty. Yet few, if any, of those who today have recourse to the Fifth Amendment for maintaining the death penalty would argue for reinstating slavery.

46. Steiker and Steiker, *Courting Death*, 77.

47. Ibid., 72. See also Zimring, *Contradictions of American Capital Punishment*, 89–92.

48. See Obama's remarks regarding the Connecticut school shootings (http://www.whitehouse.gov/blog/2012/12/16/president-obama-prayer-vigil-connecticut-shooting-victims-newtown-you-are-not-alone), and the commentary by George Monbiot (http://www.theguardian.com/commentisfree/2012/dec/17/us-killings-tragedies-pakistan-bug-splats). See also Cornel West's commentary on *Democracy Now* on July 22, 2013, pro-

voked by the not guilty verdict in the Trayvon Martin case, accusing Obama of "plantation" politics or being a "global [stand-your-ground] George Zimmerman" in his reckless disregard for Pakistani, Somalian, or Yemeni children's lives: http://www.democracynow.org/2013/7/22/cornel_west _obamas_response_to_trayvon

49. See also Ernst Kantorowicz, *The King's Two Bodies: A Study in Mediaeval Political Theology* (Princeton: Princeton University Press, 1970).

50. See Giorgio Agamben, *State of Exception*, trans. Kevin Attell (Chicago: University of Chicago Press, 2005), 2–3, 86–87.

51. See http://www.justice.gouv.fr/histoire-et-patrimoine-10050/proces -historiques-10411/le-proces-de-louis-xvi-22604.html.

52. Maximilien Robespierre, *Oeuvres de Maximilien Robespierre*, ed. Marc Bouloiseau et al. (Paris: Presses Universitaires de France, 1958), IX:121.

53. Ibid., 129.

54. Thomas Hobbes, *Leviathan*, ed. C. B. Macpherson (London: Penguin Books, 1985), 255.

55. Ibid., 667. The Peace of Westphalia ended the Thirty Years War in Europe in 1648. Hobbes's English background context, of course, was the ongoing Civil War (1642–51), which ended the year *Leviathan* was published.

56. Carl Schmitt, *Political Theology: Four Chapters on the Concept of Sovereignty*, trans. George Schwab (Chicago: University of Chicago Press, 2005), 5.

57. Jacques Derrida, *The Beast and the Sovereign*, Vol. I, trans. Geoffrey Bennington (Chicago: University of Chicago Press, 2009), 26.

58. Ibid., 16–17.

59. See Jacques Derrida, *Rogues: Two Essays on Reason*, trans. Pascale-Anne Brault and Michael Naas (Stanford: Stanford University Press, 2005).

60. Derrida, *Beast and Sovereign*, I:208–9.

61. See *Rogues*, 102–6, and Giovanna Borradori, ed., *Philosophy in a Time of Terror: Dialogues with Jürgen Habermas and Jacques Derrida* (Chicago: University of Chicago Press, 2003).

62. See Jacques Derrida, "Unconditionality or Sovereignty: The University at the Frontiers of Europe," trans. Peggy Kamuf, *Oxford Literary Review* 31 (2009), esp. 121–27.

63. Only two drones strikes are known to have taken place outside the Afghanistan theater of war before Derrida's death in October 2004. The first recorded strike was in Yemen in November 2002, and the subject of a report by the Special UN Rapporteur on Extrajudicial, Summary or Arbitrary Executions in January 2003, in whose opinion it constituted "a clear case of extrajudicial killing." The second was in Pakistan in June 2004. See https:// www.thebureauinvestigates.com/projects/drone-war.

64. Derrida, *Beast and Sovereign*, I:1.

65. "Secret 'kill list' proves a test of Obama's principles and will," *New York Times*, May 29, 2012.

66. David Zucchino, "Drone pilots have a front-seat on war from half a world away," *Los Angeles Times*, February 21, 2010.

67. See my *Inanimation* (Minneapolis: University of Minnesota Press, 2016), 179–90.

68. Carl Schmitt, *Theory of the Partisan*, trans. G. L. Ulmen (New York: Telos Publishing, 2007), 69.

69. Ibid., 16.

70. Ibid., 22. Chamayou extrapolates Schmitt's "telluric" partisan to the "stratospheric" (*Drone*, 61).

71. Cf. Schmitt, *Partisan*, 25–27.

72. Carl Schmitt, *The Concept of the Political*, trans. George Scwhab (Chicago: University of Chicago Press, 1996), 26.

73. Schmitt, *Partisan*, 95, 80.

74. Concerning precision, see in particular *Drone*, 142.

75. "Typically, power based on a slavery system is a striking example of zoopolitics [*le pouvoir esclavagiste représente la zoopolitique par excellence*]," 269n; cf. Chamayou, *Théorie du Drone* (Paris: La Fabrique, 2013), 358n.

76. Chamayou also discusses debate over whether drone operators should be awarded medals for valor (*Drone*, 101–2), and reports—and responses to those reports—regarding operators' PTSD symptoms (106–11). See also http://www.spiegel.de/international/world/pain-continues-after-war-for -american-drone-pilot-a-872726.html.

77. http://www.aljazeera.com/programmes/headtohead/2015/07/blame -isil-150728080342288.html. See also the likelihood that terrorists themselves will, or already do, possess drones of their own (see http:// foreignpolicy.com/2016/04/28/terrorists-have-drones-now-thanks-obama -warfare-isis-syria-terrorism).

78. James Brown Scott, ed., *The Proceedings of the Hague Peace Conferences: The Conference of 1899* (New York: Oxford University Press, 1920), 343.

79. See Glenn Greenwald, "Obama killed a 16 year-old in Yemen, Trump just killed his 8 year-old sister," https://theintercept.com/2017/01/30 /obama-killed-a-16-year-old-american-in-yemen-trump-just-killed-his-8 -year-old-sister.

80. Eyal Weizman, *Hollow Land: Israel's Architecture of Occupation* (London: Verso, 2007), 9.

81. Ibid., 241.

82. Ibid., 241, 250.

83. Pragmatic copresence is intended to resolve the problem of a "distance" that "covers several dimensions that are confused in our ordinary experience but which teletechnologies both disaggregate and redistribute

spatially" (*Drone*, 116). The argument of "originary prosthesis" works from a similar problematic but tends to treat distance as necessarily technological and disaggregating, while nevertheless acknowledging effects of disaggregation specific to drone warfare such as Chamayou describes on 116–19. One wonders whether a pragmatics of copresence could account for the secret or prayer, which are in no way immune from technology, discussed below.

84. Hobbes, *Leviathan*, 81. See also Chamayou, *Drone*, 218–21.

85. Derrida, *Beast and Sovereign*, I:27.

86. Ibid., 215.

87. Ibid.

88. See again "Secret 'kill list' proves a test of Obama's principles and will," and https://theintercept.com/drone-papers.

89. On "double-taps," see http://www.thebureauinvestigates.com/2013/08 /01/bureau-investigation-finds-fresh-evidence-of-cia-drone-strikes-on -rescuers. For further, empirically based analysis of how "spaces of constructed visibility are also always spaces of constructed invisibility," see Derek Gregory, "From A View to Kill: Drones and Late Modern War," *Theory, Culture & Society* 28, nos. 7–8 (2012): 188–215 (quote at 193).

90. For a different perspective, and triangulation of sovereign with terrorist, see Adi Ophir, "Disaster as a Place of Morality: The Sovereign, the Humanitarian, and the Terrorist," *Qui Parle* 16, no. 1 (2006): 95–116.

91. Jacques Derrida, *The Gift of Death and Literature in Secret*, trans. David Wills (Chicago: University of Chicago Press), 108. The Matthew 6 section of the Sermon on the Mount has as its refrain, regarding the "privacy" of almsgiving, prayer, and fasting, "Your Father who sees in secret will reward you." For an excellent, sustained discussion of this topic, see Charles Barbour, *Derrida's Secret: Perjury, Testimony, Oath* (Edinburgh: Edinburgh University Press, 2017).

92. Ibid.

93. Glenn Greenwald, "Three key lessons from the Obama administration's drone lies," *The Guardian*, April 11, 2013: http://www.guardian.co.uk /commentisfree/2013/apr/11/three-lessons-obama-drone-lies.

94. See Glenn Greenwald, "The bombing of Mali highlights all the lessons of western intervention," *The Guardian*, January 14, 2013: http:// www.guardian.co.uk/commentisfree/2013/jan/14/mali-france-bombing -intervention-libya.

95. Cf. Derrida's discussion in *Beast and Sovereign*, I:7–11.

96. See http://livingunderdrones.org/wp-content/uploads/2012/09 /Stanford_NYU_LIVING_UNDER_DRONES.pdf

97. See Derrida, *Beast and Sovereign*, I:203. On this subject, see also Derrida, "Faith and Knowledge," trans. Sam Weber, in *Religion*, ed. Jacques

Derrida and Gianni Vattimo (Stanford: Stanford University Press, 1998), 47–48; and the superb, sustained analysis undertaken by Michael Naas in *Miracle and Machine: Jacques Derrida and the Two Sources of Religion, Science, and the Media* (New York: Fordham University Press, 2012), esp. 119, 150–51.

98. Jacques Derrida, *The Beast and the Sovereign*, Vol. II, trans. George Bennington (Chicago: University of Chicago Press, 2011), 203.

99. Paul Celan, *The Meridian: Final Version—Drafts—Materials*, trans. Pierre Joris (Stanford: Stanford University Press, 2011), 9. For another reading of Celan's Meridian address, see my *Inanimation*, 139–51; and for a different rhetorico-polemical conclusion to the present discussion see the earlier version of it published as "Drone Penalty," *SubStance* 43, no. 2 (2014): 174–92.

100. Derrida, *Beast and Sovereign*, II:233–34, my emphasis.

101. Maximilien Robespierre, *Oeuvres de Maximilien Robespierre*, ed. Marc Bouloiseau and Albert Soboul (Paris: Presses Universitaires de France, 1967), X:422, my translation.

102. Ibid., 424, my translation.

103. Georg Büchner, *Complete Works and Letters*, trans. Henry J. Schmidt (New York: Continuum, 1986), 123. *Danton's Death* quotes liberally from historical documents such as those discussed earlier, for example Robespierre's invocation of terror, and the trial of Danton just referred to.

104. Celan, *Meridian*, 3, 4. See also the commentary by Philippe Lacoue-Labarthe in his *Poetry as Experience*, trans. Andrea Tarnowski (Stanford: Stanford University Press, 1999), 50–51.

6. lam time

1. "What is an act?" is one of the fundamental questions Derrida poses at the beginning of *The Death Penalty*, Vol. II, trans. Elizabeth Rottenberg (hereafter *DP II*; Chicago: University of Chicago Press, 2009), showing how—along with "What is an age?" and "What is a desire?"—it complicates the operation of criminal justice and the death penalty in particular (3–17).

2. Michel Foucault, ed., *I, Pierre Rivière, having slaughtered my mother, my sister, and my brother*, trans. Frank Jellinek (Lincoln: University of Nebraska Press, 1982). The English translation promotes Foucault to an editorial position that remains more discreet in the original (his name appears on the cover but not on the title page, and the copyright page presents the work as a collective effort); it also omits a series of pages at the end of part I that include a Rivière family chronology, and a map and detailed description of the criminal's wanderings prior to his arrest.

Further reference to the English edition will be included in text, preceded where necessary by the abbreviation *PR*. As required, the page reference to the French edition, *Moi, Pierre Rivière* (Paris: Gallimard, 1973), is added, preceded by the abbreviation *Moi*.

3. See again the case of Henry McCollum (*McCollum*, 1994), whose conviction was obtained thanks to a confession.

4. Cf. Foucault, *Moi, Pierre Rivière*, 234–37.

5. See Foucault's discussion of how the introduction of a verdict relating to insanity (Article 64 of the 1810 penal code) evolved from preempting guilt to allowing that someone could be both mad and guilty, which, following the introduction of extenuating circumstances, required psychiatric expertise. *Discipline and Punish: The Birth of the Prison*, trans. Alan Sheridan (Harmondsworth: Penguin Books, 1979), 19–21.

6. Following the period of the Revolution and the final defeat of Napoleon, the French monarchy was restored with the accession, in 1814, of Louis XVIII, brother of the guillotined Louis XVI (whose own son and successor had died in prison). Louis XVIII died childless and was succeeded by his brother Charles X, who reigned from 1824 to 1830. Charles was deposed in the "July Revolution" of 1830 by Louis-Philippe, ending the succession of Bourbon kings in favor of the line of Orléans. In turn, Louis-Philippe's own increasing authoritarianism led to his destitution in the 1848 Revolution and the constitution of the Second Republic, followed, from 1852 to 1870, by Louis-Napoléon's Second Empire.

7. Corporal punishments for various crimes had been reintroduced in the period 1810–1825. Indeed when an Anti-Sacrilege Act was introduced under Charles X, the penalty for profanation of the consecrated host was first intended to be the same as that for parricide—mutilation followed by execution—but ultimately reverted to the death penalty alone. See Francis Démier, *La France de la Restauration (1814–1830)* (Paris: Gallimard, 2012), 749.

8. Hugo writes in 1832 that readers of the anonymous 1829 edition supposed it was an English or American story. *The Last Day of a Condemned Man*, trans. Arabella Ward (Mineola, NY: Dover Publications, 2009), xiv.

9. Hugo, *Last Day*, xiii–xiv. Cf. Victor Hugo, *Le dernier jour d'un condamné* (Paris: Hatier, 2012), 8.

10. Ibid., xvi. Coincidentally, Hugo's word *serpe* is French for pruning bill, Rivière's murder weapon (cf. Hugo, *Dernier jour*, 12).

See Derrida's extensive analyses of Hugo's abolitionist militancy in *The Death Penalty*, Vol. I (hereafter *DP I*; Chicago: University of Chicago Press, 2009), first on the basis of the guillotine's bloody history, and second regarding Hugo's casting the question of capital punishment as a question of onto-theological sovereignty, specifically Christianity (*DP I* 181–83, 207–15).

11. See Derrida regarding Hugo's view that extenuating circumstances should be considered as the first step on the way to abolition (*DP I*, 102–4).

12. Morel was appointed director of the Asile d'Aliénés de Maréville in 1848, where he expanded the more humane treatment of the insane begun by Philippe Pinel in the late eighteenth century. He introduced the concept of *dementia praecox*, often credited with being the first description of schizophrenia. See his *Traité des dégénérescences physiques, intellectuelles, et morales de l'espèce humaine* (Paris: Baillière, 1857).

13. Cf. *PR*, 210–11n. The lamentation is not reproduced in the English translation. It begins: "If, in the splendors of memory famous warriors are inscribed, one [also] preserves the names of certain brigands from history; that of young Pierre Rivière . . . will figure there forever" (my translation). See Foucault, *Moi, Pierre Rivière*, 227.

14. *Moi, Pierre Rivière* (1973) was published two years before *Discipline and Punish*, in the French original *Surveiller et punir* (Paris: Gallimard, 1975). *The Archeology of Knowledge*, originally published as *L'archéologie du savoir* (Paris: Gallimard, 1969) and "The Order of Discourse," originally *L'ordre du discours* (Paris: Gallimard, 1970) had been published four and five years before that, respectively.

15. See the groundbreaking codification of narrative temporalities by Gérard Genette, *Narrative Discourse: An Essay in Method*, trans. Jane E. Lewin (Ithaca, NY: Cornell University Press, 1980).

16. One might compare Rivière's narrative mediation of his crime with contemporary interest on the part of some criminals in filming their acts, which would again call for comparative analysis of prephotographic and twenty-first-century mediatic contexts.

17. See also Friedrich Nietzsche, *Thus Spake Zarathustra*, trans. Adrian Del Caro (Cambridge: Cambridge University Press, 2006): "But thought is one thing, and deed another, and the image of a deed yet another. The wheel of motive does not roll between them" (26). I thank Paul Patton for reminding me of this passage.

18. The memoir is organized as follows:

p. 54 (*Moi*, 73), headed "Particulars and explanation"

p. 55 (*Moi*, 74), beginning of "Summary"

p. 100 (*Moi*, 123), "end of the summary of my father's afflictions")

p. 101 (*Moi*, 124), "summary of my private life and the thoughts that have busied me to this day"

p. 105 (*Moi*, 128), first mention of "the fearful design which I executed"

pp. 105–6 (*Moi*, 130–31), "Having therefore taken these fatal resolutions I resolved to put them into execution. I intended first to write down . . ."

p. 112 (*Moi*, 137), "I committed that fearful crime"

pp. 112–121 (*Moi*, 137–48), description of wanderings and eventual arrest

p. 121 (*Moi*, 148), "The End" and signature

19. Two other works by Maurice Blanchot deserve mention here in view of attention paid, in Chapter 4, to his thinking. The first is exactly contemporaneous with "Literature and the Right to Death," and is entitled precisely *Death Sentence*, trans. Lydia Davis (Barrytown, NY: Station Hill Press, 1998); cf. *L'arrêt de mort* (Paris: Gallimard, 1948). It is in two chapters, and stages the instant of death of a young woman—very different from the *L'instant de ma mort*—understood as an opposition between "lightning" and "final immobility" (29); it also foregrounds the question of the narrator's culpability in relation to his account of that death. The second chapter is a complicated story involving the narrator: it recasts a number of elements from the first chapter, and is similarly both dramatically decisive and mired in indecision. The second work, a much shorter piece entitled *The Madness of the Day*, originally *La folie du jour* (Paris: Gallimard, 1973), could be read in company with either Kafka's *The Trial*, discussed below, or the Rivière case. It has in common with the latter a desire or demand for a narrative recounting (*récit*) and an uncanny convergence of medical and juridical authority, which "constantly gave our conversation the character of an authoritarian interrogation" (18/31). Space does not permit the extensive analysis that those texts call for in the context of the questions I am raising here.

20. See Derrida's remarks concerning the problematics of abolitionist literary fiction (*DP II*, 196–98); and the forthcoming book by Peggy Kamuf, *Literature and the Remains of the Death Penalty* (New York: Fordham University Press, 2018).

21. See information provided by the Oklahoma Department of Corrections at http://doc.ok.gov/death-row-monthly-roster. The status of all prisoners on that roster appears currently to be "indefinite stay."

22. Franz Kafka, "In the Penal Colony," trans. Willa and Edwin Muir, *The Complete Stories* (New York: Schocken Books, 1971), 144.

23. Ibid., 149.

24. Ibid., 150.

25. Ibid., 160. Cf. Kafka, "In der Strafkolonie," *Gesammelte Schriften* (Berlin: Schocken Verlag, 1935), 1:205.

26. Ibid. 164.

27. Ibid. 165; cf. "Strafkolonie," 211.

28. Ibid., 166.

29. Franz Kafka, "The Metamorphosis," trans. Willa and Edwin Muir, *Complete Stories*, 89.

30. Ibid., 110, 120. Cf. Kafka, "Die Verwandlung," in *Gesammelte Schriften*, 1:95, 107.

31. Ibid., 134. Cf. "Verwandlung," 123.
32. Ibid., 135. Cf. "Verwandlung," 125.
33. Franz Kafka, "Before the Law," trans. Willa and Edwin Muir, *Complete Stories*, 3.
34. Franz Kafka, *The Trial*, trans. Breon Mitchell (New York: Schocken Books, 1998), 164–65.
35. Ibid., 167–68.
36. Ibid., 166.
37. Ibid., 168.
38. Ibid., 179.
39. I thank Wolf Kittler for information regarding the etymology of the German word (cf. "Verwandlung," 69).

White, Edward Douglass (Justice), 24, 44
Wilkerson v. Utah, 20–24, 26–29, 36–38, 41, 222n6
Wisconsin, 190
Woodson v. North Carolina, 50, 224n19

Yemen, 42, 150, 153, 154, 169, 171, 179, 182, 184, 221n2, 240n3, 244nn48,63

Zimmerman, George, 244n48
Zimring, Frank, 164, 221n5
Zola, Émile, 5

CPSIA information can be obtained
at www.ICGtesting.com
Printed in the USA
LVHW041738300119
605816LV00002B/277/P

9 780823 283491